Dear New Student:

Welcome to FYE 121! This class is designed as a resource to help with your transition into college. Along with this course, Owens Community College offers other helpful programs throughout campus to guide your success. For example, the Success Mentors program provides students with friendly, accessible advisors who help students plan their schedules, find help when it is needed and navigate the Owens system. This program offers advising through scheduled mentoring sessions to help you with goal development, academic and career planning, registration assistance, and connections and information to on and off campus resources.

Another valuable resource is the Supplemental Instruction (SI) program. Supplemental Instruction is offered in traditionally difficult classes, and is led by students who have already successfully completed the class. These students meet regularly with students in each class to talk about the lectures, the readings and the assignments. They offer a comfortable, engaging learning environment for all skill levels.

The Learning Centers offer a wide variety of help for all students attending Owens. Friendly, free-of-charge tutors offer help for all levels of ability, no matter what type of coursework or stage in the learning process. The Learning Center Labs: the Writing Center, the Math Center, the Natural Sciences Lab, and the Study Skills/IST/Accounting/Computer Skills Lab offer up-to-date course texts, software, and other resources for you to use.

As you can see, Owens offers numerous programs to help you throughout your college experience. Along with a lot of hard work and motivation, these resources will provide you with the tools and the guidance that you need to succeed.

Happy Learning!

A Former FYE Student and Supplemental Instructor (SI)

D1412159

Dear First Year Experience Student (and probably New College Student),

Welcome to Owens Community College and the First Year Experience Course. Congratulations; you have made one of the most important decisions of your life...to attend college! It will be an exhilarating experience for you, as college is a time for growth, self-discovery, and change. This course, the First Year Experience (FYE for short), will be a huge help as you begin your college journey; it will give you the tools needed to be successful in your first year of college and beyond. You will learn in this course, among many other things, the language of college, how to use your college catalog, your learning style, and what and where the resources on campus are located.

Speaking of resources, I want to highlight a few of them for you that will be essential for you, as a college student— The Learning Centers, Supplemental Instruction, and Success Mentoring.

The free professional tutors at **The Learning Centers** are there to help you, no matter your ability, in one-on-one or small group sessions in writing, math, natural sciences, study skills, accounting, and computer skills. The tutors can help whether you are struggling to begin a project, prepare for a quiz or test, or finish an assignment.

Supplemental Instruction (SI for short), which is led by students, provides extra support in traditionally difficult classes and can help whether you need a little or a lot of review. The Supplemental Instruction Leaders have already taken the class successfully, and lead the SI sessions by modeling effective study skills, using group participation, and empower students, like you, to take control of the learning process.

The **Success Mentors** are professionals who offer proactive advising through scheduled mentoring sessions and/or other mediums such as texting, chatting, and emailing. Success Mentors help you with goal development for academic, professional, and personal success, academic and career planning, along with registration assistance, and connections to campus and community resources.

Throughout your first year, you will experience new interests and ideas that will challenge you; enjoy it, and remember to use The Learning Centers, Supplemental Instruction, and the Success Mentors to help you be as successful as you can. Thank you for choosing the Owens community; it is a pleasure to help make this year the most excellent it can be for you! Best wishes for a wonderful first year and beyond!

Sincerely,

Jen Hazel
Full-Time Instructor, English Department
First Year Experience (FYE) Instructor
Mentor, Bridge to Success Program
Manager, Supplemental Instruction
Critical Thinking Faculty Facilitator, Student Learning Assessment

Foundations for College

FYE 121

SECOND CUSTOM EDITION FOR OWENS COMMUNITY COLLEGE

Taken from:

The Community College Experience: PLUS, Second Edition
by Amy Baldwin

The Prentice Hall Planner for Student Success
by Charles Muse

Learning Solutions

New York Boston San Francisco
London Toronto Sydney Tokyo Singapore Madrid
Mexico City Munich Paris Cape Town Hong Kong Montreal

Cover Art: Courtesy of Owens Community College

Taken from:

The Community College Experience: PLUS, Second Edition
by Amy Baldwin
Copyright © 2010, 2007 by Pearson Education, Inc.
Published by Prentice Hall
Upper Saddle River, New Jersey 07458

The Prentice Hall Planner for Student Success
by Charles Muse
Copyright © 2008 by Pearson Education, Inc.
Published by Prentice Hall

This special edition published in cooperation with Pearson Learning Solutions.

All trademarks, service marks, registered trademarks, and registered service marks are the property of their respective owners and are used herein for identification purposes only.

Pearson Learning Solutions, 501 Boylston Street, Suite 900, Boston, MA 02116
A Pearson Education Company
www.pearsoned.com

Printed in the United States of America

2 3 4 5 6 7 8 9 10   VOZU   15 14 13 12 11 10

000200010270579125

LL

ISBN 10: 0-558-81099-3
ISBN 13: 978-0-558-81099-3

Brief Contents

Contents

CHAPTER 3 Understanding Others in College and Diversity   48

Part II   Learning

CHAPTER 6   Learning, Memory, and Thinking   120

CHAPTER 7   Reading   144

CHAPTER 8   Listening and Taking Notes Effectively   166

CHAPTER 9   Writing and Presenting College Assignments   186

CHAPTER 10 Studying and Taking Tests   212

Part III Planning

CHAPTER 11 Planning for Next Semester   236

CHAPTER 12 Preparing for a Career and a Life   260

Preface

Nothing is more rewarding than teaching in a community college, especially working with students who are new to college and maybe even the first in their family to earn a college degree. At times, though, the work can be challenging because there is so much we feel they need to know to be successful. We mean well, but it is often hard to teach them everything that we think is important. Enter *The Community College Experience PLUS*. The idea behind the book was to address that very dilemma. I found that my students needed to know much more than "traditional four-year university students" (What is "traditional" anyway?). There were so many things that even I didn't know they didn't know! This book was written to provide that basic information to these students as well as a realistic picture of what it will take to succeed in college. There is no candy-coating or hand-holding in these pages. Why? Because these students are successful in their own right already—many of them hold down full-time jobs, take care of their family, and participate actively in their communities. They just need a little more—a little more basic information that we often take for granted they know (What is a credit hour?); a little more realism (Your relationships *will* change when you are in college, and sometimes it is not for the better); and a little more support (You already are an effective time manager, so let's build on that foundation with these tips!).

The first edition of *The Community College Experience PLUS* was an effort to provide more practical information to students who are new to college; the "plus" was additional topics and opportunities for reflection and critical thinking. The "plus" is still part of this edition, but it is a more streamlined "plus" in that only the essential information for student success has been kept. The extras, such as exercises, tables, and in-depth topics, can be found in the Instructor's Manual.

The second edition of *The Community College Experience PLUS* is organized around three principles: acclimating/relating, learning, and planning. These three principles are key to our students' success and they mirror the stages students go through in their first semester. Several of the chapters have been combined into one and moved ahead to coincide with the time in the semester when students will most need the information and skills. Most significantly, there is more information on time management strategies that are crucial to students' success from day one. The students have spoken: Time management is a major issue for them, and they will find more ideas for improving time management in Chapter 4.

Another notable addition is the section on memory and learning in Chapter 6, which is based on recent brain research. Readers can learn more about how they learn—and how to improve their learning in and out of class. The other chapters have been streamlined to present the essentials of student success and updated to provide the latest information.

Author Bio

Community College Connections

Amy Baldwin earned a B.A. in English Literature at Rhodes College (Memphis, TN) and an M.A. in English and British Literature at Washington University (St. Louis, MO). Since 1996, she has been teaching student success, composition, and literature Pulaski Technical College (North Little Rock, AR).

In 2007, she co-founded the National Student Success Institute with Steve Piscitelli at Florida State College at Jacksonville and Dr. Robert Sherfield at the College of Southern Nevada, which provides faculty development and resources to community colleges. Since 2009, she serves on the Advisory Board for the newsletter *Student Health 101*, an online publication, which also publishes a community college version, that is sent to students all over the country and focuses on maintaining a healthy lifestyle while in college. Her other community college connections include serving as co-director of her college's Achieving the Dream initiative and the recent appointment as a technical assistance provider (TAP) to the new Developmental Education Initiative (DEI), funded by the Bill and Melinda Gates Foundation. She also serves on the Executive Committee of the Two-Year College English Association-Southwest Region. In 2006, she won the TYCA-SW Teaching Excellence Award.

Innovation

Amy Baldwin was one of the first instructors at her college to teach online in 1999, and from 2003–2006, she served as the distance education coordinator, assisting in the growth of online classes and training faculty to teach online. In 2007, she set out to help develop a professional development program for faculty and staff and took on the role of the college's first professional development coordinator. In an effort to share student success strategies beyond the boundaries of her college, she created and co-chaired the first statewide conference that focused on promoting student success at Arkansas colleges and universities. As part of her role as co-director of Achieving the Dream and professional development coordinator, she started the college's first New Faculty Academy to help new faculty learn more about what they can do to be successful instructors.

Service

Amy's service to the college includes creating the first student literary magazine, *The View from Here*, in 1998, which is now in its tenth volume; serving on the editorial staff for *Milestones*, the student academic journal; serving as the self-study editor for accreditation; developing online professional development classes for K-12 teachers; and serving as co-liaison for the Foundations of Excellence® self-study on improving first-year students' experience. She also serves on the Pulaski Technical College's Leadership Class Steering Committee, a program she helped start in 2007 that provides leadership training and education for potential leaders at her college.

Personal

Amy lives in Little Rock, Arkansas, with her husband and two children. She is currently a higher education doctoral student at the University of Arkansas at Little Rock where she is focusing her studies on student retention. In between her work, family, and studies, she has provided nearly 100 professional development workshops at conferences and community colleges on student success, engaging activities, academic integrity, online learning, and research writing.

Photo by Lennon Parker

New Features

- **Student stories** is a new feature that replaces the Community College Student Profiles. In these vignettes, readers are provided with a true-to-life short narrative of four students' experiences in college that illustrate common challenges, dilemmas, and situations that can be explored further in the PLUS critical thinking exercises.
- **My Story** is another new feature that allows students to relate their own story to the chapter's topics.

Returning Features

- **Collaboration, Critical Thinking, and Reflection exercises** are included in each chapter so that students can take some time to think about, talk about, and reflect on what they have learned. The most effective exercises have been retained for this edition, while the ones that appeared in the first edition will be available in the Instructor's Manual.
- **The PLUS critical thinking exercises** tie to each chapter's opening story by asking readers to determine the best course of action for the main character. In addition, readers are asked to apply what they have learned about personality and learning styles to their own situation.
- **Integrity Matters** will continue to provide students with a look at how integrity plays a part in their success in college and life.
- **Path of Discovery Journal** topics give students a way to connect with the material in the chapter.
- **Chapter Review Questions** provide students with a way to check reading comprehension and understanding.

Acknowledgements

I would like to acknowledge my family for their love and support. Thank you, Kyle, Emily, and Will.

Thank you also to Jeffery Johnston, Sande Johnson, Jennifer Gessner, Amy Judd, Kerry Rubadue, and Lynda Cramer for their enormous help and support. The people at Pearson are the most generous souls. In addition, thanks to Shawnie Shade, Tanika Henderson, David Ploskonka, James Garza, Diane Lorenzo, Candace Rowley, and Kerry Rubadue for their assistance with the photo shoot.

In addition, I appreciate the feedback from the various students, faculty, and administration who helped shape this second edition: Allison Perrin, South Plains College; Ellen Vician, College of DuPage; and Rick Woodard, Rose State College.

MyStudentSuccessLab

*"Teaching an online course, offering a hybrid class, or simply introducing your students to technology, just got a whole lot easier and **EXCITING!**"*

To help students build college success and career development skills, students must *apply* what they learn. MyStudentSuccessLab (www.mystudentsuccesslab.com) offers students a self-paced, interactive, virtual lab designed to offer *application* and *practice* of their skills. By developing strategies that work best for them, students experience greater relevance, motivating them to achieve success.

Working with a number of our authors and faculty members, we created a lab experience that provides interactive critical-thinking cases, a goal setting and journaling tool, reflection exercises, video with applications, interactive simulations, and more. MyStudentSuccessLab is a unique, valuable learning tool that offers:

GENERAL Student Success TOPICS, including:

- Welcome to College/College Culture, Academic Skills, Life Skills, and Career Skills

Within EACH TOPIC:

- Objectives, Pre-Assessment, E-book (with Multimedia features), Interactive Case Study, Interactive Activity, Goal Setting and Journaling tool, and Comprehension Test

Posted to the COURSE RESOURCES Section:

- Understanding Plagiarism guide, Prentice Hall Planner, Student Reflection Journal, *10 Ways to Fight Hate,* Student Success Supersite, and Dictionary of Contemporary English Online

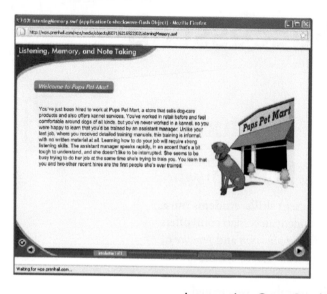

Chapter features to support your course objectives:

- **Pre-Assessment**—Students have the opportunity to take a pre-test before reading each chapter. Their test results identify chapter topics they must master. The assessment feedback identifies students' strengths and weaknesses so they can learn more effectively.

- **E-book with multimedia**—*The Community College Experience PLUS,* Second Edition, is available on this site with MSSL links embedded throughout for ease of use. Gain access to content, including interactive chapter features, video, weblinks, journal prompts, self-assessments, chapter exercises, and more.

- **Interactive Case Studies**—Students can practice their decision-making skills with these interactive cases. Each case requires them to apply skills and strategies they've learned in the chapter—such as time management, critical thinking, and listening—to solve problems. At the end of the scenario, students receive constructive feedback relating to each choice they made as they worked through the case.

- **Goal Setting and Journaling tool**—Our unique Goal Setting and Journaling tool will help your students learn to set "SMART" long-term and short-term goals as they move through each chapter—and keep track of how well they are meeting those goals. The journaling activity will help them discover obstacles preventing them from attaining their objectives—and what will help them succeed. This tool's features allow you and your students to monitor their progress and identify areas for potential improvement. As the instructor, you also have the option of reviewing their journals for completion or content.

- **Comprehension test**—After reading a chapter, students take a post-test to check comprehension. Choose from multiple choice, true/false, fill in the blank, short answer, and essay questions, and results will be imported to Gradetracker.

- **Portfolio Exercises**—Students can build an electronic portfolio containing artifacts of their work with these classroom-tested exercises. Students demonstrate skill mastery with actual work that can be shared with future instructors or employers.

- **Weblinks**—Looking for current issues in student success and career development? Weblinks offer quick access to relevant, reliable links that update course content.

NOTE—A way to search for ALL media within the site is to use the *Index of Multimedia.* Students can choose from many icons, such as *Explore* or *Watch. Explore* refers to Interactive features such as our Time Management Activity: Interactive calendar; *Watch* links to Videos. Videos include study skills, workplace tips, and role-playing videos to help students see how other students cope with the demands of college or show how the course content relates to this class and beyond.

MyStudentSuccessLab is integrated into the text to reinforce the content! Wherever the **MSSL** icons appear in the margins, your students can follow the link instructions to access the **MyStudentSuccessLab** resource that corresponds with the chapter content. *Activities & Exercises* are assignable and give students the opportunity to understand each chapter's material by applying content in an engaging way.

Margin Note Icons for Exercises include:

- *Practice* identifies opportunities for students to demonstrate skill level and reflect on the reading.

- *Explore* points to multimedia interactive exercises that reinforce the material.

- *Interactive Reading* highlights features where students read and respond to specific material.

- *Case Study* spotlights features that focus on student real world scenarios with probing questions.

- *Profile* indicates exercises that aid students in developing their personal portfolio.

MyStudentSuccessLab is available as a supplemental package option, as well as for stand-alone purchase. It is available in CourseCompass, Blackboard, and WebCT course management platforms, as well as a version to use for other learning platforms.

    MyStudentSuccessLab is easy to use and assign. It allows students to set their own pace, build self-awareness, and practice what *they* need to set personal goals and achieve success in college, career, and life. Visit www.mystudentsuccesslab.com to explore this exciting new online teaching resource, contact your local sales professional, or send an inquiry to Student.Success@pearson.com for additional support.

Supplemental Resources

INSTRUCTOR SUPPORT

Resources to simplify your life and engage your students.

Book Specific

Print

Instructor's Manual with Test Bank

Online Computerized TestGen
Online PowerPoints
Online Instructor's Manual with Test Bank

Technology

*"Easy access to online, book-specific **teaching support** is now just a click away!"*

Instructor Resource Center—Register. Redeem. Login. Three easy steps that open the door to a variety of print and media resources in downloadable, digital format, available to instructors exclusively through the Pearson/Prentice Hall Instructor's Resource Center. Click on "Educator," then click on "Download Instructor Resources" to access online resources.

http://www.prenhall.com

Are you teaching online, in a hybrid setting, or looking to infuse exciting technology into your classroom for the first time?

Then be sure to refer to the **MyStudentSuccessLab** section of this Preface to learn about our revolutionary resource that **helps students build college success and career development skills, and to *apply* what they learn. MyStudentSuccessLab** (www.mystudentsuccesslab.com) offers students a self-paced, interactive, virtual lab designed to offer *application* and *practice* of their skills. By developing strategies that work best for them, students experience greater relevance, motivating them to achieve success.

*"Choose from a wide range of **video resources** for the classroom!"*

Prentice Hall Reference Library: Life Skills Pack, 0-13-127079-6, contains all 4 videos, or they may be requested individually as follows:

- Learning Styles and Self-Awareness, 0-13-028502-1
- Critical and Creative Thinking, 0-13-028504-8
- Relating to Others, 0-13-028511-0
- Personal Wellness, 0-13-028514-5

Prentice Hall Reference Library: Study Skills Pack,   0-13-127080-X, contains all 6 videos, or they may be requested individually as follows:

- Reading Effectively, 0-13-028505-6
- Listening and Memory, 0-13-028506-4
- Note Taking and Research, 0-13-028508-0
- Writing Effectively, 0-13-028509-9
- Effective Test Taking, 0-13-028500-5
- Goal Setting and Time Management, 0-13-028503-X

Prentice Hall Reference Library: Career Skills Pack, 0-13-118529-2, contains all 3 videos, or they may be requested individually as follows:

- Skills for the 21st Century—Technology, 0-13-028512-9
- Skills for the 21st Century—Math and Science, 0-13-028513-7
- Managing Career and Money, 0-13-028516-1

Complete Reference Library - Life/StudySkills/CareerVideoPack on DVD, 0-13-501095-0

- Our Reference Library of thirteen popular video resources has now been digitized onto one DVD so students and instructors alike can benefit from the array of video clips. Featuring Life Skills, Study Skills, and Career Skills, they help to reinforce the course content in a more interactive way.

Faculty Video Resources

- Teacher Training Video 1: Critical Thinking, 0-13-099432-4
- Teacher Training Video 2: Stress Management & Communication, 0-13-099578-9
- Teacher Training Video 3: Classroom Tips, 0-13-917205-X
- Student Advice Video, 0-13-233206-X
- Study Skills Video, 0-13-096095-0
- Faculty Development Workshop (DVD), 0-13-227192-3

Current Issues Videos

- ABC News Video Series: Student Success 2/E, 0-13-031901-5
- ABC News Video Series: Student Success 3/E, 0-13-152865-3

MyStudentSuccessLab PH Videos on DVD, 0-13-514249-0

- Our six most popular video resources have been digitized onto one DVD so students and instructors alike can benefit from the array of video clips. Featuring Technology, Math and Science, Managing Money and Career, Learning Styles and Self-Awareness, Study Skills, and Peer Advice, they help to reinforce the course content in a more interactive way. They are also accessible through our MSSL and course management offerings and available on VHS.

*"Through partnership opportunities, we offer a variety of **assessment** options!"*

LASSI—The LASSI is a 10-scale, 80-item assessment of students' awareness about and use of learning and study strategies. Addressing skill, will, and self-regulation, the focus is on both covert and overt thoughts, behaviors, attitudes, and beliefs that relate to successful learning and that can be altered through educational interventions. Available in two formats: Paper, 0-13-172315-4, or Online, 0-13-172316-2 (Access Card).

Noel Levitz/RMS—This retention tool measures Academic Motivation, General Coping Ability, Receptivity to Support Services, PLUS Social Motivation. It helps identify at-risk students, the areas with which they struggle, and their receptiveness to support. Available in Paper or Online formats, as well as Short and Long versions. Paper Long Form A: 0-13-0722588; Paper Short Form B: 0-13-079193-8; Online Forms A, B & C: 0-13-098158-3.

Robbins Self Assessment Library—This compilation teaches students to create a portfolio of skills. S.A.L. is a self-contained, interactive, library of 49 behavioral questionnaires that help students discover new ideas about themselves, their attitudes, and their personal strengths and weaknesses.

Readiness for Education at a Distance Indicator (READI)—READI is a Web-based tool that assesses the overall likelihood for online learning success. READI generates an immediate score and a diagnostic interpretation of results, including recommendations for successful participation in online courses and potential remediation sources. Please visit www.readi.info for additional information. 0-13-188967-2.

Pathway to Student Success CD-ROM, 0-13-239314-X The CD is divided into several categories, each of which focuses on a specific topic that relates to students and provides them with the context, tools and strategies to enhance their educational experience.

*"Teaching tolerance and discussing **diversity** with your students can be challenging!"*

Responding to Hate at School—Published by the Southern Poverty Law Center, the Teaching Tolerance handbook is a step-by-step, easy-to-use guide designed to help administrators, counselors, and teachers react promptly and efficiently whenever hate, bias, and prejudice strike.

*"For a terrific one-stop shop resource, use our **Student Success Supersite!**"*

Supersite—www.prenhall.com/success—Students and professors alike may use the Supersite for assessments, activities, links, and more.

*"For a truly tailored solution that fosters campus connections and increases retention, talk with us about **custom publishing**."*

Pearson Custom Publishing—We are the largest custom provider for print and media shaped to your course's needs. Please visit us at www.pearsoncustom.com to learn more.

STUDENT SUPPORT

Tools to help make the grade now, and excel in school later.

*"Today's students are more inclined than ever to use **technology** to enhance their learning."*

    Refer to the **MyStudentSuccessLab** section of this Preface to learn about our revolutionary resource that **helps students build college success and career**

development skills, and to *apply* what they learn. **MyStudentSuccessLab** (www.mystudentsuccesslab.com) offers students a self-paced, interactive, virtual lab designed to offer *application* and *practice* of their skills. By developing strategies that work best for them, students experience greater relevance, motivating them to achieve success.

"Time management is the #1 challenge students face." We can help.

Prentice Hall Planner—A basic planner that includes a monthly and daily calendar plus other materials to facilitate organization. Paperback, 8 1/2 x 11.

Premier Annual Planner—This specially designed, annual 4-color collegiate planner includes an academic planning/resources section, monthly planning section (2 pages/month), and weekly planning section (48 weeks; July start date), which facilitate short-term as well as long-term planning. Spiral bound, 6 x 9. Customization is available.

"Journaling activities promote self-discovery and self-awareness."

Student Reflection Journal—Through this vehicle, students are encouraged to track their progress and share their insights, thoughts, and concerns. Paperback, 8 1/2 x 11. 90 pages.

"Our Student Success Supersite is a one-stop shop for students to learn about career paths, self-awareness activities, cross-curricular practice opportunities, and more!"

Supersite —at www.prenhall.com/success.

"Learning to adapt to the diverse college community is essential to students' success."

10 Ways to Fight Hate —Produced by the Southern Poverty Law Center, the leading hate-crime and crime-watch organization in the United States, this guide walks students through 10 steps that they can take on their own campus or in their own neighborhood to fight hate everyday. 0-13-028146-8

"The Student Orientation Series includes short booklets on specialized topics that facilitate greater student understanding."

S.O.S. Guides help students understand what these opportunities are, how to take advantage of them, and how to learn from their peers while doing so. They include:

- Connolly: *Learning Communities,* 0-13-232243-9
- Hoffman: *Stop Procrastination Now! 10 Simple and SUCCESSFUL Steps for Student Success,* 0-13-513056-5
- Watts: *Service Learning,* 0-13-232201-3
- Jabr: *English Language Learners,* 0-13-232242-0

Introduction

What Does the Community College Student Look Like?

What is a typical community college student like? Well, a "typical" community college student is hard to find. In fact, community colleges enjoy a richly diverse student body, perhaps more diverse than in any other type of higher education institution, because their programs, services, and reputations appeal to many people at different times in their lives. To see for yourself, walk into the student center or pass by a study area, and you may overhear a similar conversation between four new friends—students who have formed a study group—about how they chose to attend a community college.

Evan, 20, tells the group that he chose a community college because of its reputation for caring faculty and rigorous core classes that will prepare him for an engineering career. He plans to complete his associate of science degree first, because he can apply for a scholarship when he transfers if he keeps his grades up. Evan also reveals that he made good grades in high school and could have attended a four-year university out of state. However, he liked what his community college had to offer and preferred sitting in a small class that offered individual attention rather than getting lost in a sea of 200 students listening to a lecture.

For Laura, 31, the community college was a logical choice because of the learning support it offers and the flexible scheduling. She shares with the group that after her youngest son started kindergarten, she enrolled in a community college, because she envisioned something better for herself and her future. Not knowing what she wanted to do, she took classes that interested her and fulfilled the requirements for an associate of arts degree. At the end of last semester, she was inspired by her teachers to pursue social work, and she now has a "thirst for knowledge." With the help of counselors and instructors and the learning support staff, she has overcome a learning difficulty and enjoys the fact that she serves as a role model to her children when she sits down to study and complete assignments.

Michael, 42, has served in the military and has a wealth of work experience and knowledge, but he has lacked a degree and a career that he feels is his life's purpose. He tells the study group that his girlfriend convinced him to check out the nursing program at the community college, because the graduates always found high-paying jobs and were known for being well prepared for jobs. Before Michael can gain acceptance into the nursing program, he has to complete a developmental math course, which is why he asked his fellow students to form a study group. Michael has learned quickly that he can be more successful if he studies with others.

Juanita, 18, is the youngest of the group, but she is the most experienced community college student at the table, because she has been taking concurrent classes through her high school for over a year. Juanita's high school counselor first told her about the program that provides college-level classes to high school students so that they can earn college credits while still in high school. As Juanita explains to the study group, she chose to take concurrent classes because she wants to earn a master's degree, and the sooner she can reach her goal, the more time she will have for a family and a career. However, she admits that it has been challenging to keep up with the demands of her classes. She is expected to read, write, and study more than she has done in her high school classes that were not taught at the college level.

These stories are representative of students who attend community colleges everywhere. Enrollments nationwide are skyrocketing, changing the face of the college graduate. Today's college students come from a wide variety of backgrounds, represent numerous ethnicities, and possess various abilities.

What do all these people have in common with you? They discovered that an education is key to realizing dreams and achieving goals. They know, as you do too, that the first step to a satisfying career and a life filled with possibilities is enrolling in college. In addition, like you, they chose to start their academic careers at a community college.

The reasons that students like you are choosing to enroll in a community college are just as diverse as the community-college population. A resounding reason, though, is that community colleges offer services, classes, and an intense level of personal attention not typically found at a four-year institution. You will see these "extras" in the types of classes and degrees offered, as well as in the personalized attention and assistance you will receive.

No doubt, you have your own story as to why you are attending a community college, but the common denominator you share with your classmates and the students profiled in this text is that you all took an important step to improving your lives through education. With guidance, determination, and hard work, you will succeed in your quest.

Why Choose a Community College?

Whatever your reason for starting your education at a community college, The College Board lists its own reasons to attend a community college, which are adapted and added to in the list below:*

You are excited about your community college. You know your community college well—it has a great reputation for academics and professional services and you want to go there. This is what attracted Michael to his community college: a strong program that will prepare him for a job.

You don't want to pay a lot for college. Historically, community colleges' costs have averaged less than four-year universities' tuition and fees, in part because their missions include providing education to people who cannot afford to go to a four-year institution.

You don't want to pay a lot when you get to a four-year institution. Many four-year colleges and universities offer generous transfer scholarships for students who earn high grades at the community college. This is what Evan wants to earn when he completes his associate of science degree, and he knows that the four-year institution of his choice will accept all of his courses at the community college because of a strong articulation agreement.

*"Six Benefits of Community Colleges." Copyright © 2008 The College Board, www.collegeboard.com. Reproduced with permission.

You took a few concurrent classes in high school and loved the experience. More and more, high school students are enrolling in community colleges before they reach 18 years of age—just as Juanita did before she started taking college classes on campus. These classes, often called concurrent or dual-enrollment classes, allow students to earn college credit before they graduate from high school. Juanita is an example of such a student.

You are not sure what degree you want or if you even want to get a degree. Community colleges are a great place to start taking classes if you are unsure of your future goals. Because community colleges offer technical, business, and industrial classes as well as a university-transfer curriculum, you have more options to choose from. You can take classes in computers, music appreciation, welding, and business communication—all in the same semester. If you decide that college is not for you, you won't have a large tuition bill looming over you.

You want to work on improving your academic skills and your grades. Community colleges are well known for their open admission policies, smaller classes (one-on-one attention), and student services. Thus, a community college is the best place to improve your reading, writing, and math abilities, because you have more contact with your instructors and the opportunity to take classes that help you refine basic skills.

You need a flexible schedule because of work and family responsibilities. Just as community colleges cater to students who need help developing their skills and students who cannot afford high-priced colleges and universities, community colleges are also more likely to offer classes that fit the busy schedule of a working student. Many community colleges offer online courses; telecourses; early-morning, evening, and weekend classes; and accelerated classes. Laura has chosen to attend the community college because the classes can be taken around her family's schedule.

Other reasons you decided to enroll in a community college may include:

- The college is near your workplace, which makes it easier to get to class and back to work.
- The school has on-site day care that is affordable and accredited.
- You know someone who went to a community college, and now she has a great job.
- You took one class for fun, such as creative writing, and now you want to take more.
- You received a scholarship to attend.
- You want a "practical" degree.
- The college is closer to home so you can spend more time with your family.
- The community college has fewer distractions, such as fraternities and sororities, so you can concentrate on academics.

The Benefits of Higher Education

Certainly, the list could continue, and you will definitely find that there are many more reasons to love your experience in college, but consider for a moment what your experience can do for you personally and professionally.

Perhaps the most important reason people enroll in college is to get a better job. No doubt, higher education can help you find career success, but there are other reasons completing a degree (or just taking a few classes) can improve your life. The more formal education you have, the more likely you are to earn more money. Earning more money allows you to provide better for yourself and your family. Education can improve your life by increasing your understanding of yourself and the world around you. The more you know and understand other people, other cultures, and yourself, the better able you are to influence your community in a positive way. Knowing more about yourself also improves your self-esteem and personal happiness. Moreover, higher education gives you the lifelong learning skills necessary for your health and well-being. Life, liberty, and the pursuit of happiness may be a cliché these days, but they are the primary results of an education.

- Going to college improves your life through a better career, more money, and better lifestyle choices, because you are more informed.
- Going to college improves your freedom to make those choices—the more you know, the better choices you make, and the more liberty you have to make those choices.
- Going to college makes you more satisfied with your life, because you feel proud of your achievements.

Why Read This Book?

After reading the reasons why over five million students are attending a community college, you may be able to add a few more. But whatever your reason, you can be sure that you made the right choice. Your community college experience will enrich your life regardless of how long you stay, what degree or certificate you complete, or where you go afterward.

The purpose of this book, then, is to help you make the most of your community college experience. In the chapters, you will find information about college life and culture, the expectations of professors, study and test-taking skills, and managing your financial and educational future. You will also discover practical information to help you prepare to transfer to a four-year college or university or enter the workforce directly.

Remember, though, that this book is only one source of assistance for you as you make your way through decisions and deadlines. You can also look to your instructors, peers, counselors, advisors, friends, and family to help you with all of the challenges of being in college while juggling work, family, and extracurricular activities.

Remember, you are not alone: More than five million other students are experiencing what you are going through—the anxiety, the uncertainty, the exhilaration, and the pride that come from starting on such an important and life-changing journey. No matter how many classes you take or what degree you finally complete, you have now taken the first step to bettering yourself by improving your education.

Reference

The College Board. (2008). Six benefits of community colleges: It might be the right path for you. Retrieved February 20, 2008, from http://www.collegeboard.com/student/csearch/where-to-start/8169.html

Read This First

Welcome to college! You have made the first step on the journey to realizing your dreams and achieving your goals. For sure, it is a time to be excited and maybe even a little nervous, but you are in good hands.

Before you begin reading the chapters in this book, take about 20 minutes to read and complete the following inventory that will help you determine how and under what conditions you best like to learn. The information you provide will be used to build an individualized learning plan that you can use throughout this course—and beyond.

To see how this works, Chapter 1 will introduce you to four students with certain learning preferences, and you will see how that information affects their unique situations and the choices they will need to make. Throughout the chapter, by completing the chapter exercises, you can explore how you and your classmates think about certain topics and reflect on your own experiences. You will also be able to answer specific questions related to learning preferences with the PLUS exercises (Personality + Learning Preference = Understanding Situation) within each chapter. Finally, at the end of each chapter, you have the opportunity to create your own story by completing the individualized learning plan so that you can move from where you are now to where you want to be.

Learning Plan Inventory

There are numerous ways to see yourself and understand your behavior in certain situations, and many education specialists and psychologists have provided theories on how we think, different inventories, and personality profiles for enhancing your understanding of yourself. Theories about the two hemispheres of our brain, known as the left brain and the right brain, have given us insight into how people think, learn, and see the world. People who have strong left-brain tendencies are more likely to be logical, to see the parts rather than the whole, and to prefer to do activities step by step. They are also more analytical, realistic, and verbal than their right-brained companions. The right-brain preference shows up in the preference to see the whole picture rather than the details, to work out of sequence, and to bring ideas together.

The Myers-Briggs Type Indicator® (MBTI®), on the other hand, is a personality test that provides you with information about how you prefer to think and act. For example, one dimension of the personality test asks you how outgoing or extroverted you are in certain situations or how reserved or introverted you are in social settings. These questions indicate whether you are Extroverted (E) or Introverted (I). There are 16 type combinations, which are explored further in Chapter 2.

Other inventories, such as both the Dunn and Dunn Learning Styles Assessment and the PEPS Learning Styles Inventory, focus not only on how a person prefers to take in information, but also on a person's social and environmental learning preferences. These types of inventories provide a thorough view of how you prefer to learn, whether it is the temperature of the room, the amount of light and sound, or the preference for moving about as you learn.

TABLE 1   Learning Plan Categories

Time of Day Preferences: morning, afternoon, night

Intake Preferences: visual, auditory, kinesthetic

Social Preferences: individual, peer(s), mentor (professor, expert, leader, etc.)

Task Management Preferences: logical/analytical, spontaneous/creative

The following inventory is adapted from the models discussed above. It will help you discover your learning style preference in four areas: task management, time of day, intake, and social learning (see Table 1). The purpose of the inventory is to provide you with a basic understanding of how you learn so that you can use that information to create an individualized and flexible learning plan for the various tasks and assignments that you will experience while you are in college.

To complete the inventory (Table 2), read each statement in each category and circle the number that corresponds most closely to how much you identify with the statement. The number 1 means the statement is least like you while the number 5 means that the statement is most like you. You will calculate your answers after the inventory.

TABLE 2   Learning Plan Inventory

Time of Day Preference

	Read each statement and circle the number on the scale that best represents you.	Scale 1 (Least like me)—5 (Most like me)				
1	I feel most energized in the morning.	1	2	3	4	5
2	My energy level soars late at night.	1	2	3	4	5
3	I get more accomplished in the afternoon.	1	2	3	4	5
4	I concentrate best before noon.	1	2	3	4	5
5	Late at night is my most productive time.	1	2	3	4	5
6	Afternoon is the best time for me to complete important tasks.	1	2	3	4	5

Intake Preference

	Read each statement and circle the number on the scale that best represents you.	Scale 1 (Least like me)—5 (Most like me)				
1	When I am trying something new, I like to "see" it in my head before doing it.	1	2	3	4	5
2	I can understand a concept best when I hear it explained.	1	2	3	4	5
3	I don't really understand something unless I do it or experience it myself.	1	2	3	4	5
4	I explain my ideas best by talking through them.	1	2	3	4	5
5	I figure out what I think about a topic by experiencing it firsthand.	1	2	3	4	5
6	I like to draw out what I'm thinking so others will understand.	1	2	3	4	5

(continued)

TABLE 2   Continued

Social Learning Preference

	Read each statement and circle the number on the scale that best represents you.	Scale 1 (Least like me)−5 (Most like me)				
1	I work best alone.	1	2	3	4	5
2	I feel comfortable asking my boss/professor questions when I'm not sure what to do.	1	2	3	4	5
3	I rely on friends or coworkers to help me complete work or figure out what to do when I am stuck on a task.	1	2	3	4	5
4	I need little interaction with others to complete a task.	1	2	3	4	5
5	I'm most comfortable working in groups on a project.	1	2	3	4	5
6	I'm most at ease working on a task that my supervisor monitors closely.	1	2	3	4	5

Task Management Preferences

	Read each statement and circle the number on the scale that best represents you.	Scale 1 (Least like me)−5 (Most like me)				
1	I enjoy thinking up and starting new projects.	1	2	3	4	5
2	It is easy for me to complete important tasks.	1	2	3	4	5
3	I like to be spontaneous when I work on a project; I go wherever the mood takes me.	1	2	3	4	5
4	I like to have a detailed schedule before I begin a project.	1	2	3	4	5
5	I like to have a general idea of the main goal and then discover what needs to be done as I work toward the goal.	1	2	3	4	5
6	I like to consider the steps to a project first before thinking about the overall picture.	1	2	3	4	5

Calculating Your Score

For each learning preference category, write the number you circled for each statement. Then, add up the numbers for each type of question. The higher numbers will indicate your preferences.

Time of Day Preference

STATEMENT	YOUR NUMBER	TYPE
1		Morning
2		Night
3		Afternoon
4		Morning
5		Night
6		Afternoon
Total Morning _____	Total Night _____	Total Afternoon _____

Intake Preference		
STATEMENT	**YOUR NUMBER**	**TYPE**
1		Visual
2		Auditory
3		Kinesthetic
4		Auditory
5		Kinesthetic
6		Visual
Total Visual _____	Total Kinesthetic _____	Total Auditory _____

Social Learning Preference		
STATEMENT	**YOUR NUMBER**	**TYPE**
1		Individual
2		Mentor
3		Peer
4		Individual
5		Mentor
6		Peer
Total Individual _____	Total Mentor _____	Total Peer _____

Task Management Preference		
STATEMENT	**YOUR NUMBER**	**TYPE**
1		Spontaneous/creative
2		Logical/analytical
3		Spontaneous/creative
4		Logical/analytical
5		Spontaneous/creative
6		Logical/analytical
Total Spontaneous/creative _____	Total Logical/analytical _____	

Your highest numbers will be where your preferences are strongest. Complete the Table 3, "My Learning Preferences." You will use this information to complete your own learning plans.

Learning Plan in Action

Table 4 shows a learning plan in action for a student who works best at night, who is both a strong visual and auditory learner, who works best with her peers, and who prefers to break down assignments into manageable parts. Once you have determined your learning style, you, too, can use the Learning Plans at the end of each chapter to create a plan for tasks that you will need to complete.

TABLE 3   My Learning Preferences

Time of Day
Intake
Social
Task Management

TABLE 4   Learning Plan Example

Learning Task: Study for biology midterm	
Time of Day	Night—after dinner
Intake	Visual and auditory—review notes and talk through them with study group
Social	Peers—biology study group
Task Management	Sequence, parts, and starter—go in order of the chapters and work with classmate who can tell me what steps I may have missed.

Final Thoughts on Learning Styles

There are many ways of viewing yourself and creating a plan of action for your work in college, but no single inventory, assessment, or work plan will reflect the exceptional person you are or your unique circumstances. The goal, then, of this learning plan is to provide you with an adaptable, flexible model for putting your learning style preference into action. It also gives you a roadmap for accomplishing the many goals that you will set for yourself. When reading this book and learning more about the characters whose stories begin each chapter, take time to reflect on how you would act in the same situation and consider how you will meet similar challenges. Reflecting on who you are and how you will get where you want to go will help you create your own story of success.

References

Dunn and Dunn Learning Styles Assessment. Learning Styles. 2008. Retrieved July 16, 2008, from http://www.learningstyles.net/

Edwards, Betty. (1999). *Drawing on the right side of the brain.* Tarcher.

Lawrence, G. (1995). *People types and tiger stripes.* 3rd ed. Gainesville, FL: CAPT.

PEPS Learning Styles Inventory. Human e-Sources. Retrieved July 16, 2008, from http://www.humanesources.com/lsi.html

The Community College Experience
PLUS

1 Understanding College Culture and Your Campus

Four Student Stories: Orientation

Passports, disposable cameras, and plastic leis are scattered all over the tables; fake palm trees rustle from the movement underneath them; and the smell of coconut fills the air in the student center. "Destination: Degree," the travel-themed orientation, is winding down after an afternoon of skits, presentations, and door prizes of pink flamingo keychains and T-shirts.

"If everyone will score their inventories, we will explain how learning style preference affects your study habits," says Jason, an orientation leader who is wearing an orange "Ask me!" T-shirt and a camera around his neck.

Dozens of students are gathered next to tables where student leaders and counselors hand out T-shirts, water bottles, and welcome packets.

"Hey, I am 'kinesthetic,' which means I learn best by using body movements. That kind of makes sense. I teach kickboxing and learned how to do it by working out almost every day," Evan tells the group.

"I thought I would be more of a social learner, but my learning style preference is individual," says Michael as he rubs his head. "I spent so much time leading troops when I was in the military."

"I am definitely 'aural,'" Laura says to the group. "I got through all my classes in high school by listening to the lectures. I rarely took notes because I liked to listen."

"Yeah, I can see that. You talked during every presentation!" Evan jokes.

Juanita, the youngest of the group, twists her mouth and wrinkles her forehead. "Will you be able to do that in college, just listen?" she asks. "I mean, I have heard that the professors expect so much more of you when it comes to being in class. Seems like there is more to do than just listen."

"I am sure you will," says Michael. "My girlfriend graduated last year with a degree in nursing, and it seems like all she did was read for class and then study her notes every night."

"Yeah, that makes sense. If anyone needs someone to study with, let me know. I am an early morning person. I took dual enrollment classes in high school and did best in my earliest classes," Juanita says.

Evan, who has been looking over his orientation information, looks up when he hears Juanita's offer. "If you want to learn a few kickboxing moves in exchange for help taking notes, let me know," Evan says to Juanita.

"Sounds good!" Juanita laughs.

With neon green note cards in her hand, Jasmine approaches the group's table. She passes cards to Laura, Michael, Evan, and Juanita. "Take these cards," Jason says, "and write down what you think will be your biggest challenge in college."

"If anyone wants to exchange a home-cooked meal for some babysitting while I study, let me know, too," says Laura, continuing the conversation. "Balancing family, a job, and college full-time," she prints on the card.

Michael writes his down: "Worried I am too old to go back to school. Can't teach an old dog new tricks." Juanita writes, "Not sure what degree or career I want," and Evan records, "Meeting new people."

As the four of them hand in their cards, they gather their backpacks and the college planners they received when they signed in for orientation.

Michael gives the group his number before they leave. "I know Laura is the talkative one, but give me a call if you ever need anything. Good luck to everyone!" he says.

In This Chapter

Evan, Laura, Michael, and Juanita will soon discover the expectations of college, and after participating in orientation, they should be well prepared to handle the changes they may encounter from their previous roles and routines: Evan has worked full-time for the past two years; Laura has been a stay-at-home mother; Michael has been in the military; and Juanita has just graduated from high school. Just as these four students have been oriented to college life, the purpose of this chapter is to introduce you to this new culture, to reveal the truths about higher education, to debunk the myths, and to prepare you for meeting the challenges that you will inevitably face. This chapter also provides you with information about what this new environment will look like and what you can expect in terms of communication between the college and you.

More specifically, at the end of this chapter you will be able to do the following:

- Describe what college will be like and what the expectations are.
- Explain the differences between high school/work and college.
- Identify key campus features and information.

What Is College Culture?

Every day, we are bombarded by offers to get something without effort and without sacrificing our precious time. We have come to value anything that is quick and easy. Unfortunately, the desire for "quick and easy" has spread from fast food and convenience items to higher education as well. Students who are strapped for time but who believe that a degree will give them the financial stability and career success they want often enroll in a community college because the programs are typically shorter than those at a four-year university—the "quick" that some students are seeking. Other students enroll in a community college because they believe that the courses are not as challenging as they would be at other schools—the "easy" those students are seeking.

The degree programs at community colleges are shorter, usually requiring one or two years, but the reality is that you may need to take more time to complete a degree program if you plan to enroll as a part-time student. Also, if you need developmental or remedial classes before you can start on the required curriculum, completion of the program will be delayed.

Community college classes and degree programs are as demanding as their equivalents at four-year universities. Because of technical and industrial standards and career licensing, many courses and programs are, in fact, very challenging. Instructors who teach in the technical, industrial, and business fields are expected to graduate students who can pass licensing exams, which means the standards in the class must be high. If the courses were "easy," then the graduates would be unemployable. Likewise, students who intend to transfer to four-year universities after they complete their general education requirements would not be successful after transfer if the courses they took at the community college were not challenging. Community colleges want well-prepared and successful graduates; thus, it is in their best interest to provide courses that require the best work from their students.

Making the Transition

High School to College or Work to College

For some students, the move from high school to college seems fairly simple—both require reading, writing, testing, and attending class. Students who are taking the step from work to school may also see some similarities between their jobs and their classroom work—both require working hard, keeping yourself motivated, and following the rules. If the differences between high school or work and college are that similar, then why do so many college students have difficulty making a successful transition?

The answer to that question can be given by the instructors who see smart, competent students have trouble adjusting to the climate and culture of college because they do not understand what is expected of them. In other words, in order to be successful, students must know what is expected of them beyond the questions on the next test; they need to know how college works and how to navigate through not only their courses, but also the common challenges that they will face as they work toward a degree or certificate.

Table 1.1 illustrates some of the differences and similarities among high school, a full-time job, and college. Notice that the greatest differences occur between high

TABLE 1.1   Differences Among High School, Full-Time Work, and College

High School	Full-Time Work	College
Attendance is mandatory in order to meet requirements	Attendance is mandatory in order to stay employed	Attendance may not be mandatory
At least 6 continuous hours spent in class each day	At least 8 continuous hours spent at work each day	Different amounts of time spent in class and between classes each day
Very little choice in what classes you take and when you take them	May have little choice in work assignments and when the work is to be completed	More flexibility in when you work on assignments and how soon you complete them before the due date
Moderate to no outside work necessary to be successful	Moderate to no overtime work necessary to complete job duties	Substantial amount of outside work to complete assignments and to be successful
Teachers check homework and keep you up-to-date on progress; they will inform you if you are not completing assignments and progressing well	Supervisors check completion and quality of work at regular intervals; they will inform you if you are not meeting the standards for the position	Professors may not check all homework or provide feedback on progress at regular intervals; they may not inform you if you are not meeting the standards of the course
Teachers go over material and expect you to remember facts and information	Employers provide basic information, expect you to use it to complete the job effectively	Professors provide concepts and theories and expect you to evaluate the ideas, synthesize the ideas with other concepts you have learned, and develop new theories
Frequent tests over small amounts of material allow for grades to be raised if needed	Supervisors create employee improvement plans to allow you to improve your ratings if needed	Professors provide the standards and grading criteria but often allow only a few chances (through infrequent testing/assignments) to meet them

school and college. There are some similarities between a full-time job and college, although there are also distinct differences.

Go for the Gold by Remembering S.I.L.V.E.R.

Making a successful transition will not only include comparing where you have just come from (home, work, or another institution of learning) to college life, but it will also involve breaking down the experience into parts that you can master. To remember what you need to start and end well, remember this simple acronym: **S.I.L.V.E.R.** This stands for Supplies, Instructors' Expectations, Learning, Vocabulary, Effort, and Responsibility.

Supplies, or "The Right Stuff." Making sure you are adequately prepared for the journey you are about to take is the first step in being successful. You wouldn't head out on a trip to unknown lands without a map, proper gear, and plenty of food and water! Think of your college supplies as part of your survival gear, too. The most important items that you will need at the beginning of the semester are required textbooks and course materials. You can find out what books and materials you will need either through the bookstore or through your professors. Usually an exact list of course materials is included in your syllabus. In high school books and course materials are provided for each student, but in college, you will be responsible for obtaining and purchasing your own materials—and you will need to do that before or at the very beginning of the semester. Trying to get by without the textbook or required calculator or software can seriously hurt your chances of success and is not recommended. If you find yourself unable to acquire or buy your materials, then you will need to talk to your instructor immediately to ask about alternative arrangements.

In addition to books and materials, you may also need access to a computer. Your professors will expect that you have a working knowledge of how to use one. If you do not have the skills needed to use a computer, then seek help from computer lab technicians, special computer classes, and classmates. Most colleges provide computer labs, email accounts, and printers for student use, but their hours may be limited; they may be crowded at busy times during the semester; and you may have to pay for the pages that you print. Thus, having the necessary computer skills as well as regular access to a computer will be integral to your success, and if you need some help honing those skills, your college may offer computer classes.

Other "right stuff" items include paper (for both note-taking and printing purposes), pens, a dictionary, a writing handbook, and a thesaurus. As you take more classes, you may need specialized reference books and supplies, such as a specialized calculator, to help you study and complete assignments. A good, sturdy backpack that allows you to carry all the books and notebooks will also be essential. Since you will not have a locker or place to store your things between classes, you will have to find a bag that holds up to the task of carrying heavy materials over a period of weeks. One other item that new students need, which is becoming more essential each year, is a portable storage device that will hold your computer files and allow you to access them at any computer. Thumb drives, also known as flash drives and pin drives, are increasingly popular because they hold a large amount of files and because they are easy to carry.

Instructors' Expectations. In addition to your supplies, knowing and meeting your instructors' expectations will make a great foundation for success. One essential expectation that instructors have is preparation—yours. You should be prepared *before* you get to class by reading the assigned pages or completing the homework. Instructors who assign reading or homework expect students to prepare—they may even administer quizzes to ensure that students have prepared—and to ask questions about anything they did not understand. Instructors may assume that if you don't ask questions or participate in a discussion, you understand the assignment. They may also hold you accountable for the assigned reading on exams even though it was not discussed in class.

Another expectation is that out-of-class assignments must be typed; in fact, unless otherwise stated, assume that all outside assignments should be word-processed, because they are easier to read and they look more professional. If you don't know how to use a word processor, now is the time to learn; relying on others to word-process your work could put you at a disadvantage. You may not be able to control when the person can complete the work, which can make you miss assignment due dates.

Instructors also expect that college students are able to access technology regularly and use it competently. What this means is that your professor will assume and expect that you have consistent access to a computer and the Internet. She will also believe that you have an email account and can send emails—even messages with attachments—successfully. If these are skills and equipment that you do not have, you will need to find out where you can access a computer on campus or off campus and make sure that you have the ability to use it properly.

One last expectation—but not the only one left—is that instructors expect you to use their office hours, the time they are scheduled to be in their offices, to meet with them if you have any questions or need anything. This is a time not only to address any concerns you may have about your progress, but it is also a wonderful time to get to know your professors better.

Collaboration

Working with a group, create a list of 10 expectations of your instructors that you have discovered so far this semester. Divide your list into expectations that you feel you can meet and those that may be challenging for you.

EXERCISE 1.1

Learning. Taking responsibility for your learning is the cornerstone for college success, and in college you will be actively involved in the learning process. Being an *active* learner means that you are no longer a passive participant in your education, listening to a lecture or reading recreationally. Instead, college classes require that you participate in your own learning by reading actively and critically (see Chapter 7), by listening actively and critically (see Chapter 8), by completing assignments, by working with other students, and by making connections among the courses you are taking and your life. Active learners also seek out more information about topics and look for ways to improve their understanding of concepts by seeking help when needed. In essence, active learners make their education a top priority.

One of the most important shifts in thinking about your learning experience in college is the various ways and places that learning and student support can take place outside the classroom. In Chapter 6, Michael will face his fear of asking for help by seeking help in the tutoring center, and as he discovers, the classroom is not the only place meaningful learning experience happens! Professors routinely direct students to learning labs, tutors, or supplemental instruction to help students bolster the learning that takes place in the classroom. Consider, then, that classroom learning is only a fraction of the time and activity that you will experience. In fact, if you follow the

Critical Thinking

EXERCISE 1.2

Tutoring and student learning support services are often provided on college campuses. Although tutors provide students with great help, students may not always think they need tutoring or may not realize they need it until it's too late in the semester. What could the college do to encourage more students to get help with their classes?

PRACTICE

model of how many hours you are in class a week and how many hours a week you should spend studying, class time is only one-fourth of the time you should be spending learning. The rest of that time, of course, will be spent preparing for class, but it can also be spent working one-on-one with a tutor or reviewing notes and studying with a group. That means that 75% of your time should be spent on activities that contribute to your learning when you are in class.

Vocabulary. With a new environment comes a new language. It won't be too long before you are talking about an AA, GPA, and FERPA all at one time. Knowing what terms mean when they are used will make communication clearer. For example, do you know what a credit hour is? It is the unit of measurement that colleges use that usually equals the amount of time you are in class each week during a 16-week semester. What about FERPA? This initialism stands for Family Educational Rights and Privacy Act, and it is important to know because it determines who can access and discuss your grades or other official records. In college, if you are age 18 and over, only you

TABLE 1.2   Common College Terms

Term	Definition
AA	Associate of Arts; a degree program that community colleges offer that consists of about 60 credit hours; usually transfers to a four-year institution as part of the core curriculum
AAS	Associate of Applied Science; a degree program that community colleges offer that consists of about 60 credit hours; usually does not contain as many core courses as an AA and is not intended for transfer, but is intended for students who will enter the workforce after graduation
Academic integrity	Doing honest work on all assignments and tests
AS	Associate of Science; a degree program that community colleges offer that consists of about 60 credit hours; usually transfers to a four-year institution as part of the core curriculum; emphasizes science courses
Core curriculum	Also called general education requirements or basic courses; the common courses that almost all students who earn a bachelor's degree complete
Credit hour	The unit of measurement that colleges use that usually equals the amount of time you are in class each week during a 16-week semester
Degree plan	A list of classes that you must complete successful in order to be awarded a degree
FAFSA	Free Application for Federal Student Aid; a form that is completed each year to determine financial aid eligibility
FERPA	Family Educational Rights and Privacy Act; Federal law that regulates the communication and dissemination of your educational records
GPA	Grade Point Average; each grade that is earned is awarded grade points that are multiplied by the number of credit hours taken; the result is the grade point average

will be the one who discusses your grades with your professor. If others, such as a spouse, parent, or employer, wants to know how you are doing, then you can allow them access to that information by letting a college official know. Table 1.2 provides just a handful of the vocabulary that you will learn in college.

Effort. Woody Allen once said, "Eighty percent of success is showing up." Definitely, in college classes, you can't be successful unless you attend regularly. College professors may not take attendance or may not make an issue of students who do not attend; however, it is still your responsibility to attend. If you are receiving financial aid through grants or loans, your attendance may be important to your continuing to receive funds in the future. Some colleges require students to pay back funds received if they fail to attend classes regularly.

Irregular attendance will not only mean missed lectures and jeopardized financial aid, but also mean missed information about assignments, tests, and grading. Especially in courses that build on concepts (such as math, foreign languages, and writing), your lack of attendance can lead to problems with successfully doing assignments and performing on tests later in the semester.

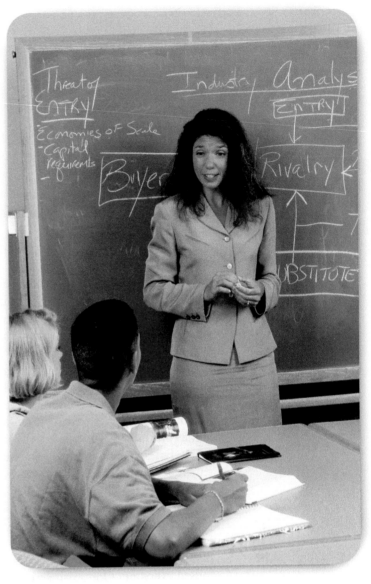

Students who are well prepared for class improve their chances of success.

If you miss a class or intend to miss a class, you should mention this to your professor. Although you may not need a doctor's excuse, you should be prepared to justify your absence, especially if you have missed an exam. Most professors, though, may not care why you were absent or may not distinguish between excused or unexcused absences. Instead, they may be more interested that you do not miss very many classes and that you keep up with the work.

Attending class is just part of the effort you will put forth; you will also need to produce quality work. Writing a paper and turning it in is only part of the requirement. You also have to adhere to the standards of the course. If your professor asks for a 10-page paper that argues a contemporary topic and uses five sources, you must follow those guidelines. In some instances, you may receive no credit for completing an assignment if you have not followed these requirements.

The more time you work to complete an assignment *usually* translates to better quality, but this is not always the case. For example, someone who types 30 words a minute will need less time to produce the same typographical-error-free assignments as someone who "hunts and pecks" at the keyboard. The quality of your work is what you will be graded on, not the number of hours you spend doing it.

Reflection

EXERCISE 1.3

Why do you think attendance is important to success in college? Besides information and assignments, what can students miss when they do not attend class regularly?

PRACTICE

Responsibility. No doubt you already juggle numerous responsibilities, and going to class and studying are just more tasks that you must complete each week. Handling your responsibilities skillfully will take a positive attitude, respect for yourself, and maturity. Laura knows how important being responsible for herself and her son is. She has had many years of relying on herself and a few family members to meet her responsibilities. Obviously, as a student she has the responsibility to take notes, study for tests, and attend classes regularly. But she also has the responsibility to ask questions when she doesn't understand or to resolve any conflict that may occur.

With responsibility also comes maturity, which is the foundation for many of the other components of college culture. Without a mature attitude and outlook, the other parts are unattainable. There are, however, less obvious actions that can help you present yourself as a dedicated, mature student. The first one is paying attention during lectures, presentations, talks by guest speakers, and videos. Although this sounds obvious, it is sometimes forgotten after the first few weeks of the semester. Chapter 4 will help you acquire skills for improving your ability to pay attention, but for now, work on looking at the front of the room and avoiding distractions. A common barrier to paying attention, besides staring out the window, is doing homework in class. Instructors frown on students who use class time to study for other classes or complete assignments that were due at the beginning of class. Just remember that the instructor sees what you are doing—that you are not paying attention—and will make note of it.

Small actions, but equally important ones, that convey maturity and readiness to meet college expectations include staying for the duration of the class, limiting off-topic conversations with classmates, refraining from eating or participating in distracting activities, and getting ready to exit class only after the instructor has dismissed everyone. One small activity that causes big problems in class is the use of cell phones, headsets, and other electronic communication devices. In some classes, such as a chemistry lab, the distraction can be dangerous. Some colleges have strict policies forbidding the use of cell phones and pagers in class. There may be exceptions, however. For example, if you work in a field that requires your immediate attention in the event of an emergency or if you have a gravely ill family member, ask if you may leave these electronic devices turned on. If your college does not have a policy, turn off your cell phone and pager in class anyway. Students who answer social calls in class appear immature and unconcerned about their education.

A more important way to demonstrate maturity in college is to understand and appreciate constructive criticism from your instructor. When you receive advice or comments about your work or progress in the course, look at it as an opportunity to learn more about yourself and the expectations of college. The instructor's job is to educate you and help you learn more about the world; it is not the instructor's job to undermine those efforts by cutting you down.

Although it is a great confidence builder, positive feedback does not necessarily challenge you to do better or indicate where you can improve. Be open to the challenge of receiving constructive criticism about the quality of your work. It takes a mature person to value constructive criticism and learn from it and a mature person to remember that your professors, counselors, and advisors want to help you be successful, so they will often set high standards that they know you can achieve.

Chapter 3 discusses diversity and relationships in depth, but it is worth mentioning here that dealing with diversity, conflict, and controversy takes a certain level of maturity. Effectively meeting any challenge to your belief system or values will demand that you act with integrity and openness. Because the purpose of getting an education is to stretch your mind and expand your ideas, you will need maturity to help you put all that new information into perspective.

The Nitty-Gritty of College

Now you know what to expect and what is expected of you in college, but understanding a few other customary practices will help you go from being a "tourist" to a "native." In other words, the following information will provide you with a better understanding of how college works beyond what happens in the classroom.

Schedules

First, it is helpful to note that colleges organize class time around semesters or terms, which can be as short as 4 weeks, usually during the summer, or as long as 16 weeks. Many colleges have at least four semesters: fall, spring, first summer term and second summer term; the summer terms are shorter than the fall and spring terms. Other colleges organize the academic calendar around 10- or 11-week terms. If you are unsure how many weeks the semester is, count the number of weeks from the first day of class until the last day of finals. You can find the information in the college catalog or in the course outline of your syllabus.

No matter how many weeks you spend taking a course, each semester classes are scheduled at different days during the week. This arrangement may differ significantly from your high school schedule. In college, you may take classes once a week, as is the case in evening or night classes, or you may take them on Mondays, Wednesdays, and Fridays or just Tuesdays and Thursdays. Usually, colleges do not offer classes on Friday nights, so if you take classes in the evening, you will take them either once a week or twice a week, Mondays through Thursdays.

Exceptions to this schedule occur during shortened terms such as summer semesters or intercession terms in which you may go every day during the week. Also, you may have a lab or special class that meets only once a week, but is tied to another class such as biology or chemistry. The best advice for new students is to read the schedule of classes carefully before registering, and as always, ask an advisor, counselor, instructor, or fellow student if you have trouble reading your schedule.

Colleges award credit hours (remember this term from earlier in the chapter?) based on how many hours a week you are in class during a regular semester (summer or intercession terms will double or quadruple the number of hours a week as compared to a regular semester). Thus, a three-credit hour class will require that you spend about three hours in class per week—some classes may last only 50 minutes three times a week. Exceptions do exist: Labs are often worth one credit hour, but they may meet for more than one hour one day a week.

Exhibit 1.1 shows a typical schedule of a full-time student. Notice the "TR" under the "Days" column; "T" stands for Tuesday and "R" stands for Thursday. Thus, the biology class meets both Tuesday and Thursday while the lab meets on Thursday only. Labs and other special classes may meet for more than one hour a

EXHIBIT 1.1   16-week class schedule

FALL 2010 (16-WEEK) SCHEDULE

COURSE ID	COURSE NAME	DAYS	TIME	CREDIT HOURS
ENGL 030	COMPOSITION FUNDAMENTALS	MWF	8:00–8:50 a.m.	3.0
BIOL 110	BIOLOGY	TR	8:00–9:15 a.m.	3.0
BIOL 112	BIOLOGY LAB	R	9:25–11:25 a.m.	1.0
MATH 034	INTERMEDIATE ALGEBRA	MWF	10:00–10:50 a.m.	3.0
COLL 101	FRESHMAN SEMINAR	TR	12:15–1:30 p.m.	3.0
TOTAL HOURS				13.0

week, but they are usually worth only one credit hour. Although the classes in this schedule meet two and a half hours each week, they are given three credit hours. Three hours is often an approximation of the time spent in class.

If the schedule in Exhibit 1.1 reflects a 16-week semester, this student will spend over 40 hours in class for the semester. During summer or intercession terms, you will spend about the same number of hours in class, but you will attend class more often and for a longer period of time.

Because Exhibit 1.2 is a schedule for a four-week term, the classes meet for more than three hours a week. In this case, students meet for 10 hours a week for 4 weeks, which will equal 40 hours or the equivalent of the total number of hours a 3-credit-hour class will meet during a 16-week term.

Controversial Content

For the most part, college will be a straightforward experience—you will learn the expectations and when you meet them, you will be successful. There are, though, other aspects of college culture that may be uncomfortable or even shocking to you. As stated above, all colleges value diversity, whether it is in the student body population or in the

EXHIBIT 1.2   4-week class schedule

SUMMER 2011 (4-WEEK) CLASS SCHEDULE

COURSE ID	COURSE NAME	DAYS	TIME	CREDIT HOURS
MATH 101	COLLEGE ALGEBRA	MTWRF	8:00–10:00 a.m.	3.0
ENGL 101	COMPOSITION I	MTWRF	10:10–12:10 p.m.	3.0
TOTAL				6.0

backgrounds of its faculty. Most definitely, you will find diversity in ideas and theories among the subjects that are offered. Some of these ideas and theories may challenge your beliefs and values. Still other subjects may contain material that you find disrespectful, offensive, distasteful, or disturbing. Besides the reading and discussing of controversial or uncomfortable issues, your college may produce student and faculty work that contains language, images, or situations that you find offensive.

What should you do if you encounter college "culture shock"? First, remember that the purpose of higher education is to provide you with a wider worldview and understanding of diversity—even if that diversity involves different ideas, theories, and methods of representing those ideas and theories. Second, remember that you have the right to an opinion and a feeling about what you encounter in college. There is no reason you should hide your feelings or attitudes about what you are learning and encountering. With this said, the third point to remember is that with your right to an opinion, you also have an obligation as a college student to examine your previously held beliefs and evaluate how they are being challenged in your courses or as you participate in college activities. You also have the obligation to appreciate that there is more than one way to view an "offensive" idea or image. Exhibit 1.3 provides a list of possible subjects that could be controversial to you or other students.

Grades

What is a discussion about college expectations without mentioning grades? For sure, grades are an important part of your education, and at the same time they are unimportant. How can something be both important and unimportant? Grades are important because they often reflect your level of achievement on an assignment or in a course; they are also important for obtaining and maintaining scholarships and financial aid. Additionally, grades are important to family, friends, and employers who may

---

EXHIBIT 1.3   A sample of possible controversial subjects

The existence of God, higher being

Conservatism and liberalism

Nudity in art, photography

Sexuality, including homosexuality and adultery

The creation of the universe

The theory of extraterrestrial life

Evolution

The beginning of life

Scientific investigation and experimentation (stem cells, cloning)

Socioeconomic theory

be supporting you financially and emotionally. Many people view grades as a reflection of a level of success. For instance, most of the people you ask would view a student who has straight A's as someone who is smart and successful. Earning good grades can motivate you to do your best and give you more confidence as you earn them.

Although good grades feel great when you earn them, grades are not always an indication of your success or lack of success in mastering a subject. James M. Banner, Jr. and Harold C. Cannon (1999), in their book *The Elements of Learning*, define grades as the following: "Grades are evaluations of your work, not of your character or intelligence. You may be a wonderful person but a failure as a biologist. You may find it impossible to do satisfactory work in history but may excel in all other subjects" (p. 160). Banner and Cannon assert, therefore, that grades have limitations. They are a necessary part of evaluation, much as you are evaluated on your job. However, as Banner and Cannon point out, grades do not show the whole picture of who you are. Grades, then, are only part of the story of your education.

If grades only sometimes indicate a level of success in a course and sometimes not, what are you to do? How will you know when to worry about your grades and when to concentrate on learning the material? The purpose of this chapter is to help you answer these questions for yourself by explaining how professors grade and how you can make good grades in college. The chapter also discusses what you can do to de-emphasize making a good grade and increase your attention on mastering the material of the course. This is not to say, however, that grades are never important. They are important because they are a way to describe the work you have done in a class. However, grades alone are not the magic carpet to success in college; they are only part of the story of your achievements. Your goal should be to strike a balance between caring about your grades and caring about improving your skills and increasing your knowledge.

As stated earlier, college professors grade a student on his or her ability to meet the standards of the course or of a particular assignment. Effort is definitely a necessary part of earning good grades—and you will earn the respect of your professor and fellow students by demonstrating an intense effort to master the concepts of a class—but it is only one part of achieving success in a course. College professors expect that you also meet the standards, sometimes called grading criteria, of the course. Exhibit 1.4 shows a potential set of criteria for a college-level paper. In this case, the criteria are for an A paper.

EXHIBIT 1.4   Grading criteria for an A paper

- An excellent introduction with engaging hooks, setup, plan for essay, and/or main idea
- An original, significant thesis that offers insightful interpretation or thought
- An inventive and logical organizational plan
- Smooth and varied transitional expressions, phrases, and sentences that provide unity and coherence
- Strong conclusion that ends the essay effectively
- Expressive, clear style with sophisticated sentence structure and word choice
- No more than three major grammatical errors

Knowing how your college assesses student performance is a start to improving your overall outlook on grading. The following is a typical grading scale in college:

90–100   A
80–89   B
70–79   C
60–69   D
50–59   F

Some colleges may use a + or − next to a letter grade such as A− or C+. Usually, colleges that allow for +'s and −'s will also alter the grading scale to designate the different grades. Here is an example of a grading scale that includes +'s and −'s:

94–100   A
90–93   A−
87–89   B+
84–86   B
83–80   B−

Each semester, the registrar will calculate your grade point average, or GPA, and post it to your transcript. Because the calculation of your GPA requires a little mathematical skill, it is important to know how your registrar figures it. Hours are the number of hours you are in class each week. As discussed above, classes are usually three-credit hours. Science or specialized classes that have labs usually carry four-credit hours. Depending on the course and the program, credit hours can be as many as six or as few as one. To know how many hours a course carries, check the description in the college catalog, because some classes meet for more hours a week than they are worth in terms of credit.

Letter grades carry a point value called quality points. Exhibit 1.5 shows how many quality points each letter grade is worth.

Courses that are designated developmental or remedial usually do not figure into your grade point average, so they do not carry any quality points. If you audit a course or receive AP or CLEP credit for a course, you will not receive quality points either. In other words, while you receive credit on your transcript for taking the course or taking an equivalent of the course, the course will not factor into your

EXHIBIT 1.5   Grades and quality points

LETTER GRADE	QUALITY POINTS
A	4
B	3
C	2
D	1
F	0

EXHIBIT 1.6   GPA calculation table

HOURS	GRADE (QUALITY POINTS)	HOURS × GRADE (QUALITY POINTS)
3	A (4)	3 × 4 = 12
3	B (3)	3 × 3 = 9
3	C (2)	3 × 2 = 6
3	C (2)	3 × 2 = 6
3	C (2)	3 × 2 = 6
15 Hours		**39 Grade Points**

grade point average. Before you figure your GPA, you will need to figure your grade points for each class. You arrive at your grade points by multiplying the quality points for the grade you received by the number of hours the class is worth. For instance, if you took a four-hour class and you made a B, then you will multiply 4 (hours) by 3 (quality points for a B).

Evan is taking 15 hours (5 three-hour courses) this semester; if he receives an A, B, and three C's, then his grade would be calculated as shown in Exhibit 1.6. Finally, divide the grade points total by the hours total (39/15). Evan's GPA would be 2.6.

What Does Your College Look Like?

Now that you have a better understanding of college culture and what is expected of you, it is time to examine how your college looks. Getting to know the layout of the campus and the people who work there is important to understanding the culture. For example, knowing where to go when you need to use a computer will make your ability to complete an assignment a little easier. Finding your professor's office may save you time and stress when you need to talk to him about an upcoming test. Of course, the more you are on campus, the better able you will be to find people and places that will help you no matter what you need.

The Campus

Find a map of your campus and study it for a few minutes. How many buildings does it have? How much parking space? How much "green" space or landscaping? Are there any unique features to your campus that make it an inviting and exciting place? Familiarizing yourself with your campus is probably the first activity you did when you enrolled in classes. If you have not taken a tour or simply walked around the campus, do so within the first few weeks of the semester. Locate the library, the student center, student parking, the bookstore, the business office, and the registrar's office—just to name a few destinations.

TABLE 1.3 Campus Layout Checklist

Building or Area	At My College	Not Sure
Student center or union		
Library		
Bookstore		
Administration building		
Theater or auditorium		
Snack bar or food court		
Athletic training facilities (indoor or outdoor)		
Science labs		
Technical and industrial training facilities		
Computer labs		
Separate divisions (such as technical and industrial, computer information systems, allied health, business, general education)		
Individual departments (such as accounting, drafting, welding, natural sciences)		
Student parking		
Benches and tables for meeting outside		
Quiet study space inside		

The more you know about your campus's layout, the easier it will be to find what you are looking for when you need it most. Using your map of the campus or your memory, check off in Table 1.3 the types of buildings or departments within buildings that you know are present at your college.

If your college has more than one campus, familiarize yourself with the layout of other college property. You may have to travel to a satellite campus to take a test or to pick up materials for a class. If you have the time and the other campus is not too far away, ask for a tour. At the very least, familiarize yourself with any of the items you marked "not sure" in Table 1.3.

College Publications

Knowing where to go to find services and people is only part of learning about your college. Another important aspect is finding and using the information that the college produces for students. College publications are a great place to find information about courses, programs, scholarships, activities, and policy changes. It is important that you regularly read these publications in order to stay up-to-date with what is going on.

Collaboration

Working with a group, determine what information you have already received that will help you navigate college more smoothly. As a group, organize the different sources of information by type. For example, what information have you received from email or the Internet? What information have you received from an advisor? Finally, determine which kinds of information are most useful to you and why.

EXERCISE 1.4

College Catalog

The college catalog is an essential document during your academic career. All the information that you need to apply for financial aid, to choose courses, and to graduate is contained in the catalog. You will also find out what you are required to do to complete a degree. The academic calendar is usually placed at the beginning of the catalog. There you will find the dates for registering, dropping courses, and taking final exams.

It is important to read and keep your college catalog because if the college changes any requirements of your degree program, you will be able to follow the guidelines that were published the year you began the program. For instance, if you are working on an office management degree and you have taken three semesters of courses so far, you will not necessarily have to adhere to new requirements that are made at a later date.

Student Handbook

The student handbook, which provides you with specific information about student conduct, academic standards, and services, is another valuable publication. Usually, the handbook contains descriptions of career services, the bookstore, computer labs, and financial aid offices. Academic information including probation and suspension for misconduct and qualifications for making the dean's list can also be found in the student handbook. Most schools view the student handbook as a legal document that outlines what students can do in certain situations, so be sure to read it closely and keep a copy at home or in your book bag.

Campus Safety Brochure

A smaller, but no less important, document that your college publishes is the campus safety and security brochure; in some cases, your college may publish this information on the website instead of printing the material. Whatever the form, this information can include policies on handling sexual assault, substance and drug abuse, and harassment. Also, you can find contact numbers for campus police as well as crime statistics for the campus.

College Newspaper

College newspapers differ from the college catalog and student handbook in that students are usually the ones who are responsible for the content. Within a college

INTEGRITY MATTERS

The student handbook usually contains the college's academic integrity policy, a policy that covers any act that shortcuts the learning process and calls into question a student's integrity as it relates to academic matters. If you are not familiar with academic integrity policies, be sure to read your college's policy about student cheating and plagiarism.

newspaper, you will find articles about upcoming events; reports on changes on the college campus; editorials on important student issues; profiles of programs; and advertisements for used books, performances by musical groups, and anything else that students want to announce. The college newspaper is also a forum to explore controversial topics and to discuss sensitive issues.

Newspapers always need students to interview, write, edit, and publish. If you are interested in working for the newspaper, contact the editor or visit a journalism or composition professor.

Bulletin Boards

Even with the increased use of the Internet, the bulletin board is still an important way to get a message to students. Found all over campus, bulletin boards usually advertise used books, needs for roommates and part-time jobs, and upcoming campus events. Bulletin boards within academic buildings often announce four-year university programs, summer workshops, and other types of academic activities.

Classroom Materials

Anything that professors hand out in class is a communication tool. The syllabus is one of the most important documents that you will receive in class, so be sure to read it carefully. In the syllabus you will usually find the following information:

- Instructor's name, office location, phone number, hours open to students, and email address
- Prerequisites for the course
- Course description from the catalog
- Textbook information
- Course objectives, or what you will accomplish by the time you finish the class
- Course content, or what topics will be covered throughout the semester
- Assignments and due dates
- Grading criteria
- Attendance and late-work policies
- Academic integrity statement (which also appears in the student handbook)
- Disability accommodations policy
- General policies for classroom conduct

The syllabus is considered a contract between the student and the instructor. This means that not only will the syllabus contain what is expected of you during class, but it will also contain what you can expect from the instructor. Both of you—the student and the instructor—will be bound by what is stated in the document. Reading the syllabus closely and following it regularly will keep you on top of the policies, expectations, and assignments.

Other essential information that is handed out in class includes directions to assignments, photocopied readings, study questions, and notes. Regard anything that is given to you by the instructor as important, even if you are told "This won't be on the test."

You should also consider the grades and written comments you receive as communication from your instructors. Be sure to read any comments or suggestions that are written on papers and exams, ask questions if you don't understand them or they are illegible, and save all feedback until the semester is over.

College Website

The college's website is where you can find the most current information about classes, academic programs, and contact information for professors. It is easier to update information on a website because it doesn't involve printing and distribution, so it is more likely to provide the most accurate information. College websites usually list phone numbers and email addresses of professors and deans, which makes contacting them easier.

In addition to general information about degrees and departments, your college's website may give you access to professors' syllabi and assignments. This provides a good opportunity to investigate what courses you want to take based on the course objectives and assignments.

PLUS

EXERCISE 1.5

(Personality + Learning Style = Understanding Situations)

Let's consider Laura's challenge in college: balancing work, family, and college. As she confirms in orientation, she is an aural learner. From what you have learned from Chapter 1, what should Laura know about transitioning to college full-time that will help ease her mind? What resources could help her be successful?

Now, considering your own learning style, personality type, and special circumstances, what will you do to make the transition to college easier? What have you learned from the chapter that will make the transition smooth for you?

PROFILE

MY STORY
Learning Plan

Directions: Using what you have learned in this chapter and what you know about your learning preferences, choose a task or assignment that needs to be completed soon and create a learning plan that will help you accomplish this task. Then, write your *My Story* Summary, a one-sentence synopsis that crystallizes your newly created plan.

LEARNING TASK	
Time of Day	
Intake Preference	
Social Preference	
Task Management Preference	

MY STORY SUMMARY:

Path of Discovery

Journal Entry

What is your experience so far with college culture?
What has been the biggest difference you have experienced
so far between high school or work and college?

HOMEWORK

From College to University

The Changes in Culture and College Services

If you are moving from your community college to a larger, more diverse university, you may experience a slight culture shock despite the semesters you already have under your belt. In addition to a bigger campus with more buildings to find and more students to meet, you may find that a university seems more impersonal. Many students who transfer from a smaller community college complain that professors do not seem to care about them personally and that they lack the support and guidance they received at their other school. Transfer students also note that expectations are higher—and their grades are lower—especially as they move into their majors and begin working toward a career.

Culturally, you should expect that your new university will offer more activities and groups than your smaller community college. You also should expect some kind of adjustment period as you get used to what your new professors expect of you. Statistically, transfer students do experience a slight drop in their GPA. This drop, however, is not necessarily an indication that they were not properly prepared for transfer by their community college.

All in all, the culture shock you experience when transferring to a four-year university will depend on how much bigger and how much more different the school is from your community college. Just remember that whatever differences you notice, there are people at the four-year school who can help you deal with the adjustment. Seek out counselors, advisors, faculty, and students to help make your transition smoother. Your campus map and list of faculty and administrators will point you in the right direction.

From College to Career

How the Culture Will Change Again

Just as you had to adjust to college culture, you will have to make a new adjustment to the workforce if you have never held a full-time job. When starting your first job out of college, you will experience a period of getting used to the way the office or business works. You will encounter new terms, new methods of doing things, and new people. In addition, you will experience working in groups or teams to accomplish tasks, and you will be expected to communicate orally and in a written format. You may also rely more heavily on electronic mail and computers to do your work. Certainly, integrity will be an important part of your working experience. There will be less supervision and more expectation that you do the work you say you will do.

Paying attention to how others act on the job can alleviate any anxiety that you may feel. Just as you made friends and found mentors in college, you should look for others who can offer guidance and help as you learn the ropes of a new career. Also, think about how you adjusted to college and use the same strategies to make your new working environment seem less foreign and more comfortable.

Chapter Review Questions

QUICK REVIEW

1. What differences exist between high school and college or a full-time job and college?

2. Name and explain five different characteristics that professors will expect from you as a college student.

3. How and why do colleges grade?

4. What types of documents and communication can you expect in college? What are their purposes?

Chapter 1 Case Scenarios

CASE STUDY

1. In Jennifer's literature class, she is reading Tim O'Brien's *The Things They Carried.* Although she understands that the book is about the Vietnam War, she doesn't know why she has to read a book that contains so much profanity and graphic images of death. She has made an appointment to speak to her professor about the reading assignment because she wants to get out of reading a book that is so depressing and discomforting. What advice would you give Jennifer before she speaks to her professor? Predict what the outcome of the talk will be and what the consequence of the discussion will be on Jennifer's college career.

2. Ja-Ling is taking a biology class. One of her assignments is to create a group presentation on an assigned topic. Her group's topic is the theory of evolution, a theory that Ja-Ling finds fascinating; however, when she meets with her group to prepare for the presentation, two of her group members express deep concern that they are being asked to study something that they don't believe in. They refuse to help with the project even though they know their lack of participation will lower the whole group's grade. What should Ja-Ling do?

Research It Further

RESEARCH

1. Find the University of South Carolina's (USC's) Carolinian Creed on the Internet. Try the website www.sa.sc.edu/CREED/. Using USC's creed as a basis, write your own creed that would fit your college's values. Is there anything that you would revise or add to USC's creed?

2. Find a map of your college and determine what building or landmark is the geographical center of the campus. Then, write a short paper on how that building is an appropriate "center" of your college. Questions you may want to consider include the following: What does the building house—a library? A classroom for the engineering department? A student center? What does the building symbolize? If you were to design a display or piece of art that reflects the "center" of the college, what would it look like?

3. Interview a college employee about his or her job and how it fits into the college's structure. Present the information about the person and the job to your class.

Reference

Banner, J. M., & Cannon, H. C. (1999). *The elements of learning.* New Haven, CT: Yale University Press.

2 Understanding Yourself and How You Learn

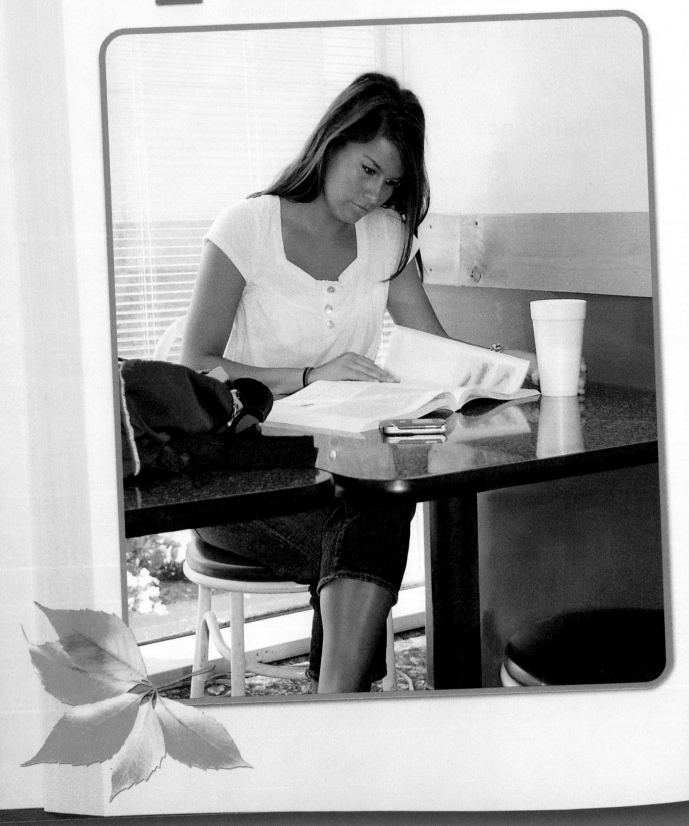

Juanita's Story

Juanita calls her mother for the second time in two hours. She often finds her mother's voice and advice exactly what she needs to hear after a day of dissections, citations, and continental drift. Her break between classes usually gives her enough time to check in on her cell phone. "Call me," she texts to her mother's cell number. Juanita's mother responds immediately to the message by calling her.

"Juanita," her mother says with a softness in her voice that indicates she is tired, "what do you expect at the beginning of the semester? It'll take time to get used to your new instructors and your classmates. It's not high school."

Juanita doesn't know if her schedule is right for her. The classes seem different from the dual enrollment classes she took in high school; even though the expectations and workload are the same, the different students—all different ages—are something for her to get used to. Only a few of her friends are attending with her, and she never gets to see them because they are taking classes at different times and in different buildings. The only time she "sees" them is on their websites where she can view their latest pictures.

"Yeah, but I didn't have to make a life decision in high school. I just signed up for a degree plan," she replies, biting her nails.

"Electrical engineering, just like we talked about, right?" her mother asks.

"Well, I wanted to talk to you about that. My biology professor talked to me about respiratory therapy. She said I could make a really good salary right after I graduate," Juanita says.

"But you don't like working with people who are sick, Juanita. Don't you want to build things instead? You were always building things in the backyard, growing up," her mother replies.

Juanita feels the conversation going in the same direction it always does, and she moves from biting her nails to chewing her cuticles.

"Juanita, you need to make a decision now. You need to get through as soon as you can and get a job. If not, I don't know if I can support you for much longer," says her mother.

Her mother's words make her stomach harden because Juanita knows that her father will not be able to work for long and her mother will have to care for him. When that happens, there may not be enough money for her to stay in college. Because of the classes she has taken in her high school's dual enrollment program, Juanita could graduate with an associate's degree next year, but if she doesn't get a scholarship to continue her education, she may not be able to transfer to a four-year university.

"We can't afford mistakes, Juanita," says her mother. "I will be proud of you whatever you decide, but make a choice and stick with it."

Juanita knows her mother is right. She has a goal of getting a degree—and nothing will keep her from that—but she is not sure how to make the right decisions between today and the day she graduates.

Before she decides between the grilled chicken sandwich or the veggie burger, chips or fries, and a diet drink or fruit punch, Juanita tells her mother good-bye and promises to pick up a prescription on her way home. She resolves to think about what she should do after she makes an appointment with her advisor.

In This Chapter

This chapter helps you answer questions that you may have right now:

- What can I gain from college? How will I understand myself better?
- What are mission statements, goals, and values?
- Why is goal setting so important?
- What are learning style preferences and how will understanding my own help me be successful in college?

Who Are You?

The question "Who are you?" sounds easy to answer. You may start by listing a variety of characteristics. For example, you are a male, age 25, married, father of a son, an electrician, and a Native American. Or, you are a single female, age 19, part-time sales assistant, full-time student, and mountain climber. But what are you beyond those labels? Where have you been? What are you doing now? Where are you going and where do you want to be? Now the questions get a little more difficult and take more time and thought to answer. The point is that you need to have some idea of who you are, or at least an idea of where you want to be, when you begin college.

Maybe you can say that you don't know who you are yet, but you hope that enrolling in classes and pursuing a degree will help you come to a better understanding of who you are. Don't worry, though, if you cannot immediately articulate the essence of you. This question—"Who are you?"—and the possible answers have been intriguing human beings for thousands of years. In his book *Who Are You? 101 Ways of Seeing Yourself* (2000), Malcolm Godwin explores the ways that we have tried to answer this question. From body types to ancient Indian mysticism to workplace dynamics, there are numerous ways you can learn more about what and how you think. The ultimate goal is to know yourself and your environment well enough to reach your goals.

Of course, who you are will change, maybe dramatically, as you take classes, encounter new subjects, and research interesting topics. But taking the time now to think and reflect about yourself will help you map your course throughout your community college experience and beyond—from returning to work, to raising a family, to attending another college, to having a fulfilling career. This chapter assists you in understanding who you are by helping you identify what you know and how you learn. This chapter also aids in your decisions about who and what you want to be while helping you make the transition into college.

What Do You Value?

Values are part of your belief system and are what make you unique. Values can be inherited from your parents, or they can come from what your culture, religion, or ethnicity regard as important. Values can also be formed from both positive and negative experiences. For example, a value of yours may be honesty, which means that you try to be truthful and straightforward in most situations and that you expect others to be honest with you. If you value hard work, then you strive to do

FIGURE 2.1   Values to Priorities Flowchart

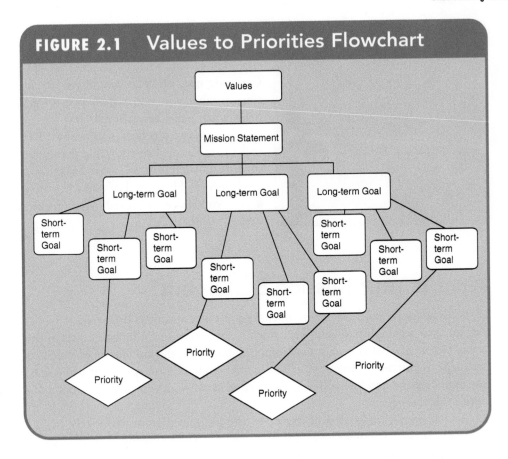

your best in your life. If a friend has treated you with compassion, you may value sensitivity to others. On the other hand, if you have been discriminated against in the past, you may now value open-mindedness in others. Figure 2.1 shows how your values influence goals, both long-term and short-term, as well as priorities. As you read the rest of the chapter, refer to Figure 2.1 to see how it all fits together.

The importance of knowing and understanding your values is that this knowledge can help you set realistic goals. If you value a satisfying career, for instance, you will set goals that support that value. Therefore, you will probably investigate careers and fields that are challenging and interesting. If you value a stable financial future, you will set goals that enable you to earn enough money to provide for your needs and wants. If you value your family, you will make spending time with them a priority. Your values should be a true reflection of who *you* are and what *you* believe.

Think about Juanita's conversation with her mother. Her mother wants Juanita to consider electrical engineering, perhaps because she values financial stability and success or career prestige. What if one reason Juanita hesitates at choosing a major and career path is that she values meeting new people and traveling? What if she also wants to learn more about ancient cultures? If she decides to adopt her mother's values and ignore her own, what kind of future can you envision for her? Although her mother's intentions may be well meaning, Juanita will have to compromise herself in order to meet her parents' goals for her, and she will probably suffer some regret in the future.

EXERCISE 2.1

Reflection

How have your values changed over the years? Compare what you valued 10 years ago with what you value now and discuss why that change has occurred.

PRACTICE

Does this example mean that you should ignore others who have helped you figure out what you want to be? Certainly not. But you should pay attention to what you want when you do get help with your educational and career goals. Be open to others' suggestions, but make sure you feel comfortable with your final decision. Those who truly want you to succeed will be proud of you when they know you have achieved your heart's desire, not theirs.

What Is Your Mission Statement?

Mission statements are declarations of what people or institutions believe in and what they hope to accomplish. Mission statements, then, are usually broad strokes of the overall picture of what you want to accomplish. Values are the foundation of a mission statement. If you are unsure of your values, then your mission statement will not be easy to understand and follow. Thus, you need to know what you value before you can write a mission statement.

As you meet your goals and learn new things, your mission will likely change and your mission statement will need to be revised. The following is an example of a mission statement that you can use as a model for writing your own.

Sample Personal Mission Statement

My mission is to have a fulfilling personal and professional life that allows me to meet new people, take on new challenges, and have flexibility in my schedule. As a mother and wife, I want to have a close relationship with my family, acting both as a caregiver and as a role model. As a teacher, I will be dedicated to providing students with the best education that will prepare them for a four-year university curriculum as well as for the demands of the world of work.

Discovering Your Dream

As you consider your goals, you will also want to think about your dreams. What do you want to do that you have not written down because you feel it is too far-fetched? There are many stories of people who denied their dreams and took jobs that provided them with financial security and prestige, only to discover that their lives were not fulfilled because those were not their values.

Why don't more people follow their dreams? First, they may not know what they are. Second, these same people may be scared. Following what one's heart wants often contradicts what one's head is saying. Third, some people need to make the "safe" choice first before they feel confident that they can fulfill their dreams. In other words, they may need to take a job that pays well so that they can save money to fulfill their dreams at a later date.

Although you may not be able to drop everything right now and follow your heart, you should at least start thinking about what you really want to do with your life as you plan your college degree.

What Are Your Goals?

To fulfill your mission in life, you will need to have a plan. Setting goals and achieving them will put you on the path to fulfilling that mission. If you are not used to writing down tasks for the day or voicing your plans for the future, you will need to start working on making lists and talking about what you want to be and do.

From your list of values and your mission statement, you will be able to formulate goals that support both what you believe in and what you want for yourself. The fact that you are reading this book is evidence that you are someone who has set a goal and is working toward achieving it. Also, the fact that you are in college says that you value education as a means of improving your life. You may have overcome many obstacles to get where you are today. You may have faced pressure from your family and friends to join the workforce upon graduating from high school rather than go to college, or you may have gotten negative feedback from others when you decided to stop working, or stop working as much, to get a degree.

Nonetheless, realize that setting and achieving goals is not as easy as writing them down and crossing them off. You will encounter obstacles, some of which may threaten to knock you off course. Flexibility and determination are the keys to achieving your goals despite setbacks.

Setting Goals

Even with the most supportive friends and family, you still need some well-defined goals to give you direction as you chart your course in college. A goal is something that you work toward—it may be to learn how to cook macaroni and cheese, to quit a bad habit, or to write a novel. Whatever your goals, they should be reasonable and attainable in the time frame that you have assigned. For instance, if you want to lose 10 pounds in one week, you may need to rethink the time in which you would like to achieve your goal. A more reasonable goal would be to lose 10 pounds in four months. Reasonable goals are more likely to be met.

As you begin to think about your goals, consider dividing them into long-term goals and short-term goals. Certainly, one of your long-term goals is to earn a degree. This goal may take one year or more, depending on how many degree requirements you need to complete or how many other responsibilities you may have. A short-term goal that would contribute to your achieving the long-term goal of earning a degree could be to complete your classes successfully, to study for an exam, or to work on a research paper.

When you make a list of your goals, consider the following guidelines:

- Make your goals attainable and reasonable.
- Break larger goals into smaller goals that will lead to fulfillment.
- Think of setting goals in these time frames: 1 week, 1 month, 1 semester, 1 year, 5 years, 10 years.

Take time to reflect on your goals and write them down.

Regularly review your goals and make changes as necessary.

Because it is difficult to plan 10 years into the future, make a list of goals that are tied to the near future. For instance, if you want to own your own business in the next 10 years, think about structuring your short-term and long-term goals this way:

LONG-TERM GOAL (10 YEARS)

* Run a successful landscape design firm.
* Provide landscaping for low-income properties.

LONG-TERM GOAL (5 YEARS)

* Work for a landscape design firm.
* Continue community service and encourage coworkers to participate.

LONG-TERM GOAL (3 YEARS)

* Complete my associate's degree in landscape design and management.
* Continue community service work.

SHORT-TERM GOAL (9 MONTHS)

* Complete two semesters of landscape design classes.
* Continue working at the garden center.
* Plant and maintain my own flower and vegetable garden.
* Participate in a community service project that landscapes low-income properties.

SHORT-TERM GOAL (1 SEMESTER)

* Complete the classes that will count toward my degree.
* Look for a community service project that landscapes low-income properties.

SHORT-TERM GOAL (1 MONTH)

* Help a friend plant new trees.
* Attend a local lecture on seasonal planting.
* Begin research for a final paper on plant diseases.

SHORT-TERM GOAL (1 WEEK)

* Study for my classes.
* Apply for a job at a garden center.

- Weed and fertilize the backyard.
- Take a hike in the park.

No matter what you want to achieve, be sure that you write down all your goals and review them every few months to assess your progress. Henriette Anne Klauser has made a career of helping people write down their dreams and goals so that they can finally realize them. In her book *Write It Down, Make It Happen: Knowing What You Want and Getting It!* (2001), Klauser states, "Writing down your dreams and aspirations is like hanging up a sign that says 'Open for Business.' . . . Putting it on paper alerts the part in your brain known as the reticular activating system to join you in the play" (p. 33). In other words, the process of writing down your goals tells your brain to start paying attention to your ambitions and makes you aware of opportunities to achieve them.

Managing Your Goals

You will see this suggestion throughout this book: To accomplish anything, set goals by writing them down. Even something as simple as spending two hours preparing for class should be written down as a goal for the day or week. Goals must be manageable, however. Too many goals and you could become overwhelmed at the thought of meeting them all, or you may feel like a failure for not accomplishing everything. Avoid the temptation to overschedule and be realistic about how long it will take to complete your goals for the day or week. Too few goals and you will likely feel like a rudderless ship, easily veering off course.

Once you have written down your goals, communicate them to your coworkers, family, and friends. Enlist them to help you meet your goals, especially if you need to schedule time to study and complete assignments. For example, tell them that you must have the evenings free of distractions, or make arrangements with them to have a weekend or weekday to yourself to study. Don't assume that because they *know* you are in school they will also *know* you need extra time and personal space to get your work finished. Managing your time will be much easier if your priorities and goals are concrete, realistic, and communicated to those around you.

Eliminating Negative Influences as You Work Toward Your Goals

As you work toward your goals, make an effort to eliminate anything that keeps you from focusing on them. If you think you don't have time to accomplish two short-term goals during the week, examine where you have been spending your time and eliminate the activities that do not contribute to your goals or that do not reflect your values.

If you watch seven hours of television a week, and you aren't achieving the sought-after short-term goal of becoming more informed or of relaxing, then spend that time doing something that does contribute to your goal. In addition to meaningless activities, anything that distracts you and is unnecessary in your life should be eliminated, including a habit that is destructive or dangerous, such as taking drugs.

TABLE 2.1   Activities That Contribute to or Distract from Your Goals

Activities That Contribute to Your Goals	Activities That May Distract You from Your Goals
Practicing car maintenance allows you to get to school and work safely.	Excessive socializing depletes the time and energy you have to focus on your goals.
Exercising allows you to remain healthy and reduce stress.	Mindlessly watching TV may not contribute to learning.
Eating and sleeping will keep you healthy and reduce stress regularly.	Using drugs and alcohol keeps you from focusing on goals and is dangerous.
Reading the newspaper keeps you informed, helps improve reading skills, and contributes to learning.	Sleeping and eating irregularly creates stress, which inhibits the ability to reach goals.

Collaboration

Working within a group, create your own list of activities that may distract you from reaching your goals. Then, as a group determine what can be done to eliminate these activities or to turn them into more productive pursuits. For example, watching TV can become an activity that supports a goal by limiting what and how much is watched.

EXERCISE 2.2

If you are unsure whether your activities contribute to your goals, take a few minutes to list what you have done this week and determine how each activity has supported or not supported one of your goals. Table 2.1 gives some examples.

Another type of negative influence that can affect your ability to achieve your goals is a pessimistic friend or family member. If you have someone in your life who belittles your efforts to go back to school and earn a degree, try to limit your time with that person or try to focus on conversation topics that are not related to you. Reducing the negative effect that disapproving people have on you may not be easy, but understand that you do have control over how they make you feel.

Lillian Glass, Ph.D., in her book *Toxic People: 10 Ways of Dealing with People Who Make Your Life Miserable* (1997), recommends limiting contact with people who make you feel hurt, stressed, dumb, or unworthy. Dr. Glass refers to people who stand in your way of being your best as "toxic" because they "are hazardous to others'

INTEGRITY MATTERS

One definition of integrity is to do what is right even in the face of adversity. Sometimes, life is difficult when other people do not want you to do what is right, especially if that means obtaining a college degree. To maintain your own personal integrity, you may have to make some tough choices about whom you hang out with and what messages you listen to. It is not always easy, but living with personal integrity, doing what is right for you despite challenges, will pay off in the long run with a more satisfying life.

mental, emotional, and physical health" (p. 12). Dealing with toxic people will reduce the time and energy you have to work on your goals and to benefit from the positive influence of those who support you.

Managing Your Priorities

A discussion of values and goals cannot be complete without also talking about priorities. Simply stated, a priority is something that is important at the moment. Today your top priority could be studying for an exam, but later in the day, it could be taking care of a sick child, which means that studying will have to come second if at all. Priorities, by their very nature, can change weekly, if not daily or even hourly.

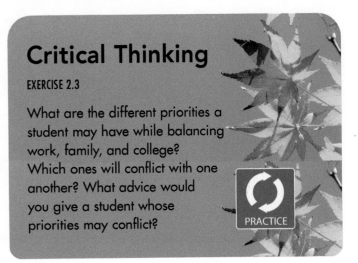

Critical Thinking

EXERCISE 2.3

What are the different priorities a student may have while balancing work, family, and college? Which ones will conflict with one another? What advice would you give a student whose priorities may conflict?

PRACTICE

Your actions also reflect your priorities. If you say that your first priority is to pass your classes this semester but you spend all your spare time playing basketball with friends, then your social life as well as a little exercise is really your top priority. You must make sure you know what your priorities are and take action to satisfy them. You may also need to express to others what your priorities are so that they can help you stick to them.

Staying Motivated to Achieve Your Goals

One of the hardest parts of setting goals is maintaining the momentum to achieve them. There will be times in your academic career when you will feel overwhelmed by the responsibilities you have, and you will feel unsure of your ability to handle it all. When you feel weighed down by all that you have to accomplish for a particular week or day, try to calm down first. If you can, talk with a friend, an instructor, or a counselor and explain your frustration and stress. Sometimes, if an instructor knows you are feeling overwhelmed by expectations in a course, he or she will assist you by giving you more time to complete an assignment. A friend may also volunteer to help by studying with you.

To stay motivated and to resist the temptation to give up because of the stress, review your short- and long-term goals. Is there anything that you can change that will make your goals more reasonable or attainable? Have you allowed enough time to achieve them? Revising your goals or your time line may be necessary to keep yourself on track.

Finally, think positively about yourself and your progress. Many students before you have successfully juggled a job, classes, and a family. That is not to say that they did not doubt themselves along the way or suffer any setbacks. The difference between these students and those who were not successful is that they persevered because they believed in themselves more often than not. Tell yourself that you can get through stressful times.

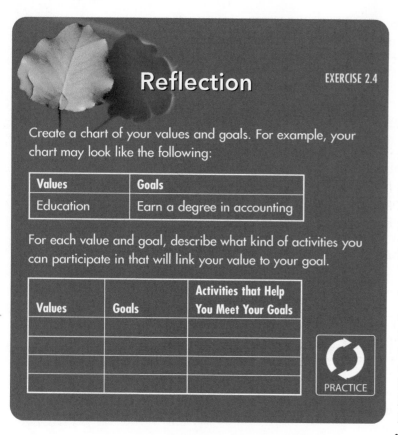

Reflection

EXERCISE 2.4

Create a chart of your values and goals. For example, your chart may look like the following:

Values	Goals
Education	Earn a degree in accounting

For each value and goal, describe what kind of activities you can participate in that will link your value to your goal.

Values	Goals	Activities that Help You Meet Your Goals

PRACTICE

Learning Styles and Personality Types

Learning Style Preferences

As you may recall from the "Read This First" section in the front of the book, knowing your learning style preferences provides a foundation for understanding yourself in other aspects of your life. Information about what you like and dislike, how you relate to others, and how to work productively will help you achieve your goals and, as Gordon Lawrence (1995) states in his book *People Types and Tiger Stripes,* help you make "dramatic improvements in the effectiveness of [your] work" (p. 5). You have already completed an inventory in the "Read This First" section that precedes Chapter 1, and the appendix offers Neil Fleming's VARK* learning styles inventory, which focuses on four learning style preferences: Visual, Aural, Read/Write, and Kinesthetic. In the next few pages, you will complete a personality preference inventory, which can help you see another side of who you are. Your values, dreams, mission statement, goals, learning style, and personality preferences work together to create a more complete picture of who you are and how to get where you want to go.

Although learning preferences are not necessarily directly linked to college majors or careers, you can easily see that your learning style preference will come into play when you choose your major and your career. Kinesthetic learners, for example, may be drawn to majors or careers that allow them to move about or use their bodies to complete tasks. Landscape design, auto body repair, culinary arts, and nursing are just a few community college degree programs that would appeal to kinesthetic learners. Review Table 2.2, which lists possible majors and careers for some of the

TABLE 2.2   Learning Style Preferences, Majors, and Careers

Learning Style Preference	College Majors	Careers
AUDITORY	Music, communications, counseling	Musician, music educator, marketing director, public relations director, counselor
KINESTHETIC	Sciences, sociology, computer technology, culinary arts, massage therapy	Nurse, doctor, therapist, networking specialist, computer technician, chef, massage therapist
VISUAL	Art, graphic design, drafting, architecture, interior design	Art teacher, artist, graphic designer, architect, interior design stylist

learning style preferences, but note that it is not considered an exhaustive list. Also, some majors and careers may speak to more than one learning style preference; for example, an advertising executive who writes, edits, and directs commercials may rely on almost all the learning style preferences that are part of the inventory at the beginning of the book on a daily basis as she creates commercials and ads for clients. For sure, she will need to work individually, with peers, and with her boss on different aspects of a project, and she may find that she is needed to complete tasks at different times of the day, even late at night when filming continues long after the typical work day ends.

The learning styles inventory in the "Read This First" section that precedes Chapter 1 provides you with a helpful way to consider how you take in information and learn new concepts, but there are other learning styles inventories and intelligences questionnaires. Harvard psychologist Howard Gardner is well known for his theory of multiple intelligences, which is another term for "what we know, understand, and learn about our world" (Lazear, xiv). Gardner has created eight categories of how we can know and learn.

Verbal/linguistic intelligence is evident in people who can use language with ease. People who demonstrate the verbal/linguistic intelligence enjoy reading and writing and may be journalists, novelists, playwrights, or comedians. The **logical/mathematical** intelligence is demonstrated by an ease and enjoyment with numbers and logic problems. People who have a strong leaning in the logical/mathematical intelligence like to solve problems, find patterns, discover relationships between objects, and follow steps. Career choices for logical/mathematical people include science, computer technology, math, and engineering.

Visual/spatial is an intelligence that is characterized by anything visual—paintings, photographs, maps, and architecture. People who have a strong visual/spatial sense are usually good at design, architecture, painting and sculpture, and map making. **Body/kinesthetic** is an intelligence that focuses on body movement. Body/kinesthetic people enjoy using their bodies to express themselves. Obvious career choices for this intelligence include dancing, sports, and dramatic arts. **Musical/rhythmic** intelligence encompasses the mind's proficiency with the rhythms of music and hearing tones and beats. People who have strong musical/rhythmic intelligence may use musical instruments or the human voice to express themselves. Career choices for this intelligence include all types of musical performers.

How you relate to others and yourself is part of the interpersonal and intrapersonal intelligences. People with strong **interpersonal** intelligence relate well with others. They read others' feelings well and act with others in mind. **Intrapersonal** intelligence centers around the ability to understand oneself. People who possess intrapersonal intelligence know how and why they do what they do. **Naturalistic,** the eighth intelligence, refers to people who enjoy and work well in an outdoor environment. Naturalistic people find peace in nature and enjoy having natural elements around them.

Personality Types

In addition to discovering your learning style preference, knowing your personality type provides another way to think about who you are and how you can achieve your goals. People who are shy or introverted, like Laura, may find themselves choosing majors and careers where interaction with others is minimal. In Laura's case, she may find that working one-on-one with someone is preferable to having a job that requires her to speak in front of hundreds of people at a time.

TABLE 2.3   MBTI□ Types

Extraversion (E), likes to focus on people, is active in the world	**Introversion (I),** reflective, thinks before acting, attuned to inner world
Sensing (S), observing, using all five senses, in touch with physical realities	**Intuition (N),** imagining, thinking about possibilities
Thinking (T), using logic, being objective and skeptical	**Feeling (F),** using emotion, caring about others, being tactful, appreciating harmony
Judgment (J), goal-oriented, planning, controlling	**Perception (P),** curious and open-minded, taking in information

There have been almost as many personality tests and categories as there are personalities, but one that has stood the test of time is the Myers-Briggs Type Indicator, or MBTI□. The MBTI□, a popular personality test that has been around since the 1970s, was developed by Isabel Briggs Myers and Katharine Briggs. The "four dimensions of type" that the MBTI□ uses are listed in Table 2.3.

Sixteen personality combinations result from an MBTI□ inventory: ESTJ, ISTJ, ENFJ, INFJ, ENFS, INFS, ISFJ, ESFJ, ISTP, ESTP, INFP, ENFP, ISFJ, INTJ, ESFP, ISFP. Each type carries with it a distinct set of characteristics.

ACTIVITY   Personality Preference Survey

Directions: There are several pairs of sentences for each indicator. For each pair, place a check in front of the sentence that is more true of you. Select the choice that comes closest to your preference when you are relaxed at home. Try to avoid choosing how you wish you behaved or how you may be forced to behave in work situations. When you have made your selections for each indicator, total the checks and record your personality preference.

Indicator I: Do you focus your energy and attention on the outer world of people and things or the inner world of thoughts and ideas?

EXTROVERSION	INTROVERSION
_____ I am primarily concerned with the well-being of others.	_____ I am primarily concerned with developing my own potential.
_____ After a hard day's work, I like to spend time with family and friends.	_____ After a hard day's work, I like to spend time alone.
_____ When someone asks me a question, I'll usually have an answer for them.	_____ I usually need to mull over a question in my mind before answering.
_____ I enjoy it when the phone rings or coworkers stop by to chat.	_____ I like to concentrate on my work; I don't appreciate interruptions.

_____ I tend to think out loud.	_____ I need to do my thinking internally, privately.
_____ At parties, I enjoy meeting new people.	_____ At parties, I enjoy spending time with a friend I know well.
_____ Looking back, I've pursued a lot of interests.	_____ Looking back, I've pursued a couple of strong interests in depth.
_____ I really like to talk.	_____ I really like to ponder.
_____ I have quite a few friends.	_____ I have a couple of close friends.
_____ I value the recognition I get from others.	_____ I am the best judge of my achievements.

Number of checks for Extroversion (E) _____

Number of checks for Introversion (I) _____

Preference _____

Indicator II: In new situations, how do you perceive what's going on? How do you take in information?

SENSING	INTUITING
_____ I tend to focus on facts and details.	_____ I tend to see the "big picture."
_____ I take a practical and realistic approach to solving problems.	_____ I look for imaginative solutions to problems.
_____ I take things apart to figure out the whole.	_____ I observe trends and speculate about the future.
_____ I prefer clear instructions.	_____ I prefer to go with my hunches.
_____ I like set procedures and established routines.	_____ I like change and variety and the chance to be inventive.
_____ I have great respect for hard work and perspiration.	_____ I have great respect for ideas and inspirations.
_____ I enjoy life in the present moment.	_____ I live in a state of anticipation.
_____ I have a passion for gadgets.	_____ I have a passion for possibilities.

Number of checks for Sensing (S) _____

Number of checks for Intuiting (I) _____

Preference _____

(continued)

Indicator III: How do you prefer to make decisions?

THINKING	FEELING
_____ I tend to approach decisions logically and objectively.	_____ I tend to approach decisions personally.
_____ I try to treat everyone equally.	_____ I try to consider everyone involved.
_____ I analyze situations thoroughly.	_____ I relate to others' feelings and concerns.
_____ I rely on principles and standards.	_____ I depend on my personal values.
_____ I have a tendency to "bottle" my emotions.	_____ I usually am able to express my feelings and convictions.
_____ I remain cool, calm, and impersonal in tense situations.	_____ I tend to get personally immersed.
_____ I consider the criteria.	_____ I consider extenuating circumstances.
_____ It is important that I understand my feelings.	_____ I don't analyze my feelings; I simply experience them.

Number of checks for Thinking (T) _____
Number of checks for Feeling (F) _____
Preference _____

Indicator IV: How do you approach your life and your dealings with other people?

JUDGING	PERCEIVING
_____ I usually wake up knowing what my day will be.	_____ In approaching the day, I welcome the unexpected.
_____ I am driven to finalize a decision.	_____ I gather information and consult with others as my decisions evolve.
_____ In meetings, I tend to keep people on task.	_____ In meetings, I encourage open discussion.
_____ I'm a list maker and a list follower.	_____ When I make lists, I revise them frequently as my priorities change.
_____ I work incrementally toward deadlines.	_____ I work best when under the pressure of a tight deadline.
_____ I like to get plans scheduled on my calendar.	_____ I like to keep my options open.
_____ I don't like to change my plans.	_____ I am always willing to be flexible.
_____ I like to "run" things; then I know they are being run right.	_____ I adapt easily to new situations and enjoy what comes along.
_____ I enjoy finishing things.	_____ I enjoy starting new projects.

Number of checks for Judging (J) _____

Numbers of checks for Perceiving (P) _____

Preference _____

You now have a four-letter score, with the letters representing your preferences among the indicators. Record your results here: _____ _____ _____ _____

Knowing your MBTI® type is one way to understand who you are and what your strengths and weaknesses are. However, there are many more ways of understanding yourself. Although personality tests cannot express our whole selves, they can lead us to greater reflection about who we are and how and why we choose certain things and act in certain ways.

Kit Harrington Hayes (2000), in the book *Managing Career Transitions,* created the preceding personality preference survey that helps you discover your own personality preference.

Considering Learning Style and Personality for Careers

Discovering your learning style preference and your personality type will definitely help you set realistic short-term and long-term goals. For example, confirming that you have a read/write learning preference and you work well with deadlines and staying organized (Judging) may help you realize that your long-term goal of being a writer will work well with who you are and how you learn and work. However, identifying your style and type should not limit your choices or keep you from working on areas of your learning style and personality that may be weaker or get less attention. If you are a strong visual learner, but you are taking a class that relies on listening effectively and critically, you should use that opportunity to become a better listener, to improve your aural learning style preference by following listening tips like the ones found in Chapter 8. Likewise, if you work better alone (Introversion) and have a strong kinesthetic learning style preference, choosing a career as a computer technician may play to your strengths, but you may also find yourself working with others collaboratively and communicating frequently in writing and verbally.

Whatever your learning style strength and personality preferences are, consider how other styles and types will factor into your short-term and long-term educational goals. Then, look for opportunities to strengthen those less-developed sides of your learning and personality so that you are more comfortable in a variety of situations and so that you are a well-rounded person.

PLUS

(Personality + Learning Style = Understanding Situations)

Think about Juanita's uneasiness with setting a goal to complete a certain degree. She is 18 and feels as though she will have to live with her decision the rest of her life no matter what she chooses. Using what you have learned from this chapter, what advice would you give her? How can she be sure, if she can be sure at all, that the goals she has are the ones that she will want to meet in the future? What if they are not?

Now, considering your own learning style, personality type, and special circumstances, what would you do in her situation?

PROFILE

MY STORY
Learning Plan

Directions: Using what you have learned in this chapter and what you know about your learning preferences, choose a task or assignment that needs to be completed soon and create a learning plan that will help you accomplish this task. Then, write your *My Story* Summary, a one-sentence synopsis that crystallizes your newly created plan.

PROFILE

LEARNING TASK	
Time of Day	
Intake Preference	
Social Preference	
Task Management Preference	

MY STORY SUMMARY:

Path of Discovery

Name and describe three people or situations that changed your life. What did these people or situations teach you about your values, priorities, motivations, or goals? How have they changed you?

HOMEWORK

From College to University

What You Know and How You Learn Will Change

If your beliefs, goals, and values remain relatively unchanged during your community college experience, then your move to a four-year university should be easy, right? The transition can be relatively smooth if you are willing to apply some of the ideas in this chapter to your new environment and your new challenges.

First, your definition of who you are will change when you transfer, perhaps dramatically. You will likely be more confident in your abilities and you will be better able to handle the stress of juggling numerous responsibilities. Second, your values may also change after your semesters at a community college; if you were unsure of what you valued before, you may finally have a clearer picture of your belief system. On the other hand, you may be more confused than ever about what you believe after studying different religions, psychological theories, and social ideas. Because higher education values inquiry and research, no matter what shape your values are in by the time you transfer, you will find support as you struggle to make sense of it all at both the community college and the four-year university.

Third, just as your knowledge of yourself and your values will have changed, your goals will go through a transformation. Although your main goal of graduating with a four-year degree will still be in sight, you will notice that you have already met some of your smaller goals. Perhaps you have successfully completed an associate's degree, or you have become more organized. Just the fact that you are ready to transfer credits means that you have accomplished some necessary steps to fulfilling the rest of your goals.

Finally, you will be able to revise your list of what you know because what you know will change after taking classes at a community college. You may even be able to include a career choice in your "What I Know" list. Also, you may know yourself better through application of the learning styles discussed earlier. However, you will need to be prepared to adapt to different teaching styles and new pressures after you transfer.

Now, to prepare yourself for the next step, you will need to revise, preferably on paper, your list of what you know. You will also need to realize that you may have to adapt the learning styles that you have felt most comfortable with—or to explore and use new styles—at your four-year school.

From College to Career

Goals and a Mission Will Help You Succeed

Many businesses rely on creating mission statements, strategic plans (long-term goals), and operational plans (short-term goals) to chart a course for their success. Because you have experience writing your own mission and goals, you will be able to contribute to your company's planning. You will be able to do this because you understand how the company's values underlie its mission and how its goals create its road map to success. Your experience in goal setting will also help you to write departmental or personal goals. If you understand how values, mission, and goals fit together, you will be better able to create goals that are explicitly linked to the focus of your workplace.

Chapter Review Questions

1. How do your values and background affect your goal setting?
2. Why do some people have trouble reaching their goals?
3. What steps can you take to manage your priorities effectively?
4. How does your learning style and personality preference affect goal setting?

Chapter 2 Case Scenarios

1. Peter has started college, but he is not sure what he wants to do. In fact, he is afraid to tell his parents that he wants to be a dental hygienist because his parents want him to take over the family business. Neither of his parents went to college, and they don't understand why any of their children would want to work outside the family business. Peter values loyalty to his family—he has been through many challenges that have strengthened his relationship with his parents—but he also has a strong interest in working in the health field. Peter's ultimate goal is to be a dentist, but he thinks that working as a hygienist first would be a way to make sure that he has what it takes. What advice would you give Peter? What should he do to make sure his goals are met?

2. Serena, a single parent, has started her first semester in college, but she also works full-time in a law office. Her sister keeps Serena's twin boys while she works, but she sometimes has to miss work when her sister cannot look after them. Serena wants to get a four-year degree and eventually go to law school, but she feels as though it will take too long if she doesn't start now. She is motivated by time and money. She wants to hurry and get her degree, and she wants to be financially independent so that she can take care of her boys. She works very hard, but she doesn't have any other family or friends who can help her. To add to her obstacles, her sister is not supportive of Serena's desire to get a degree and improve her life. Serena's sister thinks that she has all she needs and shouldn't "mess it up by going to college and getting all kinds of crazy ideas." What advice would you give Serena? What have you learned about setting goals and managing priorities that would help Serena? What have you learned about overcoming challenges that would help Serena?

Research It Further

1. During the Middle Ages (500–1500 A.D.), the terms *sanguine, phlegmatic, choleric,* and *melancholic* were used often to describe people. Research these descriptions further and have the class determine which category each student falls into.

2. Choose a long-term career goal and research what the qualifications would be to accomplish it. For example, if you would like to be a network administrator, check your college catalog for degree requirements and look on the Internet for job descriptions that include the kind of degree and work experience you would need. List any other skills you would need for the career.

3. Using the key word "mission statements," search the Internet for college and business mission statements. Print at least three different mission statements and determine the similarities and differences. Report your findings to the class.

References

Glass, L. (1997). *Toxic people: 10 ways of dealing with people who make your life miserable.* New York: St. Martin's.

Godwin, M. (2000). *Who are you? 101 ways of seeing yourself.* New York: Penguin.

Hayes, K. H. (2000). *Managing career transitions,* 2nd ed. Upper Saddle River, NJ: Prentice Hall.

Klauser, H. A. (2001). *Write it down, make it happen: Knowing what you want and getting it!* New York: Simon & Schuster.

Lawrence, G. (1995). *People types and tiger stripes,* 3rd ed. Gainesville, FL: CAPT.

Lazear, D. (1991). *Seven ways of teaching: The artistry of teaching with multiple intelligences.* Palatine, IL: Skylight Publishing.

Myers-Briggs Type Indicator® (2008). Retrieved 15 May 2008, from http://www.myersbriggstypeindicator.co.uk/.

3 Understanding Others in College and Diversity

Michael's Story

"Evan, are you going to be around later today? I may need some help," Michael asks his new friend and study group partner. Michael stayed after orientation to exchange numbers with Evan and, since then, they have talked a few times on campus and on the phone.

One reason Michael felt an instant connection with Evan that first day they met was that Evan is obviously different from him, someone who obviously has a different background, ideas, and experiences. From his experience in the military, Michael knows how to deal with diversity; he has met all kinds of people from different countries and backgrounds.

"Sure, man," Evan says. "Maybe you can help me, too. I have to move some furniture for my aunt this weekend. You think you can lend me a hand?"

Michael paces outside the library and drops his backpack on the wall before he sits down next to it. Although he has been through the college orientation, he is still getting used to the college experience. His philosophy professor, for example, has a very different view of the world and challenges her students to question their own views. Sometimes the debates get heated and he forgets that he is there to learn, not to get angry and shut down. His political science instructor does not agree with him on the responsibility and roles of state governments, but he does allow Michael to share his military experiences and is respectful of Michael's point of view.

"Are you sure you can use help from an old man like me?" Michael asks. Michael has never thought much about being 42 until some students he is working with on a group project said something about his being "too old" to work with.

"You may be old, man, but I'm pretty sure you can bench press more than me," Evan says as he laughs.

"Maybe when I was your age, but not anymore," Michael says. "Seriously, though, I have this group project, and, well, my group keeps meeting without me, and I have to get this project done or I am done for."

"Ah, c'mon," Evan says. "I would make you the leader of my group. I've heard you debate the professor before and win! You are fierce in an argument."

"I think that is part of the problem, too. I ran into a guy in the class and he said he saw two people in my group meeting in the library and working on the project when I was able to meet, but no one even called me," Michael says.

"So what do you need from me? Need some boxing tips?" Evan asks.

"Do you think if I talked to the professor that she would reassign me to another group or tell me to deal with it?" asks Michael.

"Man, what do you have to lose by asking?" Evan replies.

49

In This Chapter

One of the easiest parts of college can be the hardest for busy college students. The easy part to making friends and forging relationships is that people are everywhere—in class, computer labs, and the library—and everyone shares at least one thing, college, in common. As Michael will discover, getting to know those around you is essential to your well-being and happiness while you are working on your degree. The hard part, however, is making the time to cultivate relationships. As a community college student, you most likely have other activities that fill your schedule outside of class: work, family, hobbies, church, and friends. Part of this chapter's purpose is to show you the benefits of starting and maintaining strong relationships with people on campus.

In addition to making friends and connections with people in college, this chapter also discusses diversity as an issue to be explored and appreciated. You will certainly notice that the people you encounter in college are different and that you will most likely meet people who have different values, goals, opinions about politics and religion, and ways of leading their lives. An important component of being an educated individual is understanding that college is, in part, about learning to listen to others, understanding their points of view, and appreciating them in the larger context of humanity. This chapter, then, presents you with several categories of diversity—to be sure, there are as many categories as there are people—to explore and discuss with your instructor, classmates, and others. There is also discussion of instances in which a lack of appreciation for others' differences can lead to prejudging them, or worse, discrimination. All of these topics will help you create and maintain mutually respectful relationships with others and will help you broaden yourself and others in the world. More specifically, after reading this chapter, you will be able to:

- Describe the different types of people and their roles on your campus.
- List the benefits of cultivating relationships in college.
- Describe teaching types and how to learn from each type.
- Explain the importance of appreciating diversity.
- Discuss how stereotyping, prejudice, and discrimination are related.

The People on Your Campus

Research has shown that getting to know at least one person, no matter who it is, on your campus will increase the likelihood that you will stay in college and complete your degree. Whether it is the janitor or a career counselor, getting to know someone beyond just her name, title, and face is to your advantage while you are in college.

You have probably noticed already that there are many people who work at a college—and most of them are there to support and guide you through your college experience. Equally important to understanding where buildings and services, as discussed in Chapter 1, are located is knowing who does what on your campus. It saves you time when you know, for example, that to get copies of your transcript will involve speaking with someone in the registrar's office or that checking on loan applications will include contact with a financial aid officer. All of these people are charged with the task of helping you succeed each semester you are in college, and it will make your transition from either high school or the world of work much easier if you are familiar with the various common jobs on campus.

Cultivating Relationships with Professors

There may be no one more important to your college and possible future career success than a professor. She does not just provide you with access to the content and support you as you think critically about the subject matter; she also can be a mentor and a resource as you complete your degree and start your career. One way to start out on the right path to a good relationship is to greet your professor with a smile and a "hello" when you see her in and out of class. College professors see their relationships with their students outside of class as part of their advising and mentoring duties. For many instructors, their students are not only people in their classes, but they are also potential graduates from their programs or transfer student success stories. Being friendly in and outside of class is a great way to start on the path to a strong, valuable relationship during your college career (and maybe even after!).

Another way to start developing meaningful relationships with your professors is to appreciate the diversity of disciplines, personality types, and teaching styles among them. For sure, you will not love every class (although we professors wish you could), every teaching style, and every personality that you will encounter in college. When you take pleasure in the class and the instructor, enjoy every minute of it; when you don't, use the experience to keep focused on what you want: a college degree. Also realize, however, that what you "don't like" at first may just be a first impression that will not necessarily be your feelings at the end of the course. Sometimes students' initial experiences in a class are uncomfortable, but those same experiences may be ones that they reflect on as the most meaningful because they learned something about the course topic as well as themselves.

Because each instructor's expectations in terms of class preparation and policies regarding attendance, late work, and make-up exams will differ, be mindful that rules that apply in one class may be different in another. Relationships built on acknowledgement of others' boundaries (in this case, professors' expectations and policies) as well as respect and integrity are stronger and more authentic. To cultivate a solid relationship with your professor, make the most of his office hours. Office hours are best used for questions about material that was previously covered, assignments and policies that were previously explained, and anything else that does not pertain to the day's lecture or in-class activity. Sometimes students only see office hours as a time to discuss a problem; office hours should be used for positive visits as well—stopping by to say "Hello!" or to follow up on an idea that sparked your interest in class are great ways to strengthen your relationship.

It would be a perfect world if there were no conflicts in your relationship with your instructor. However, there may be a time in your college career when you don't feel as though you have a strong, respectful relationship. If you experience conflict with a professor, be sure to discuss the issue as soon as possible—and in private. Use "I" statements to explain your perspective rather than "you" statements. For example, saying "I am confused about what our exam will cover" is better than saying "You were confusing when you talked about the exam." Using "I" statements also underscores your control over your actions and reactions during the conflict. Look, too, for common ground that can help you manage the conflict maturely and respectfully.

A good relationship for its own sake is perfectly acceptable, but also remember that professors can provide a link to other opportunities beyond the classroom. You will most likely turn to a professor when you need a recommendation letter for student activities, scholarships, internships, and jobs. Getting to know at least one professor well will give you an advantage when you want to move forward in your college career. Professors in your certificate and degree program are usually tied closely to the business and industry in which they teach. Thus, a good relationship with a professor in respiratory therapy, for example, may lead to a job opportunity in the field. A professor who teaches a general education course, one designed for transfer to a four-year university, may work closely with a professor in the same discipline at the local university. She may know about special scholarships or helpful people to contact once you have completed your degree.

Although a good relationship with your professor is a key to your enjoying your education experience, remember that your professor is not an equal in the relationship and still must challenge you to learn and stretch your concept of yourself and others, as well as evaluate you during and at the end of the term. Creating boundaries in relationships is discussed later in the chapter.

Getting to Know Advisors, Counselors, and Learning Support Staff

In addition to professors, some of the most important relationships that you will forge during college will be with people whose sole job is to make sure you succeed. Counselors and advisors will be key people in your academic career, so be sure to take the time to get to know these individuals. College administrators also play an important role.

Advisors. Your advisor may be the first person you encounter at college. An advisor explains to you what courses you should take, how many hours you should take a semester, and how to plan remaining semesters. An advisor works for you; it is his or her job to see that you complete your degree with little difficulty. You may be lucky enough to have the same advisor throughout your college career. In that case, regular contact with your advisor will help keep the lines of communication open. If you have a different advisor each semester, you may wish to find one person on whom you can rely to act as regular advisor. That person may be a former professor or a counselor who has advised you in the past. The goal is to find someone on campus who has an interest in your education beyond one semester.

Counselors. You should take the opportunity to get to know at least one counselor on your campus. Whether it is a career counselor or a disability counselor, make it a point to schedule an appointment with one while you are in college. Getting to know counselors is a great way to obtain more information about the school and its services. For example, a career counselor may inform you of a career fair or recruiting day. He can also help you prepare a resume and practice interviewing. Counselors who deal with students who have personal issues are another valuable resource for you. Even if you do not need personal counseling, you may benefit from a relationship with one. This type of counselor can give you tips for managing stress and dealing with difficult people, just to name a few experiences you may have in college.

Tutors, Mentors, and Student Leaders.   In addition to the key people you will encounter in college, there are a variety of other people who work or volunteer their time to help you achieve your academic, career, and personal goals. Those people can include tutors in a learning assistance lab. Working one-on-one with them provides you with a unique relationship in that a tutor can really get to know what your learning needs are and how to help you fulfill them. A tutor can be a great resource for understanding the material for a class because he is often a student himself or has just recently taken the class.

Student or peer mentors are other types of people you will find on your college campus who can be instrumental in keeping you on track to success. Peer mentors are usually current students who have been successful in their classes and who are willing to provide support to new students who may need extra encouragement to navigate the choppy waters of the first few semesters. Peer mentors may give you advice for studying, for choosing a degree, or for balancing family, work, and college. And just think—if you are also successful, you may be a great peer mentor for a student who was just like you when you started!

One final group of people with whom you may come in contact is student leaders. You may find them in special clubs, associations, or student government. Unlike peer mentors, whose primary role is to work one-on-one with a student, student leaders work with both students and the college or organization to provide leadership in certain areas. For example, a student government representative may ask college officials to provide more family-friendly activities so that more students can attend with their children. If administrators agree, then the Student Government Association may work with students to find out what types of activities are best and may organize an event to get more students involved.

Reflection   EXERCISE 3.1

What relationships on campus have you cultivated so far? What challenges might you have in getting to know tutors, student leaders, and mentors?

PRACTICE

Getting Along with Classmates

Last, but certainly not least, getting to know your classmates can make the difference between struggling all alone and meeting new challenges with a like-minded support group. Who else can relate to the challenge of studying for a chemistry final exam than the students in the class with you? Think about it: Your classmates will be the majority of the people who populate a college campus. You may get to know well only three or four professors throughout your college career, but you have the potential of meeting and working with hundreds of students.

In addition to sharing experiences with your fellow students, you can also rely on them as study partners or emergency note-takers if you can't be in class. Another benefit to making friends with classmates is that you can learn about other classes, instructors, and degree programs from them. Their firsthand knowledge could help you choose the best classes and the most promising programs.

Getting to know your classmates can be relatively simple, especially since you will be sitting close to them during each class. Here are a few tips for creating lasting relationships with fellow students:

- Introduce yourself to those sitting around you. It may be easier to arrive early and start conversations with other students.
- Exchange phone numbers or email addresses with classmates who seem reliable and trustworthy. You may need to call someone if you miss class.
- Offer to study with someone. Not only will you help a classmate, but you will also help yourself learn the material.
- Keep in contact with friends even after the semester is over. While you may not share classes anymore, you still may be able to study and offer support to one another.

Creating Boundaries

Because you will be surrounded by a diverse group of people of all ages, it may be difficult for you to create and maintain the traditional boundaries that exist between students and their counselors, professors, administrators, and learning support staff. It almost seems contradictory, but boundaries may be necessary at the same time that you are getting to know others. Why should you refrain from close relationships with professors and advisors when you need them to get to know you if you are to ask for a referral or recommendation?

For one, some colleges discourage intimately personal relationships between professors and students, just as many companies prohibit the same type of overly friendly relationship between supervisors and their employees, because such relationships can be problematic. One possible problem is that intimate relationships can result in perceived or actual unfair evaluation or treatment. Because a professor is considered a superior, the college views the professor's role as one of authority and power. Many sexual harassment policies and laws are built on the imbalance of power between a person in authority and a subordinate.

Another possible problem is that other students may see the relationship as favoritism and feel as though they are being treated unfairly. Additionally, there is the possibility of a sexual relationship, which is sometimes strictly prohibited at colleges. If you have not already done so, check your student handbook regarding your college's policy about relationships between students and faculty. Ultimately, you will need to make the decision that is best for you and the situation as to how friendly you should be with faculty or other college officials.

If you get along well with your professor and genuinely enjoy her company, then your best move is to respect the professor–student relationship while you are in class. You can do this by meeting your professor during her office hours on campus and keeping conversations focused on your progress in your classes and your career plans. You can then continue the friendship after you have finished the semester and have no intentions of taking another class with that professor again. Some friendships between professors and students are long lasting, so consider cultivating them once the class is over.

Collaboration

Working within a group, decide whether personal relationships between faculty and students should be encouraged and supported or prohibited. Be sure to provide a list of benefits that support your stance.

EXERCISE 3.2

When a Problem Arises

A time may arise when you have a problem in one of your classes. If it does, you can be assured that the college's employees will work with you to resolve it. There are, however, rules and procedures regarding how to resolve a problem at a college. Knowing and following these procedures will ensure that a problem is handled appropriately and quickly.

The first step to resolving a conflict in class is to define the problem. Is it a communication problem? Is it a problem with the course material? Is it a problem with the course standards? Once you have defined the problem, your next step is to discuss the problem with the person directly. If the problem is with your instructor, make an appointment during her office hours to discuss the issue. If you are emotional—angry, upset, nervous—wait until you have calmed down to discuss the problem. Your goal in meeting with the instructor is to resolve the conflict.

For the process of conflict resolution to work, you will need to complete the first two steps. If you are not satisfied with the result or if you feel the problem has gotten worse, not better, move to the next step: talking to the department chair or dean. You will no doubt be asked if you have met with the instructor. Again, your goal at this step is to resolve the issue. Occasionally, the instructor may be called in to help resolve the issue. Staying calm and focused on resolving the conflict will be to your advantage. In the event that the problem is not solved at this level, your last stop is with the dean of students or vice president for instruction. Starting at the top will only delay resolution.

Integrity in Relationships

As you will see as you read the rest of the chapters in this book, integrity is an important part of college life and the world at large. Integrity is defined as "a strict adherence to an ethical code of conduct," but the definition can be expanded to show its relevance to relationships. You can have integrity in relationships by being honest with other people and demanding honesty from them. Without integrity, relationships are superficial and meaningless.

The underlying factor of integrity in a relationship is trust. If you can trust others, then you will be better able to learn, grow, expand, and improve yourself. If you do not have trust, then you may shut yourself off from others and experiences that are new to you. Trusting others takes time—it isn't an overnight event. Give people reasons to trust you and then deliver on your promises. Likewise, put your trust in others, giving them an opportunity to prove themselves trustworthy.

A specific part of trust in relationships is reliability or, expressed another way, doing what you say you will do. If your classmate asks you to take notes for him on days he cannot be in class and you fail to do so each time, then you lack reliability. Your classmate will not be able to trust you to help him. If you agree to take notes knowing that you may not be able to do it, then you are not being honest—with him or yourself.

Acting with integrity is not easy and doesn't always come naturally. Instead, it is a conscious decision to do what is right even when it makes things harder and more uncomfortable for you and others. Being reliable and trustworthy takes more work because you may find yourself doing things (such as taking notes for a friend or driving a coworker home at the end of the day) that are inconvenient and time-consuming.

INTEGRITY MATTERS

Maintaining integrity in relationships includes being honest with others and with yourself. It takes time and energy as well as conscious decisions to be honest in order to build trust in relationships. However, the rewards are great!

Moreover, the rewards for acting with integrity are not always immediate; therefore, remember that despite how you feel at the time, the effects of your action will be far reaching and positive.

Tips for Lasting Relationships

As discussed at the beginning of the chapter, community college students do have a harder time cultivating friendships because of their busy schedules and because they do not typically spend four years with the same group of people. What else can you do to forge relationships in college?

Leave time in your schedule to talk with friends or meet with instructors. If you must leave directly after class to get to work, you will not be as successful in cultivating important relationships. One way to ensure that you connect with your professors is to make an appointment with them during the semester to ask questions or get feedback on your progress. Your ulterior motive is to cultivate a relationship with them. Also, be sure to approach conflict as an opportunity to learn more about yourself, and always act with integrity. Lasting relationships are ones that are built on trust and doing what is right.

Changes in Your Relationships with Family and Friends

Entering college will be a new experience not only for you, but also for your family and friends, especially if they have not gone to college. Communication, then, will be the key to weathering any changes in your relationships. They need to know how you feel about going to college, and they need to be aware that you will be going through changes while you are there. Surely you will be experiencing changes in your outlook on life, your belief in yourself, and your attitude toward the future.

When these changes occur, people around you may react differently. Some will be supportive and excited that you have created personal goals and are achieving them. A few, however, may react negatively. These people may be jealous of your success or your new "lease on life" because they did not have the same opportunities or because they squandered the opportunities that they did have. Others who react negatively may be insecure about themselves and feel "dumb" around a person in college; these same people often fear that once the college student graduates, he or she will leave them for a "better" spouse or friend. Also, there are parents who do not want to acknowledge that their children are grown adults who are and should be making decisions on their own; parents are also often worried that their children will be exposed to value systems and beliefs that are very different from what they taught them.

Whatever the reasons that the people around you react to the changes you experience, be comforted by the fact that you will survive, and better yet, you will have more of an understanding of the **diversity** of opinions that you will encounter. Learning how to deal with different people in college will allow you to apply what you learn to your personal relationships.

Exploring Diversity

An exciting part of college is that you will meet and work with people from all ages and backgrounds. Unlike a traditional university, at your community college you may be part of a study group that includes a grandparent, home-schooled teenager,

Critical Thinking

EXERCISE 3.3

In what ways have your relationships with family and old friends changed since you enrolled in college? In what ways have they stayed the same? Why do you think they have stayed the same or changed? What can you do to maintain the relationships that matter? How will you deal with the relationships that are not supportive of your educational endeavors?

PRACTICE

veteran, administrative assistant to a dean, full-time detective, and minister. At a community college, then, it is crucial to be sensitive to others' values and perspectives, which is one of the purposes of diversity.

A simple definition of diversity is "difference" or "variety." Another term heard when "diversity" is discussed in a college setting is "multiculturalism." Although the two words have different implications, they often have the same motivation—to expose the community to a variety of ideas, cultures, viewpoints, beliefs, and backgrounds.

When people talk about diversity, they usually mean race, gender, ethnicity, age, and religion. Colleges that want to promote diversity on their campuses often look for opportunities to hire and enroll people who have different backgrounds than the majority of the campus population. They do this with the belief that diversity enriches the educational experience for all because it exposes us, faculty, staff, and students, to new ideas and challenges our preconceived notions of the world around us.

Other Kinds of Diversity

Dealing successfully with diversity includes more than working well with people from different nations, different religious or political backgrounds, and different disabilities; you will also need to consider the diversity of attitudes and work ethics. For example, not everyone you meet in college or in your career will value the same things you do. What will you do if you work with others whose values conflict with your own? What will you do if the difference between your and others' work ethics cause conflict?

You will get the opportunity to work with others in class when you are assigned a group project or presentation. Even if you all are the same gender, race, religion, and age, you will still find that each of you is different and has different expectations

The more you experience diversity, the more you will be able to appreciate the differences between you and others.

and opinions of the assignment. Being able to work with others, regardless of their learning and work styles, is a skill. The more you are exposed to diversity, the more you will be able to handle and appreciate the differences between you and everyone you meet.

Gender and Sexual Orientation Diversity

The latest educational statistics show that almost two-thirds of the college student population across the country is female. In the past few decades, women have enrolled in college in record numbers. It may seem strange to think that several decades ago, there were far fewer women in college, especially in law and medical schools. No doubt, you will encounter gender diversity at your college, and what this means for you is that you will have plenty of opportunities to work with both men and women and explore any preconceptions you may have about the differences between the sexes. You may have to pay more attention to society's assumptions about gender and be more attuned to how language, art, and sciences, among other disciplines, perpetuate gender stereotypes.

Sexual orientation is another type of diversity that you will more than likely encounter in college if you have not already. Homosexuality and bisexuality are just two categories of sexual orientation diversity. Organizations such as the Human Rights Campaign (www.hrc.org) strive to educate others about discrimination that can—and does—occur because of the stereotypes and prejudice that exist regarding sexual orientation. Why should you know more about sexual orientation as a part of diversity? Sexuality is part of the human experience, and one purpose of higher education is to help you better understand and appreciate your and others' human experience. Recognizing sexual orientation as a category of diversity gives you a more complete picture of humankind.

Sexual Harassment. Colleges and universities as well as the workforce have been aggressively educating students and employees about the definitions and prevention of sexual harassment for decades. Sexual harassment, by legal definition, refers to a superior, or a person in power, harassing a subordinate, or a person with less power than the harasser. College and employee policies often broaden the definition, however, to include any unwanted sexual advances that create an uncomfortable situation or hostile environment. This broader definition means that, in college, a student can sexually harass another student or a student can sexually harass a professor—or any other scenario that involves students, prospective students, and employees and guests of the college. To further round out the definition, women can sexually harass men and people of the same sex can experience sexual harassment.

Despite educational programs for new students and required seminars for employees, colleges—like any place in which people live and work—are not immune to instances of sexual harassment. According to Katz (2005), the American Psychological Association surveyed female graduate students about their experiences in college. The survey results found that 12.7% of female students experienced sexual harassment and 21% avoided taking certain classes for fear of being sexually harassed. Surveys about sexual harassment in the workplace paint a dimmer picture with 31% of female employees and 7% of male employees claiming to be sexually harassed at work.

Educating yourself about the seriousness of sexual harassment, your college's policy on sexual harassment, and the common behaviors that are often considered sexual harassment are steps in the right direction to minimizing incidents. For sure, sexual harassment is no laughing matter, and a review of your college's statement on the matter will reveal what lengths the college will go to discipline those who sexually harass others. Some college policies list the following behaviors as sexual harassment:

- Offensive jokes or comments of a sexual nature
- Requests or demands for sexual favors in return for favorable treatment or rewards (e.g., a good grade)
- Unwanted physical contact or assault
- Showing or distributing sexually explicit materials to others
- Posting sexually explicit images or websites in college-owned online course management systems or emailing those images or websites from college-owned computers

Although it may not be considered sexual harassment if it is not distributed to others, accessing sexually explicit websites with college-owned computer hardware and software may be prohibited conduct that will result in disciplinary action on the part of the college and possible criminal charges.

As with all forms of diversity and possible problems that can arise, be sensitive to others; treat everyone you meet on campus with respect; and be honest with others if you feel uncomfortable in a situation or with certain conversational topics.

Racial, Ethnic, and Cultural Diversity

Over the last 20 years, colleges embraced and developed multicultural studies in response to the past emphasis on "white, male, Western" history, ideas, and culture. Cultural and racial ignorance at its worst has led to the deaths of millions of people all over the world. Understanding and appreciation for the diversity in culture and ethnicity at its best create connections between peoples who have much to learn from each other. Table 3.1 provides you with activities that you can do to appreciate diversity.

Generational Diversity

The idea that our parents' generation is vastly different from our own, which will be greatly different from our children's generation, is considered a fact of life. One unifying viewpoint among the generations is that different generations view the world differently.

You will, no doubt, encounter generational diversity at your community college and in the world of work—more so than in generations past. The American Association of Community Colleges (2004) cites the following statistics from the National Center for Education Statistics: A 1999 study found that 46% of community college students are over the age of 25. Fifteen percent are over 40 years of age. These statistics mean that almost half of the students on a community college campus are not the traditional college age of 18–22.

What is a "generational cohort" and what does it mean for your college and work experience? According to Ron Zemke, Claire Raines, and Bob Filipczak, in their book *Generations at Work: Managing the Clash of Veterans, Boomers, Xers, and Nexters in Your Workplace* (2000), a generational cohort is a group of the population that was born within a certain period of time, that marked as important some of the same world events, and that hold certain common values. In their book, the authors recognize and

TABLE 3.1   Tips for Appreciating Racial, Ethnic, and Cultural Diversity

Work to eliminate all racial, ethnic, or cultural stereotypes or slurs from your thoughts and vocabulary. Stop yourself before you speak and ask, "Is this a stereotype or could it be offensive to some?"
Racial, ethnic, and cultural jokes, images, and cartoons are insensitive at best, harassment at worst. Avoid making fun of others' heritage. Be sensitive to others' backgrounds.
Learn more about your heritage and culture.
Strive to learn more about cultures that are new and different to you.
Participate in college and community cultural celebrations.
Attend seminars, guest lecturers, artistic performances about different cultures and countries.
Do not tolerate others who exhibit racial and cultural insensitivity. If you don't feel comfortable saying something to them, then avoid them and similar situations in the future.

TABLE 3.2 Generations, Birth Years, and Core Values

Generation	Birth Years	Core Values
Veterans	1922–1943	Dedication, sacrifice, patience, respect for authority
Baby Boomers	1943–1960	Health and wellness, optimism, personal growth
Generation Xers	1960–1980	Diversity, fun, self-reliance, global thinking
Nexters or Millenials	1980-present	Civic duty, morality, street smarts

describe four generations that can be found in the workplace (and college for that matter). These generations are defined and described in Table 3.2.

Each of the generational groups, the authors contend, holds certain values that influence how they work with others and how they achieve personal success. The diverse core values and attitudes can create enriching experiences for all generations that work together, or they can be a cause of conflict for those who do not understand and appreciate fellow students and coworkers of a different generation. Misunderstanding generational differences at its worst can become ageism, which is discriminating against someone because of his or her age. The key with generational diversity—as with all types of diversity—is to learn more about yourself and others and appreciate the differences.

Collaboration

Working in a group, choose one of the categories in Table 3.2 and discuss how the college or the community can help people appreciate this type of diversity. What events could help the community learn more or celebrate diversity?

EXERCISE 3.4

Personality Types and Learning Styles Diversity

As you learned in Chapter 2, there are a variety of ways to describe what we are like and even how we learn. This information is certainly important in understanding ourselves, but it is also helpful as we work with others in the classroom and on the job.

Take, for example, a couple who is trying to decide what to do on Saturday night. One person suggests they go out with friends to a club to dance. The other person suggests they stay home and watch a movie. It's not hard to imagine that the subsequent conversation contains the question "Why do you always want to . . . ?" and either one person gives in and does what the other wants or each does what he or she wants to do on his or her own. Now, consider that the couple has taken a personality test and knows that one of them is an outgoing person and the other is shy. Knowing that each has a different preference when enjoying free time may not eliminate the conflict completely, but it does provide information and insight into the other's likes and dislikes. That information makes it easier for both to appreciate the differences and opens the door to compromise.

Now, consider personality types and diversity in the classroom or workplace. Exhibit 3.1 is an example of how personality diversity can affect group work.

Without knowing why the others are acting the way they do, do you think that this group will be successful in completing their task? Even if they do complete their

EXHIBIT 3.1   Example of Personalities at Play

Michael, Juanita, and Laura are working in a group to complete a task. Michael wants to list all the possible ideas before making a decision on which one they should pursue. Juanita wants to consider only one or two ideas because she feels that going through all of them would waste valuable time. When Juanita and Michael ask Laura which action they should take, she shrugs her shoulders and says, "I don't care. Whatever you want." Michael and Juanita are frustrated by Laura's reaction, because they assume she doesn't care about the project. Laura thinks both Michael and Juanita are wrong in their approach, but they are so domineering, she doesn't think it is worth telling them what she really thinks.

task, they will not be successful in understanding one another's work personality, which may cause problems later on if they are assigned to work together again. For sure, they will not understand themselves well enough to work well with other personality types on future projects. What if, instead of trying to work together without an appreciation for the diversity of personalities, they talk about what they are like and how they like to work? If Laura tells them that she avoids conflict and would rather listen to others than offer an opinion, then they will understand why she responds to what she thinks is impending conflict. If Michael tells the others that he enjoys generating ideas and needs constructive criticism in order to help him shape ideas, he may find that both Juanita and Laura would be more willing to give it to him. If Juanita tells them that she would rather support others toward a common goal rather than come up with the goal herself, the rest of the group may decide to reorganize how they are approaching the project in order to play on each other's personality types and strengths.

Teaching Styles Diversity

You will encounter many different personality types on campus, in and out of the classroom. You will also encounter a variety of teaching styles. It has been said that most professors teach the way they learn best, but there are college instructors who use a variety of teaching methods to encourage student learning. You will be more successful if you can identify each teaching style and what you need to do to adapt to it. Gone are the days of saying, "I just can't learn in her class. She doesn't teach the way I need her to." Like the people who must work together in groups and be sensitive to one another's personalities, you, too, will need to recognize what your learning style is and how it will fit into your professor's teaching style. Ideally, your instructor will recognize that his students have different learning style strengths and adapt his material to those learning styles, but not everyone you will encounter in college will vary his teaching style to meet your needs. Your best bet is to be ready to learn no matter what the teaching style.

To help you recognize the different methods of teaching, Table 3.3 contains a description of each and tips for making the most of the different types of classroom instruction.

TABLE 3.3   Teaching Styles

Teaching Style	Description	Tips for Success	VAK Category
Lecture	Professor talks for the majority of the class; a brief outline may be included; questions are limited or discouraged; usually very structured	Practice good listening skills; record lectures with permission; take good notes during class and review them frequently	Aural
Discussion	Professor poses a question and requires students to answer and build upon an idea or theme	Practice good listening skills; record theme or question for the discussion; note repeated ideas; record essence of each person's contribution; participate in discussion	Aural
Project	Professor bases class learning on projects; provides instruction for assignment; assigns roles; monitors progress	Make connection between project assignment and course objectives; ask for feedback during project to make sure you are progressing; refer to course materials for extra help	Aural, Kinesthetic
Problem solving	Professor poses or writes a problem on the board; walks through solving the problem	Break process down into steps; identify any step that is unclear; ask for extra practice and feedback if needed	Visual, Kinesthetic

Stereotypes

A discussion of diversity is not complete without mentioning some common problems. Stereotyping is an oversimplified opinion of someone or something. We often use stereotypes to make quick decisions every day. When choosing a checkout line, we may make a quick decision as to which is the fastest based on the people in line and what they have in their carts. When playing outfield on a softball team, we may stereotype the smaller players as weaker hitters, which will cause us to move closer to the infield. Parents also encourage children, who have difficulty making complex decisions, to stereotype strangers in order to protect them. Although these stereotypes are not necessarily harmful, they can create problems for us. We may get in a line we think will be shorter, but we end up standing in line for a longer time; we may move so close to the infield that the smaller player hits the ball over our heads; we may confuse children about the characteristics of a stranger, making it difficult for them to trust adults.

Stereotypes can serve a purpose in the short run, but as the examples above illustrate, stereotypes do not take into consideration all the facts. For the most part, stereotypes keep us from having to think about the complexity of issues, and often, then, we are unable to appreciate the beauty of diversity. In essence, stereotypes are a shorthand for evaluating situations and making decisions, but if used repeatedly, they can become prejudice and discrimination.

Prejudice

Prejudice is literally "pre-judging" a person or situation without knowing the facts. Prejudice is often based on stereotyping, which is one of the dangers of stereotyping in the first place. Let's take a seemingly harmless example of stereotyping that can result in prejudice: If you assume that all smaller softball players are weak hitters, then you may take that stereotype a bit further by disliking playing with smaller players because they don't make the game very challenging.

Like stereotyping, prejudice is a judgment based on little or no information or misinformation about a person or thing. In other words, it is based on ignorance or lack of correct information. That is why education is so important—you can avoid prejudging people and things by learning about them and making decisions about them based on *knowledge* rather than ignorance. Although we cannot always avoid stereotyping, we can eliminate prejudice and subsequently eradicate discrimination by making the decision to learn about others.

Types of Prejudice. As you have read above, there are a variety of ways we can categorize and classify ourselves and others. Used as one way of understanding ourselves better, these types of diversity are useful tools. If they are used to stereotype and then make judgments about people based on these stereotypes, then the categories become means to discrimination.

Sexist Attitudes. The increased numbers of women in college has changed the culture to be more sensitive and inclusive to women, but stereotypes and prejudice about females still exist. However, sexism is not limited to prejudice against women. Men, too, can suffer from sexist attitudes that are based on stereotypes. Examples of sexist attitudes in college:

- "My welding instructor is a woman! What does she know about welding? I can't possibly learn what I need to know for a job."
- "My male psychology professor is so much more demanding than the female professor. I should have taken her class instead. Plus, she would understand that I am a parent who has to juggle raising kids and going to school."

Homophobia. Sexual orientation prejudice is often in the form of homophobia, or fear of homosexuals. Homophobia is sometimes born out of ignorance of sexual orientation diversity, and sometimes it comes from a person's own background and values. Examples of homophobic attitudes in college:

- "My algebra instructor is gay. I don't approve of homosexuality, so it makes me very uncomfortable to be in his class."
- "I am avoiding taking composition so that I won't have to take the lesbian instructor who teaches it at the time I need it. She won't grade me fairly because I am a male."

Racist Attitudes. Racist attitudes can be obvious or subtle. People can hold racist views, like all other prejudices, and not realize that they are being intolerant of others. Asking people of other races what kinds of racism they experience is one way to understand what they perceive as prejudice. Monitoring your own words, actions, and attitudes is another way to be more sensitive to other races and cultures. You may think you don't mean any harm by what you say or do, but the recipients of racism don't always agree. Examples of racist attitudes in college:

- "I am going to study with the two Asian Americans in my physics class. They are super smart and maybe that will rub off on me."
- "The Hispanics at this college are only here to keep from being deported back to their own country. I resent having to take classes with them."

Ageist Attitudes. As you read earlier in the chapter, different generations have different values and viewpoints. An environment in which people from different generations work closely together can be exciting or tense, depending on how much people are willing to recognize, understand, and appreciate their generational differences. Problems arise, though, when people have prejudicial attitudes about a certain age group. We usually think of ageist attitudes as ones that stereotype people older than us, but people can hold prejudicial views against those younger than they. Examples of ageist attitudes in college:

- "I don't want to be in a study group with him. He could be my grandfather, and I am sure that he doesn't know one thing about computer networks."
- "I can't relate to the girls in my project group. All they talk about is going out and getting drunk. They have no real responsibilities and they don't take this class seriously."

Discrimination

Discrimination occurs when an action is taken on the basis of the prejudice. If, for instance, you decide that you do not want to play softball with teams with smaller players because you believe they are not as fun as teams with bigger players, then you have discriminated against smaller players and their teams. Because of recent laws and lawsuits, colleges and other places of business are sensitive to discrimination issues and spend a large amount of time and resources educating employees about it. Sexism, racism, and ageism are types of discrimination that are the most common in the workplace. It will be an important part of your education to understand how and why people discriminate so that you can avoid similar problems that stem from discrimination, which is why this chapter spends a considerable amount of time on this subject.

Even though most workplaces strive hard to eliminate sexual, racial, and age discrimination, there are still other types that can appear in everyday situations. For example, a coworker may declare that she won't hire anyone from a certain college because she believes that all its graduates are more interested in partying than working. Your boss may state his disdain for people from a certain part of the country and then refuse to promote an employee who is originally from the same area. Although you may not be able to change everyone's mind, you should be attuned to these more subtle, and sometimes acceptable, forms of discrimination and make an effort to eliminate them.

PLUS

(Personality + Learning Style = Understanding Situations)

Consider Michael's situation with his classmates. Although he is outspoken in class, confronting another person one-on-one is not his strength, and because he is not sure if his study group is shutting him out intentionally, he doesn't want to make the situation worse. He is also a visual learner, so what he sees or visualizes has a greater effect on him. Using what you have learned from this chapter, what advice would you give him? How can he combat the stereotypes that some in his group seem to have or that he has about others?

Now, considering your own learning style, personality type, and special circumstances, what would you do to resolve a conflict with your classmates in which you were required to work together on a project? How would you deal with any stereotyping, prejudging, or discrimination that may occur in the group?

PROFILE

MY STORY
Learning Plan

Directions: Using what you have learned in this chapter and what you know about your learning preferences, choose a task or assignment that needs to be completed soon and create a learning plan that will help you accomplish this task. Then, write your *My Story* Summary, a one-sentence synopsis that crystallizes your newly created plan.

PROFILE

LEARNING TASK	
Time of Day	
Intake Preference	
Social Preference	
Task Management Preference	

MY STORY SUMMARY:

Path of Discovery

Journal Entry

HOMEWORK

Reflect on how the information about diversity and relationships in this chapter has made you think about how you have treated others in the past. What mistakes have you made? What have you done well in terms of treating others with respect? What will you do in the future?

From College to University

The Relationships You Foster Now Will Open Doors after Transfer

Your relationships with advisors, counselors, and professors should yield more contacts at your new school. Advisors and counselors will be able to recommend certain programs and administrators. Professors will be able to put in a good word with the people they know at your transfer school, which may mean extra consideration for admission into a program or for a scholarship.

Those same relationships may also prove fruitful if your advisors, counselors, or professors have inside knowledge of little-known internships and aid, or if they know about deadline extensions and special transfer scholarships. The closer the relationships you have, the better able you will be to use your connections to make a smooth transfer. Advisors, counselors, and professors can also provide advice about the particular challenges you may face once you have completed the move.

From College to Career

Dealing with Diversity Is a Key to Success on the Job

We sometimes think that once we reach our ultimate educational goal and have started our dream career, we will be magically transported to a world in which everyone gets along. Unfortunately, we are brought back down from the clouds as early as the first day on the job.

Certainly, you will never stop needing to make positive connections with others or to redefine the relationships you already have. You will also encounter diversity on a daily basis and will have to rely on what you have learned in college (and life in general) in order to consider others' feelings, beliefs, and attitudes. What you have learned in college about other cultures, time periods, and philosophical and political ideas should provide you with a well-rounded view and will make it easier to work with and appreciate your diverse coworkers.

Chapter Review Questions

1. Name and explain four different categories of diversity.

2. How will you use what you have learned in this chapter to start and improve relationships with people on campus? Whom will you seek out and why?

3. What strategies can you use to deal with difficult people?

Chapter 3 Case Scenarios

1. Jonathan has been raised in a very religious household. He believes that homosexuality is wrong, and he is struggling with an assignment in one of his classes in which he must write about the issue from a sociological perspective. The professor cautioned the students that they must be objective in their papers, but Jonathan doesn't think he can. What should Jonathan do?

2. Marie has been married for 14 years. She and her husband have twin girls who are 12. Since Marie started college, she has noticed that her husband seems less interested in her and what she is learning in her classes. He has started belittling her desire to earn a degree. Although he first encouraged her to enroll at the nearby community college branch in their town, he now seems to be against her continuing her education there. Marie has been discouraged by his reaction and is thinking about not enrolling next semester. What would you tell Marie to do?

3. One of Willis's professors has missed three night classes in a row without telling the students beforehand and without providing a plan to make up the missed material. Willis really needs this class for his major in business, and he is worried that he won't be successful in subsequent classes. He is also worried that if he complains to the instructor, his grade will be lowered in retaliation. Because he may have to take the professor again later, what should he do?

Research It Further

1. Review the section on teaching styles and determine what styles might be missing. Interview classmates in different courses to get ideas for other teaching styles. Write your own descriptions of the new styles and provide tips for being successful in those classes.

2. What does your college do to promote cultural appreciation on the campus? Collect examples of the college's promotion of multiculturalism and determine what, if anything, the college could do to enhance racial, ethnic, and cultural sensitivity and understanding.

3. What is your college's policy regarding relationships between students and faculty? In addition to reviewing your student handbook, interview students, faculty, and administrators about their opinions on the faculty-student relationship.

References

American Association of Community Colleges. (2004). Retrieved July 13, 2005, from www.aacc.nche.edu

Katz, N. (2005). Sexual harassment statistics in the workplace and in education. Retrieved July 5, 2005, from http://womenissues.about.com/cs/sexdiscrimination/a/sexharassstats.htm

Zemke, R., Raines, C., & Filipczak, B. (2000). *Generations at work: Managing the clash of veterans, boomers, xers, and nexters in your workplace.* New York: Amacom.

4 Managing Your Time

Laura's Story

Pouring her fourth cup of coffee at 11:00 p.m., Laura searches for her history paper assignment that she copied from the board. It's due at 9 a.m. tomorrow. She sinks into her chair at the kitchen table to go through her backpack one more time and debates whether or not to call a classmate for help. As she begins to tremble from the caffeine, her mind races. Is it too late to call? Will he know how to help her? Laura doesn't normally procrastinate about her school work, but her middle child has been sick for two days and she's been home caring for him and taking him to doctor's appointments. Because of her dyslexia, Laura has taken good notes during class. Her study routine includes recording each lecture, listening to each one repeatedly, and then writing and rewriting what she hears. For information that her professor emphasizes as important, she rewrites her notes in red. Although she still can't find the assignment with the specific requirements, she does have her lecture notes to work with to begin the paper.

At midnight, she is still working. Even though she has downed another cup of coffee, she is tired and her eyes begin to water. She listens to the recorded lecture in which her professor introduces the assignment.

Three hours; two more cups of coffee; a bag of spicy corn nuts; a 68-ounce, fruit-flavored sports drink; and one rerun of *Judge Judy* later, Laura's paper is finished. As she prints her final copy, the printer begins to screech loudly and stops with her last page clutched in its mouth. The ink light blinks at her like her mother's pointing finger saying, "You shouldn't have waited to the last minute, Laura Leigh. This is what happens when you procrastinate."

Frantic, she rips the page from the printer and shakes the ink cartridge in hopes that she can get the last page printed before she hits the bed. When she presses print, the first three words barely appear on the page before the ink completely disappears. The only thing she can do is to save her paper to a thumb drive and hope that tomorrow provides her with a solution.

Exhausted, she shuffles to bed. She sets her alarm an hour earlier so that she can call her mother to come over and watch her son. Before her head reaches the pillow, she remembers a flyer she found for the campus computer lab, which opens at 7 a.m. This may be the solution she was hoping for if she can get to the campus early.

After several hours of deep sleep, Laura has a renewed determination to get the assignment finished and submitted. Because she gets to campus early, she is able to print off the remaining page in the computer lab—thanks to some help from the lab assistant. As she slides into her seat in her history class, she pulls her completed paper out, looks it over one more time, and turns it in. It may not be her best work, she thinks, but it is finished.

"I will return your papers next week," says her professor. He turns to write on the board and says, "In the meantime, you may want to get started on your next paper assignment on Greek culture."

Laura reaches into her backpack, replaces her pen with a red marker, and writes "IMPORTANT" at the top of her page as she copies the assignment from the board.

In This Chapter

In Laura's story, she is feeling the effects of "life getting in the way" as she manages her time and tries to minimize her stress. Would you have done the same as Laura? Would there be anything you would have done differently, either during the same situation or before it even happened? To help you answer those questions, this chapter focuses on the different time and stress management options that can help you stay on task throughout your college career and handle tough situations. Your goal in reading this chapter will be to find the method that works best for you and that helps you keep time and stress more manageable. Specifically, you will be able to:

- Determine what steps are needed to get organized.
- Consider different time management strategies.
- Examine goals and priorities as they relate to time management.
- Explain how your energy levels are an important part of time management.
- Identify time and energy zappers.
- Identify strategies to eliminate procrastination.
- Recognize methods for minimizing stress at work, home, and college.

Is Time on Your Side?

Is it surprising that the number one issue that community college students say is their biggest challenge is **time management?** Why do so many students identify time management as one of the areas that they need more help with? The answer may be that for many of them, they are adding another responsibility to their busy lives. Another answer could be that they are now expected to do things they haven't done before or haven't done for a long time. Being a student demands more than just showing up for class. There is plenty of work to do outside of class—at home, in the library, on the computer, and in study groups. Being aware of how you spend your time and choosing the most effective strategies for you will not only help you complete more tasks in a *timely manner*, but will also help you minimize the stress that comes from trying to juggle many responsibilities.

The benefits of managing time effectively include not only getting tasks completed, but also experiencing the success of accomplishment. Darwin B. Nelson and Gary R. Low (2003), in their book *Emotional Intelligence: Achieving Academic and Career Excellence,* state that "[a]n important by-product of good Time Management is a feeling of self-control—we are managing our responsibilities, not being managed by them" (pp. 100–101). You will certainly feel more in control of your time after you complete this chapter!

Getting Organized

The first aspect to consider when it comes to managing your time and stress is getting organized. Seems like a simple idea, but think about how much time you have wasted before when you couldn't find something or how you missed an important event because you didn't write it down. Nothing is more stressful than knowing you could have done better if you had been organized! Getting organized for success, however, doesn't have to take a lot of money and time. If you use a few simple strategies, you can save yourself both time and energy in the long run. To help get organized, think of the three S's: Supplies, Space, and Same Time. The three **S's** consists of getting the right **supplies** (including a calendar), keeping your **space** clean and organized, and checking your "to do list" or calendar at the **same time** each day.

Supplies for Success

Pens, pencils, calculators, paper, notebooks, and thumb drives, oh my! There are so many items you will need in college to get organized and complete assignments—not including books, lab manuals, and computer access. What you *need* will depend on what you are taking and what your instructors' expectations are. What you *want* to get in addition will depend on your preferences and your budget. At the very least, a good, sturdy backpack that can accommodate all your books and notebooks—and that doesn't break your back—should be high on your supply list.

Many a good student has fallen victim to "assignment amnesia." This disorder occurs when otherwise smart students believe they can remember all of their assignments and appointments without writing them down and without consulting their syllabi or course outlines. Fortunately, there are measures you can take to prevent an attack of assignment amnesia: using a calendar or a device, like a cell phone, that keeps track of your assignments, especially one in which you also add all the tasks you need to complete from your personal, professional, and college life.

If you use a paper calendar, you have many different types from which to choose. Once you determine the type that works best for you—a monthly, weekly, or daily calendar—make a habit of writing down your tasks, no matter how big or small. Here is an example of a typical list of a day's activities for a student like Laura:

THURSDAY

- Make appointment to have oil changed
- Pick up medicine for Terrence
- Take Phillip to baseball
- Study for history quiz on Friday
- Read 30 pages for English
- Get book from library

A typical monthly calendar, as Exhibit 4.1 shows, allows you to see several weeks at once so that you can remain aware of upcoming events, but often there is little space on a monthly calendar to write down detailed lists such as the one above.

A weekly calendar, such as the one in Exhibit 4.2, allows you to glance at one week at a time. A benefit to a weekly calendar is that you have room to write details of each activity; however, a drawback to a weekly calendar is that it is difficult to anticipate what you must do the next week.

Daily calendars usually provide the most space to write your day-to-day tasks and appointments. This kind of calendar may be the most difficult to work with if you need to plan ahead. Because you cannot see the rest of the week or month, you may overlook important events or be surprised by them. Use a daily calendar, like

EXHIBIT 4.1   Lightly Scheduled Monthly Calendar

SUNDAY	MONDAY	TUESDAY	WEDNESDAY	THURSDAY	FRIDAY	SATURDAY
					1	2
3	4	5	6	7	8	9 picnic—noon
10	11 work late	12	13	14	15 pay bills	16
17	18	19	20	21 play rehearsal 7:00	22	23
24	25 nutrition exam 10:00	26	27	28	29	30 birthday party 2:00

EXHIBIT 4.2   Heavily Scheduled Weekly Calendar

MONDAY	TUESDAY	WEDNESDAY	THURSDAY	FRIDAY	SATURDAY	SUNDAY
8:30 Work	9:00 English	8:30 Work	9:00 English	8:30 Work	8–10 Clean house	3–8 Work on paper
2:00 Geology	11:00 Acct.	2:00 Geology	11:00 Acct.	2:00 Geology	3–4 Exercise	
3:00 Trig	6:00 Help sister with painting	3:00 Trig		3:00 Trig	6–11 Study	
5:00 Pick up dinner				7:00 Movie with friend		
7:00 Study for Accounting						

the one in Exhibit 4.3, if you are extremely organized and can plan ahead effectively, or use it in addition to a monthly calendar.

Space Considerations

The right stuff and the ideal calendar are first steps to managing your time well, but there is more you can do. To manage your time effectively and efficiently, create a clutter-free space where you can study and complete assignments. If you don't have a place in your house or apartment that you can call your own, a comfortable chair or seat at the kitchen table may be all that you can spare. Make sure it is comfortable and quiet and has adequate space for books, notebooks, and other supplies. It has to be a place where you *want* to be or it will be difficult to go there to stay on task.

EXHIBIT 4.3   Daily Calendar

FRIDAY
MARCH 12, 2010

7:00	Wake up, shower, get ready for school
8:00	Drive to school, arrive early, study in the library
9:00	College Algebra
10:00	English 2
11:00	Study for Biology exam
12:00	Eat lunch and review notes for College Algebra
1:00	Biology—EXAM!!
2:00	Drive to work
3:00	Work
4:00	Work
5:00	Work

Same Time, Same Place

A good system for writing down your daily tasks and establishing a place to complete your assignments are a good foundation to managing your time well and reducing the negative effects of stress. However, there is one last tip: Create a routine. In other words, every evening write down your goals for the next day and every morning review what you need to do for the day. Knowing what to expect for the day will make surprises less likely. As you complete each task, scratch it off the list. You will get the satisfaction of a completed job and can focus on the next task.

Making Time for College

How much time should you devote to college? Some first-time students seriously underestimate the amount of time that is needed to prepare for a class, study for tests, and complete assignments. Unfortunately, they often realize their error when an assignment is due or a test is given. A common formula for calculating the amount of study time is to multiply the number of credit hours for the course by three. For example, a demanding class that carries three credit hours and meets three times per week for 1 hour each time will require 9 hours per week of out-of-class work. These 9 hours plus the 3 hours in class means you will spend a total of 12 hours studying and attending that one class each week. Multiply 12 hours by 4 classes and you will have a 48-hour college work week. Add 40 hours of work on the job and you will be spending 88 hours per week working on your job and your classes!

EXHIBIT 4.4   Student College Schedule

RESPONSIBILITY	CONTACT HOURS PER WEEK	OUTSIDE HOURS PER WEEK	TOTAL HOURS PER WEEK
College Algebra	3	6–9	9–12
Composition 101	3	6–9	9–12
U.S. History	3	6–9	9–12
Reading	3	6–9	9–12
Work	25		25

Total Hours per Week: 61–73 Hours

Looking at Exhibit 4.4 can be overwhelming for students, especially if they work more than 25 hours and take more than 12 credit hours per semsester. A full-time student who also works full time can expect to spend half her hours a week working on classes or at work (and that doesn't include time to sleep!). Studies have shown that the reality of how much time students spend outside of class is much lower than the recommended number of hours, but students often find that how much time they spend varies from semester to semester, depending on what kinds of classes they take.

To see how the recommended study hours look when they are scheduled throughout the week, check out Laura's calendar in Exhibit 4.5. She works full-time, a 40-hour week, and is in class 12 hours each week.

Given Laura's schedule in Exhibit 4.5, will she be able to reach the 48 hours that are needed to take and study for college classes? If she were to add two hours a night after class—and if she felt like studying after a long day—she would study an additional 10 hours during the work week, which leaves 22 hours and 15 minutes of studying to be completed in her "spare time."

Look at the calendar again. In order to reach 48 hours of studying and class, where will Laura include additional study time? Will she need to study every waking moment that she is not at work, in class, or taking care of herself and her other responsibilities? If she could not devote that much time to her college classes, would Laura need to take fewer classes, ask for help with home responsibilities, or cut back on her hours at work? Despite what some may think, Laura doesn't have to give up her dream to be in college, but she will need to rearrange her schedule. Without doing so, she will not be able to meet the demands of her classes. However, she can feel some comfort in knowing that getting up a little earlier, multitasking, and using her weekends for studying at longer intervals will be short-term changes to her schedule.

But What Do I Do?

The question sometimes arises as to what you should be doing for those 6–9 hours each week. For one, you will need to read any assigned material *before* class. Another activity that will need to be part of your outside study time is reviewing your notes

EXHIBIT 4.5   Laura's Weekly Calendar

MONDAY	TUESDAY	WEDNESDAY	THURSDAY	FRIDAY	SATURDAY	SUNDAY
6:30–7:30 Get ready for school	6:30–7:30 Get ready for school	6:30–7:30 Get ready for school	6:30–7:30 Get ready for school	6:30–7:30 Get ready for school	7:00–10:00 Clean house, shop	7:00–10:00 Study
7:30–7:45 Travel to work	7:30–7:45 Travel to work	7:30–7:45 Travel to work	7:30–7:45 Travel to work	7:30–7:45 Travel to work	10:00–11:30 Soccer	10:00–11:00 Go to church
8:00–12:30 Work	8:00–12:30 Work	8:00–12:30 Work	8:00–12:30 Work	8:00–12:30 Work	11:30–12:15 Lunch with team	11:15–12:30 Lunch with parents
12:30–1:15 Eat lunch and run errands	12:30–1:15 Go to doctor's appointment	12:30–1:15 Eat lunch with friend	12:30–1:15 Eat lunch and walk 1 mile	12:30–1:15 Eat lunch and study	12:15–2:00 Run errands	12:45–3:45 Study
1:15–4:45 Work	1:15–4:45 Work	1:15–4:45 Work	1:15–4:45 Work	1:15–4:45 Work	2:00–6:00 Go to library and do research	3:45–5:45 Do yard work
4:45–5:00 Travel	4:45–5:00 Travel	4:45–5:00 Travel	4:45–5:00 Travel	4:45–5:00 Travel	6:00–7:00 Fix and eat dinner	6:00–7:00 Eat dinner
5:00–5:45 Eat dinner and study	5:00–5:45 Eat dinner and study	5:00–5:45 Eat dinner and study	5:00–5:45 Eat dinner and study	5:00–7:00 Eat dinner with friends	7:00–9:00 Study	7:00–8:00 Walk 3 miles
6:00–9:30 Classes	6:00–9:30 Classes	6:00–9:30 Classes	6:00–9:30 Classes	7:00–9:30 See movie	9:00–10:00 Answer email and watch TV	8:00–10:00 Do laundry, get ready for next week
10:00 Go to bed	10:00 Go to bed	10:00 Go to bed	10:00 Go to bed	10:00 Go to bed	10:00 Go to bed	10:00 Go to bed

from class and filling in any gaps in information that you were not able to get by working with a classmate. Rewriting your notes after the discussion of the chapter or topic is another very important way you can spend an hour for the week. Of course, you will need to budget time to complete assignments, whether they are review questions at the end of a chapter or a research project.

The plan in Exhibit 4.6 is for *one* college class. If you have more than one, you will need to add an hour each day of the week for each 3-credit-hour class that you are taking.

EXHIBIT 4.6   One-Hour-a-Day Time Management Plan

DAY OF THE WEEK	TIME	ASSIGNMENT	COMPLETED	
Sunday	3:30–4:30 p.m.	Read Chapter 5 and take notes while reading. Review notes after reading the chapter once.	Yes	No
Monday	7:00–8:00 p.m.	Review reading notes as well as class notes. Define all vocabulary terms that are key to the chapter and that are unfamiliar.	Yes	No
Tuesday	11:15–12:15 p.m.	Answer study questions that accompany the chapter.	Yes	No
Wednesday	8:00–9:00 p.m.	Create sample test questions on flash cards and write the answers on the back.	Yes	No
Thursday	7:00–8:00 p.m.	Complete homework questions for the chapter.	Yes	No
Friday	5:30–6:00 a.m. and 3:30–4:00 p.m.	Review flash cards.	Yes	No
Saturday	3:30–4:30 p.m.	Rewrite notes from the entire week of class. Include any material that was assigned in the reading but not covered in class.	Yes	No

Even with the best intentions, many students, however, opt to cut back on studying because the other activities, such as running errands and participating in their children's activities, are necessary parts of their lives and cannot be eliminated or rearranged. Realistically, you may be able to cut back on studying in some classes at slower times; however, you should not eliminate study hours for all classes throughout each semester. Your best bet is to recognize that taking college classes is a tremendous time commitment and to work your other responsibilities (except maintaining your health) around them as best you can. You won't always be able to put college as your first priority, but you will need to make a conscious effort to put studying near the top of your list most of the time.

Managing Your Time

Despite our many differences, what we all have in common is that we have the same number of hours each day and the same number of days each week. Why, then, does it seem as though some people are more accomplished than others? Are they able to magically extend the day by a few hours or sneak eight days into a week? Do they forgo all sleep, meals, and personal needs just to get things done? We would like to believe that high achievers have superhuman strength, but the truth is they usually do not do anything to achieve their goals that we cannot do as well. When you talk to very productive people, they usually tell you that the secret to their success is that they have learned to manage their time efficiently. Effective time management is not a talent; it is a skill, one that gets better as you practice over time.

EXHIBIT 4.7   Time Log Example

TIME	WEDNESDAY'S ACTIVITIES
7:00 a.m.	Get ready for classes; eat breakfast
7:30 a.m.	Review notes for business class
8:00 a.m.	En route to school
8:30 a.m.	Business Communications
9:00 a.m.	Class, continued
9:30 a.m.	Class, continued
10:00 a.m.	See advisor to plan next semester's classes

Analyzing Your Time

After recognizing that we all have the same number of hours, analyzing your time is another step to effective time management. Tim Hindle (1998), in his book *Manage Your Time,* suggests keeping a time log of your day that is divided into 30-minute increments (p. 9). Separate from your calendar, the purpose of a 30-minute time log is to help raise your awareness of what you are doing throughout the day. You can make your own time log like the one in Exhibit 4.7 and keep up with one day's worth of activities, but be sure to give yourself time to write down your activities either every few hours or at the end of the day. Keeping an eye on how you spend your time will help you make realistic time management goals and will keep you from wasting too much time or miscalculating how much time it takes you to complete tasks.

Asking the questions "Where did the time go?" and "What do I do with my time?" is a start to analyzing your time. You will also need to analyze your time management skills—or how well you use your time wisely to meet your goals and stay healthy in the process. The assessment in Activity 4.1 asks 10 questions about time management abilities.

Back-Dating Time Management Plan

If there is one piece of advice that experienced students want to pass along to new students that would help them manage their time better, it is that even though they sound the same when spoken aloud, the words "due" and "do" *don't* mean the same thing. Starting the night before an assignment is due may create more stress than is necessary. Therefore, the method of creating "do" dates before

Critical Thinking

EXERCISE 4.1

Look at all the calendars and time management strategies in this chapter. Which ones seem to be easier for you to use? What are the characteristics that make the calendars easier or harder for you to use?

PRACTICE

ACTIVITY 4.1   Personal Time Assessment

Circle the number (1—Never, 2—Sometimes, 3—Usually, 4—Always) that best describes your experience.

STATEMENT	NEVER	SOMETIMES	USUALLY	ALWAYS
1. I arrive at class prepared.	1	2	3	4
2. I review my notes within 24 hours of class.	1	2	3	4
3. I spend my time on campus taking care of personal business, talking with professors, studying, or doing research.	1	2	3	4
4. I have study goals, and I achieve them each week.	1	2	3	4
5. I feel prepared for tests.	1	2	3	4
6. I spend enough time on writing assignments.	1	2	3	4
7. I get enough sleep each night.	1	2	3	4
8. I spend some time each week doing something I enjoy.	1	2	3	4
9. I have enough time to take care of most of my personal needs.	1	2	3	4
10. I get support from others to help me meet my educational goals.	1	2	3	4
Score each column.				
Add each column's total.			Total	

SCORE RANGE	MEANING
40–32	You do a good job of managing your time. For the most part, you are satisfied with how you manage your time and what you accomplish each week.
31–26	You are doing a good job managing your time for most activities. Identify your weaker areas and create a plan to improve time management in those areas.
25–19	You may be dissatisfied with your time management and find only a few goals are met each week. Review what you are doing right with some of your time and make a plan that will draw upon your time management strengths.
Below 18	You may feel as though you are not meeting the majority of your goals during the week. An honest look at your goals, your necessary activities, and your priorities is needed.

EXHIBIT 4.8   Back-Dating Time Management

SUNDAY	MONDAY	TUESDAY	WEDNESDAY	THURSDAY	FRIDAY	SATURDAY
		1	2	3	4	5
6	7	8 1:00 p.m. Receive paper assignment	9 6–7:30 p.m. Choose paper topic; brainstorm or freewrite on topic	10	11 9–10:30 p.m. Reread brainstorming list; create a draft outline	12
13 3–5:00 p.m. Write first draft of paper	14	15 11–12:00 noon Visit writing lab for assistance with paper	16	17	18 8:30–10:30 p.m. Write second draft of paper, incorporating tutor's advice	19
20 3–4:30 p.m. Write final draft of paper	21	22	23 8–9:00 p.m. Edit paper; print on quality paper; place in backpack	24 2:00 p.m. Turn in paper	25	26
27	28	29	30			

your assignment is "due," or back-dating assignments, is an essential one to use if you are going to create habits of completing assignments successfully. To see how this works, let's say you have a career exploration paper that is due on the 24th of this month (see Exhibit 4.8). In order to build enough time into your schedule, you can use a calendar to divide the possible steps to your paper and fill in the calendar with the time that you have to work on the paper. When back-dating assignment tasks, remember to provide adequate time between tasks so that you can reflect on the work that you have done and approach the assignment with "fresh eyes" each time.

Making Time for Relationships

No doubt you are getting the connection between college success and time management. Remember from Chapter 3 that a good relationship with at least one person at your college can mean the difference between completing a degree and dropping out. Then, it should be no surprise that cultivating and maintaining good relationships takes time and takes making time to work on them. Experienced students will tell you that when they were new students they underestimated how much time they would need to devote to meeting with advisors, counselors, and professors outside of class. Some think that unless there is an academic problem, they will not need to see their professors regularly during their office hours. Nothing could be farther from the truth: If your goal is to make solid connections during the semester with your professors, you will need more time than just before class or right after. Moreover, if you find that you will need to work closely with a counselor or tutor, you will have to find enough time during the week to make that happen. Some students schedule their classes and work or family obligations with so little wiggle room that substantial amounts of time to get extra help or to plan out their degrees are nonexistent.

With this said, it is a good idea to look at your schedule now (and consider this when you plan for next semester) and see what days and times work best for meeting with people on campus. Try to keep those times free and clear in case you need to use them at the last minute. If you find you do not need that time that day to take care of personal business on campus or to talk to your professor, then you have a little extra time that can be used for studying, completing assignments, or even relaxing a bit. It is hard to make any relationship work if you don't spend enough time nurturing it; likewise, relationships in college, whether they are with professors, counselors, advisors, or fellow classmates, need time to develop. The benefits of taking the time to cultivate strong relationships are endless and can certainly help you stay on course and possibly provide you with new opportunities for connections you couldn't have imagined.

Reflection

EXERCISE 4.2

Consider what you have read so far about managing your time. Write down what you think will be your greatest challenges in managing your time in college.

PRACTICE

Managing Your Priorities

Managing your time and priorities when you are in college can be a game of strategy, action, and patience. In the following exercise, consider what should be top priority; what can be completed if there is time; and what can be delegated, modified, or rescheduled for another day.

It is Monday morning and you have 10 items on your "to do" list (Exhibit 4.9) that you would like to get accomplished today, but you don't have enough time to complete all the items. Determine which activities are top priorities and which are not. Then, list what you have eliminated from the list and explain why you decided to make it a low priority item. Finally, describe how you will accomplish the low priority items the next day.

From the list in Exhibit 4.9, determine what three items should be top priority.

Top Priority _____

Top Priority _____

Top Priority _____

Why did you determine these priorities to be the most important?

_____

_____

With the time remaining, determine what else can be accomplished in the same day.

Additional activity _____

Additional activity _____

EXHIBIT 4.9   To Do List

MONDAY'S TO DO LIST—FOURTH WEEK OF CLASSES

- Pick up sister from airport at 7:30 p.m. (Airport is 15 minutes away.)

- Attend two classes, one at 2:00 p.m. and one at 4:00 p.m. (You have a one-hour break in between.)

- Complete paper for 4:00 class. (You will need an hour to finish.)

- Prepare dinner for family at 6:30 p.m. (It will take at least 30 minutes.)

- Study for Tuesday's psychology exam. (You would like to spend two hours.)

- Take children to school at 7:45 a.m. (School is 10 minutes from your house.)

- Get up at 6:00 a.m. and go to gym for an hour's workout.

- Call your cousin who had surgery last week. (30 minutes)

- Help children with homework. (1 hour)

- Meet study group at noon to start working on final project in business communications class.

Additional activity _____

Additional activity _____

Why did you determine that the above activities could be completed if time allowed?

_____

_____

What items can be low priority, modified, or rescheduled?

Low priority _____

Low priority _____

Low priority _____

Why did you choose these items as low priority?

_____

_____

How could you modify the low-priority items so that they could be completed in the same day?

_____

_____

Before you can begin to manage your time, you will need to make sure that your goals and priorities are clear. As you learned in Chapter 2, writing down your goals and setting your priorities, which may change frequently, are the first steps to realizing your dreams; they are also the first steps to figuring out how much time you need to spend on each goal. Before you can think about time management, take time to review what you have written down as your short-term goals and priorities.

If you were to list your priorities right now, college would be near the top of the list. Certainly, your enrolling in college and reading this book mean that you are committed to furthering your education. Nevertheless, you will need to figure out where the priority of going to college fits in with your other priorities. Perhaps attending classes is your only priority because you live alone and do not work; more likely, however, college will compete with other priorities. If you are going to succeed in college, your education must be a top priority the majority of the time.

In addition to college, you may need to consider your family as a priority. Depending on your situation, you may have family members who need you for emotional, physical, and financial support. You may even be the only one they can rely on. Because family is often a first priority for many students, it will be important to manage your time with them wisely and effectively.

If you have not done so yet, you should talk to your family about the new responsibilities that you will have. Be honest in your descriptions of what you will be doing and what you will need from them. If you think your time will be limited for family trips and weekend activities, let them know. If you think you will need to cut out some basic duties such as planning meals, cleaning the house, and running errands, be sure to communicate this to your family. The more they know about what to expect, the better able they will be to support your decision to enroll in college.

Time is valuable only if you plan and use it well.

Another priority that you may have is your job. Most community college students work as well as attend classes. For some, their jobs supplement their household income and are not necessary for survival; for many others, their jobs are more important than college because they provide the primary or sole income for the family. If your job is your top priority, then you should know where the other priorities must fall, and you should be prepared to make sacrifices in other areas to ensure that your job remains at the top.

With all the other responsibilities you have, it is easy to overlook the priority of relaxing; without it, the other priorities can run you down. Don't forget that you can have fun while in college, and you certainly want to allow yourself to participate in activities that you enjoy. Without them, your college career will seem stressful and dull. Scheduling "down time" to play and rejuvenate will be an important part of effective time management. Get outside, read for pleasure, or participate in the types of activities you enjoy. Relaxing and having fun will recharge your body and mind to concentrate on the demands of your other priorities.

Managing Your Energy

Just as important as managing your time is managing your energy. Think about this scenario: You have all weekend off from work and your spouse has taken the kids to visit their grandparents. Therefore, you have 48 hours of complete solitude to write a research paper that is due on Monday. Sounds ideal, doesn't it? But what if you have the flu for those two days? Does the time mean anything when you don't have the energy to do any work? What if, instead of having the flu, you pulled two double shifts and haven't slept more than 5 hours in two days? Will you be able to use your free 48 hours productively or will you need to take care of yourself?

Time, in other words, is only valuable if you have the energy to use it well. Thus, you need to be aware of how you feel, how energetic you are, and how willing you are to use your time wisely. To determine which times of the day you feel the most energetic, place an "X" in the appropriate column of Activity 4.2 for each time of day. If you work nights and sleep during most of the day, create your own chart with the times that you are awake.

In addition to the time of day, your energy levels rise and fall during the week. Do you find yourself tired on Monday mornings, but full of energy on Fridays? Or do you feel worn out by Thursday evenings, but rejuvenated on Sundays? Depending

ACTIVITY 4.2   Time of Day Energy Levels

TIME OF DAY	HIGH ENERGY	NEUTRAL	LOW ENERGY
6:00 a.m.			
8:00 a.m.			
10:00 a.m.			
12 noon			
2:00 p.m.			
4:00 p.m.			
6:00 p.m.			
8:00 p.m.			
10:00 p.m.			
12 midnight			

ACTIVITY 4.3   Day of Week Energy Levels

WEEKDAY	HIGH ENERGY	NEUTRAL	LOW ENERGY
Sunday			
Monday			
Tuesday			
Wednesday			
Thursday			
Friday			
Saturday			

on your work, school, and personal schedules, you will find that you have regular bursts of energy at certain times of the week. To determine which days of the week you feel most energetic, write an "X" in the appropriate columns in Activity 4.3.

Identifying Time and Energy Zappers

Despite your best efforts in managing your time and energy, there will be times when you find your best-laid plans are interrupted by needy people and last-minute changes in plans. A few distractions during the day can be a nice break from the mundane tasks of going to school and working or caring for a family. However, if they take so much time away from your studies that you can't seem to keep up with the pace of your classes or that you are stressed out, you will need to find ways to lessen the frequency of or eliminate the intrusions altogether.

You may be able to create your own list of time and energy zappers, but here are a few common ones:

- People who want your attention and time, but who don't need it
- Interruptions such as unnecessary phone calls
- Fatigue and illness
- Personal problems
- Mindless television watching
- Internet surfing that serves no purpose
- Continuous "chatting" online
- Playing video or computer games
- Inability to say "no"
- Procrastination
- Poor organization
- Inability to concentrate because of learning difficulty, medication, or stress

Now is the time to block out the zappers. You won't be able to afford the time that they waste, and you will need to be proactive in getting rid of them. Some will be easy to reduce or get rid of, such as playing video games or hanging out all day with friends; others will be more difficult, such as learning to say "no" to people or eliminating procrastination. The key to getting rid of the energy and time wasters is to take on the easiest ones and work on the others through goal setting. Of course, one person's time waster is another person's stress reliever. If you find that playing a video game or going to a movie with friends is necessary to refresh yourself before tackling other important tasks, schedule it as part of your weekly routine. When those activities keep you from finishing others, then it may be time to reassess how often you do them.

One way to help yourself manage your energy is by becoming aware of what activities relax you when you are stressed and what activities allow you to refill your energy reserves. In Activity 4.4, place an "X" in the appropriate column next to each activity. If the activity does both, place an "X" in both columns. If the activity neither relaxes nor energizes, then leave both columns blank. Use this chart when planning your time. If an activity rejuvenates you, helps you recharge, you may want

ACTIVITY 4.4   Time and Energy Zappers

ACTIVITY	RELAXING	ENERGIZING
Watching television		
Spending time with family/friends		
Pleasure reading		
Doing housework		
Exercising (light to moderate)		
Gardening		
Talking on the phone		
Writing		
Cooking		
Shopping		
Napping		
Participating in a hobby		
Surfing the Internet		
Organizing closets, drawers, files		
Enjoying a nice meal		

Collaboration

Working within a group or with another classmate, describe the types of activities that can zap students' time and energy, then create solutions for managing them. Present your ideas to the class.

EXERCISE 4.3

to schedule times to do it when you need more energy. If an activity helps you wind down, you may want to schedule it after you have completed major tasks.

Running Low on Time and Energy

There will be times when you find yourself with goals for the day or week still left on your list, but you don't have the time and energy reserves that you hoped to have. Sometimes life throws us a curveball, and our beautiful plans are mangled if not completely destroyed. If you find yourself in such a situation, then you will benefit from changing goals and priorities quickly and eliminating unnecessary items from your "to do" list. For example, you had planned to bake a friend a birthday cake from scratch, but you don't have two hours to do it. What can you do? How about buying a cake on the way to your friend's house? The outcome is still the same: Your friend has a cake for his birthday. You hoped to get all the bills paid by the end of the day, but you don't have the time and energy left? Pay the bills that are due the soonest and complete the task the next day.

There will be some days that you just can't do it all. You may find that you cannot read the assigned chapter in your sociology class the night before. If this happens to you—and it will at some time in your college career—then create a back-up plan like the ones offered above. Avoid giving up completely if you run out of time or energy; do something, even if it is just a little bit. Can't get to the library to start looking for sources for your research paper? Create an outline or a task list instead, and go to the library the next day. Do something that keeps you moving forward, but don't give up. You will have more energy and time the next day to complete new tasks.

Putting Procrastination in Its Place

One would think that all college students routinely participate in cramming and "pulling all-nighters." Putting off studying and completing projects will certainly add to your stress, but procrastination does not have to be a necessary part of going to college. Realistically, community college students probably delay beginning projects and studying because they are pressed for time, not because they are wasting time hanging out with their friends or goofing off. However, in order to maximize your time, you can follow the same rules as for procrastinators.

There are many humorous sayings about procrastination:

"If it weren't for the last minute, nothing would get done." —Anonymous
"I never put off till tomorrow what I can possibly do . . . the day after." —Oscar Wilde

Kidding aside, procrastination can be, American author Elbert Hubbard remarked, "the father of failure." Postponing an activity or task because you do not want to do it or can find more interesting activities to do can have serious consequences. For example, if you put off researching your legal terminology paper until the night before, you might find that the library has closed early or the access to online databases is down. You may even discover, like Laura, that your computer won't work and your printer is out of ink.

Procrastination can be the barrier between you and your goals, and it can cause you undue stress. Managing your time and planning ahead will, however, minimize the likelihood that you will procrastinate. Writing down your tasks and goals, too, will make them visible and instill the joy of crossing them off your list.

FIGHTING PROCRASTINATION

- Create a time line of when you want to complete each part of your project. Make adjustments if needed, but try to stick to the schedule.

- Give yourself enough time to complete each part. It is easy to assume that you can find all the resources you need for a paper in one day, for example. A more realistic goal is to find two sources during one trip to the library.

- Just do it. Start right here, right now, and don't think about finding a better time to begin.

- Recognize that behind every procrastinator is someone who fears—the unknown or failure. Acknowledge that fear by writing down what the fear is. Once you recognize your fear, you are more likely to move past it.

- Reward yourself for completing a particularly difficult or boring project.

- Write a list of consequences for *not* doing the project on time and a list of consequences for doing the project on time. Decide which list you can live with.

- Remind yourself of the reason that you are in college and think about how this project supports that reason.

> ## Critical Thinking
>
> ### EXERCISE 4.4
>
> Using what you have learned about your energy levels, your priorities, and your stressors (Chapter 3), as well as the exercises you completed in this chapter, create a plan for handling stress over the next week and schedule your "stress-relieving" tasks on a calendar that works best for you.
>
> PRACTICE

INTEGRITY MATTERS

One way to eliminate stress and anxiety is to make integrity a top priority. Even though it may seem less stressful to take the easier path, in the long run, your negative stress will be less when you maintain your integrity.

PLUS

(Personality + Learning Style = Understanding Situations)

Let's revisit Laura's dilemma. She is an aural learner and introverted; she also takes longer to complete assignments because of her dyslexia; and she has to juggle family and college because she is a single parent. What time and stress management strategies can she use the next time that she has an assignment due?

PROFILE

Now, considering your own learning style, personality type, and special circumstances, what would you do to avoid the stress of completing an assignment the night before when you find yourself challenged by unexpected events?

MY STORY
Learning Plan

Directions: Using what you have learned in this chapter and what you know about your learning preferences, choose a task or assignment that needs to be completed soon and create a learning plan that will help you accomplish this task. Then, write your *My Story* Summary, a one-sentence synopsis that crystallizes your newly created plan.

LEARNING TASK	
Time of Day	
Intake Preference	
Social Preference	
Task Management Preference	

MY STORY SUMMARY:

Path of Discovery

What energizes you the most? What could you do for hours and not notice that time has passed? Describe the activity and discuss why you think you find so much pleasure in the activity that you don't mind spending time doing it.

HOMEWORK

From College to University

How to Handle the New Pressures on Your Time

A good time management strategy that works now for you will serve you well when you transfer to a university. Yes, there will be more work and more expected of you when you get closer to completing a bachelor's degree, but there may also be less direction from professors. They will assume you have solid time management skills. The more you practice now, the better you will be able to handle even more restrictions on your time. Try out a few strategies and find what works, but also talk to students who have already transferred to find out what new expectations you will encounter.

From College to Career

Improving Time Management on the Job

If you decide to go directly from college to work, or back to work, your time management skills can be the difference between a dreaded job and a life-fulfilling career. Time management will be even more important on the job because your actions will affect more people. Just like a move from college to university, the more you practice good time management skills, the more likely you will be able to complete assignments on time. Beware, though, that on the job, the stakes will be much higher than they were in college. Using a calendar and writing down daily tasks will help you keep up with your work. Also, being honest about *not* meeting deadlines will keep you on top (and will help minimize stress). There may be times when you won't be able to manage your time as effectively as you wish, but if you can be honest and speak up quickly, you may be able to save others time as well.

Chapter Review Questions

1. What should you consider when you begin working out a time management plan for a semester?

2. What stresses you? In what ways can you eliminate or reduce the amount of stress that you have?

3. What activities zap your time, and what can you do to eliminate the amount of time they take from you?

4. What strategies are available to eliminate procrastination?

Chapter 4 Case Scenarios

1. Janice has been doing very well in her classes. She has been able to manage her time wisely and adjust her schedule any time something unexpected has come up. However, Janice has had a hectic week. Her boss expects her to stay late for the week to finish a special project; she has an important exam on Thursday evening; her daughter has been sick with a stomach virus; and her husband has been out of town for the last two weeks. Her goal is to take care of each problem without jeopardizing her job, her grade, or her daughter's welfare. What do you recommend she do? Is it realistic that she can take care of each of her problems?

2. George has a 20-page research paper in his Abnormal Psychology class due at the end of the semester. The professor has asked for an annotated bibliography, an outline, and a rough draft to be turned in at the same time as the final draft. George is feeling overwhelmed. Help him map out a plan of action so that he can fulfill his requirements without unnecessary stress.

3. Barbara has been sick for two weeks and has fallen behind in her classes. She is worried that she won't be able to catch up or that she will not be allowed to make up her work. What should she do?

Research It Further

1. Keep a journal of how you spend your time for the next seven days. Write down how long you spend on each activity. Make sure you are honest and that you write in your journal every few hours. Then, create a report for your class as to how you spend the majority of your time.

2. Create a survey that asks your classmates how students spend their time. Once you collect your data, report the results to your class and determine which activities are most prominent among students.

3. Create a "toolbox" for students who are plagued by procrastination. Make the toolbox creative and fun.

References

Hindle, T. (1998). *Manage your time.* New York: DK Publishing.

Nelson, D. B., & Low, G. R. (2003). *Emotional intelligence: Achieving academic and career excellence.* Upper Saddle River, NJ: Pearson.

5 Handling Stress and Making Healthy Choices

Evan's Story

Evan is a student by day and a kickboxer by night, usually competing several times a semester. At 20 years old, he can already tell that it takes him longer to see the results of regular strength training than it did three years ago. Even if he is a little slower in the ring, he has made up for it with smarter moves, the result of years of training both his body and his mind.

Because he is dedicated to the sport, he spends hours each afternoon and evening working as hard, or sometimes harder, than he does for his college classes. Sometimes he wonders if he can do both and be successful in and out of the ring. A few years ago, he saw a doctor because of depression, and he feels the symptoms creeping up on him again.

When he steps out of his car to enter the metal building that he calls his second home, a strong hand squeezes his shoulder.

"Evan, man, you're a little late today," his coach says. "What gives? You are usually early to practice."

"Hey, Coach. I hit some heavy traffic on the way in because I didn't leave at the time I usually do. Had too much homework to do," Evan replies.

"Evan, I know you are committed to college. That's great, but you have to do your time at the gym. If you don't, you won't be ready for your next fight. No offense, but I don't train second place."

The words sting Evan. He is highly competitive— you have to be, in this sport—and he prides himself on his athletic ability. True, he isn't getting any younger, but a winning title is still possible for an "old geezer" like him.

Then, there is college—another goal that he wants to achieve. When he registered for college, he really thought he could do both kickboxing and college and succeed at both. Most definitely, his workouts at the gym provide him with the energy release he needs. What better way to relieve stress and stay in shape than to box every day?

Evan packs his sweatshirt into his gym bag, stretches, and thinks about the homework he still has to complete before going to bed tonight, which will be around 2 a.m. if he gets home by 11:00. A few energy drinks and a protein bar will be needed to keep him awake to get his work done.

"I've got some extra drills we need to work on tonight," his coach says. "Can you stay another hour after you get your workout in?"

Evan hesitates. He has to finish a paper, and now he will need to stay up all night to get it done even though that will mean "sleepwalking" through his classes and maybe even his workout tomorrow.

"Sure, Coach," Evan says, and reassures himself that worrying about what he has to do won't make it any better.

In This Chapter

For most of us, minimizing the negative effects of stress and maximizing good health is a matter of making appropriate choices. How to decrease stress, how to improve your energy, what to eat, how much to exercise, and how to reconnect with ourselves are choices we make every day, yet so many of us make inappropriate choices. The choices we make now are the ones that we will literally have to live with for decades to come. We will be living longer than our ancestors did, but will our lives and our health be better? Some experts are seriously worried that we are making decisions about our health without thinking through the consequences.

The purpose of this chapter is to provide you with information so that when you know better, you will make better choices for your physical, mental, and sexual health, which will in turn help you handle stress more effectively. Specifically, you will be able to do the following:

- Define stress and determine how to minimize its negative effects.
- Determine which health issues are important to consider while you are in college.
- Describe the kinds of stress-related illnesses and how to avoid them.
- Recognize the effects of drugs and alcohol.
- Identify methods to make better choices about your health.

Understanding Stress

Stress is a physical and psychological response to outside stimuli. In other words, just about anything that stimulates you can cause stress. Not all stress, however, is bad for you. For example, the stress you feel when you see someone get seriously hurt enables you to spring into action to help. For some students, the stress of an upcoming exam gives them the energy and focus to study. Without feeling a little stressed, these students might not feel the need to study at all.

Not everyone, however, handles stress the same way, and what is a stressful situation for you may not be for someone else. How we handle stress depends on our genetic makeup, past experiences, and the stress-reducing techniques that we know and practice. There are ways to reduce stress or change our reaction, both physically and psychologically. First, though, it is important to be able to identify causes of stress. The list in Table 5.1 is not exhaustive, but it can start you thinking about different ways that you experience stress.

TABLE 5.1   Possible Causes of Stress

Self-doubt	Pressure to succeed (from yourself or others)
Fear of failure or the unknown	Speaking in public
Congested traffic	Lack of support—financial, physical, or psychological
Uncomfortable situations	The demands of a job such as a promotion/demotion, deadlines, and evaluations
Life experiences such as the death of a loved one, having a child, getting married, and moving	Too many activities and not enough time to complete them
Waiting in lines	Computer problems

Stress Patterns

Each of us has certain triggers, such as the ones listed in Table 5.1, that stress us out. Usually, however, the same situation doesn't stress us out the same way each time we are in it. Take waiting in line at the bank. One day, you might be extremely angry to be waiting 15 minutes in a line to cash a check because you are late for a job interview. The next time that you are in the same line waiting the same amount of time, you may be calm and relaxed because you are enjoying a little quiet time to think while your mother waits in the car. Thus, it is not necessarily the situation or action that causes negative stress, but more likely other factors that are involved.

When you are suffering from lack of sleep, you may be more likely to react negatively to people and situations that usually would not bother you. When you are feeling unsure of your abilities to be successful in college, you may take constructive criticism as a personal attack. Being aware of times and situations that cause you the most stress is one step to helping manage stress better. If you realize that you are sensitive to others' feedback because you are feeling insecure, then you may be less likely to react negatively.

In Activity 5.1, place an "X" next to situations that are negatively stressful for you. Consider other situations or people that cause you to react negatively. The goal is to recognize a pattern of stress and then work to overcome it. When you are able to tell your professor or coworker that you experience negative stress when you are assigned a big project, then those who work with you or assign you a big project can help you create a plan to complete it.

ACTIVITY 5.1   Situations and Stress

SITUATION	STRESSES ME	DOES NOT STRESS ME
Starting a big project		
Paying bills		
Being in a messy environment		
Receiving graded papers and exams		
Not getting enough sleep		
Taking a personal or professional risk		
Getting out of bed		
Not getting feedback on my work		
Being distracted by other people		
Thinking about the future		
Taking tests		

Minimizing Stress in College

Because you will find stress in college, at work, and at home, it is important to be able to identify the different stressors in each environment and work toward minimizing the negative stress in each area. Some weeks, you will have to contend with negative stress in only one area, but there will be times when it seems as though each part of your life is making you miserable. The more you understand what you can and cannot control, the more likely you will be able to work through stressful times and stay on track with your goals.

Stress in college is inevitable, but it doesn't have to be overwhelming if you know what you can do to minimize negative stress in the first place. There are several ways that students unknowingly cause themselves stress: failing to read the catalog and student handbook about course prerequisites and descriptions as well as degree program requirements; registering for more hours than they can handle; trying to do too much at work and home; missing deadlines; arriving late for class or appointments; and keeping the same social schedule despite more academic demands.

The information in this chapter and others in this book should help you minimize your stress in college by providing you with information and strategies for accomplishing your goals. Even if you avoid the above behaviors, you may still find that things don't go your way in college. If you realize that there will be times that you or others will make mistakes, then you will be more likely to bounce back from problems. Minimizing the negative effects of stress can include activities such as reading all information that you receive from the college; paying attention to flyers on doors, bulletin boards, and tables; and talking to your advisor, instructor, and counselor on a regular basis.

You will also want to regularly check the college's website for announcements and updates. Be sure, too, to read publications such as newspapers and newsletters that the college sends to the community. As always, ask questions when you are not sure of something, and make an effort to get involved with campus organizations and clubs because people in these groups often know what is going on around campus.

Minimizing Stress at Home

Reducing stress at home will, no doubt, be the first step for minimizing your overall stress. Because your family and friends are likely to be your most important supporters, what they think of you and the demands they place on you will need to be discussed. Some family members may be unsure of what you are doing or worried that your schoolwork will leave little time for them. Your friends may feel the same way, especially if they are used to hanging out with you after work and on the weekends. The key to minimizing stress at home is to communicate your needs. Talk to your loved ones about what you and they can expect when you are taking classes.

INTEGRITY MATTERS

One way to eliminate stress and anxiety is to make integrity a top priority. Even though it may seem less stressful to take the easier path, in the long run, your negative stress will be less when you maintain your integrity.

Some other tips for making your home life a sanctuary rather than an asylum include telling your family when you have exams or major projects due and informing them of your breaks and vacation time. They may be excited to count down the days until you are finished with the semester. Remember to explain how your responsibilities will change when you are in college. Also, be aware that you are a role model for your family—you may be inspiring other family members to go to college.

Minimizing Stress at Work

For some, stress on the job can be the most difficult to deal with because of the fear of performing poorly and being fired. Stress on the job can also be particularly tough to manage because you may feel uncomfortable confronting coworkers and being honest about your feelings. There are ways, though, to cope with the negative effects of stress at work. To help minimize the amount of stress that you have about your job, consider talking to your employer about your educational goals. Your boss may be very encouraging that you are increasing your knowledge and improving your skills. Your employer may allow you flextime to take classes, which means you may be able to arrive at work early, skip a lunch break, or stay late in order to take classes during the day.

As you would with your family, let your boss know when you have finals or other activities that may interfere with your regular workday, but avoid studying on the job. Be sure to handle any conflict that may arise from your schedule as soon as possible. Coworkers may be jealous of your success or they may misunderstand the arrangements you have made to work and go to school. If you have any concerns, address them to the appropriate person.

There is no cure-all for stress. It is an integral and important part of life and can actually be thrilling and exciting. Nonetheless, preventing it in the first place can keep you happier and healthier, which will make you better able to achieve your goals.

Reducing the Negative Effects of Stress

Because you cannot eliminate all stress, you will need to develop methods for reducing the negative effects that your body and mind experience when they are stressed out. One of the quickest, easiest ways to reduce the negative effects of stress is to take a deep breath. You may have even told someone who was upset to breathe deeply in order to calm down. The breath is, as many cultures have known for thousands of years, an important part of life; for example, in yoga, the ability to control the breath is essential to controlling the mind and body and to bringing fresh air to the lungs and other organs.

Visualization is another method for reducing the effect that stress has on the mind and body. In order to visualize a more relaxed time and place, all you need to do is to find a quiet, comfortable spot, sit down, and close your eyes. Relaxation experts suggest that you visualize a place that makes you feel warm and relaxed. Many people think about a beach because the mood there is often relaxed and the sound of the ocean is comforting. You will need to find your own special place.

Once you decide where you want to go mentally, you should start noticing the details in your place. If you are at the beach, then you should feel the sunshine's heat. Next, listen to the waves crashing on the surf and smell the salty air. Depending on how long you need to visualize this special place, you may want to stick your toe in the water or lie down on the beach and soak up the rays—leave your stress in those designated beach trash cans. The goal in this method of relaxation is to stay there as long as you need to; when you mentally return to your present location, you should feel refreshed and renewed.

Sometimes physical activity can be a better stress reliever than mental exercises. Getting outside or to the gym to work out your frustrations and stress is an excellent way of maintaining your health. By exercising, you can eliminate the physical side effects of stress while you take your mind off your troubles. If you do not usually exercise, take it slowly. Start with a 15-minute walk around the block or do some simple stretching exercises on the floor. Overdoing exercise can lead to more stress, so start small and increase the time you spend getting your blood circulating as you get stronger.

If you happen to exercise too much, you can look toward massage therapy to reduce all your stress. Although it is a little less conventional than other methods of reducing stress, a massage can improve circulation and alleviate muscle soreness. You can seek professional massage therapy or ask a family member to rub your neck, shoulders, or feet. Massage therapy can give you the rejuvenation you need to tackle the rest of the week.

You have heard the cliché that "Laughter is the best medicine," and it is also an ideal way to eliminate stress. Have you ever been in a very stressful situation when someone made you laugh and you thought, "Boy, I needed that"? You probably felt all the tension melt away as you doubled over giggling. Surrounding yourself with people who make you laugh is one way to keep stress at a minimum. Other ways include renting comedies or reading funny books. Of course, good, old-fashioned acting silly can relieve stress and anxiety as well.

Last, you can comfort yourself with familiar favorites to eliminate the negative effects of stress. A special meal or a visit with your best friend can put you at ease. Looking at old photographs, reminiscing about family trips, and watching your favorite movies can be great stress relievers. If you have enrolled in college in a new town or you have moved out on your own for the first time, you may find comfort in the familiar, whether it be an old pillow or a favorite movie. Make sure, though, that your methods of reducing negative stress are healthy. Drugs and alcohol may temporarily relieve stress, but they cause more problems in the long run.

Staying Flexible

An important method of managing stress is to remain flexible. If you try to control too many aspects of your life, you will quickly discover you can't do it all. Although it is important to manage your time and mark your progress toward your goals, you still need to plan for the unexpected and be willing to make adjustments. Good time managers plan for problems by keeping their schedules loose enough to make room for adjustments. For example, if you have a doctor's appointment at 2:00, you shouldn't schedule a job interview at 3:00. Delays in the doctor's office or traffic problems could keep you from your 3:00 appointment and cause more stress, just like with Evan. Instead, you should give yourself plenty of time in between scheduled tasks, especially if you will have to rely on others' time management skills.

Reflection   EXERCISE 5.1

What kind of stress do you have in your life now? What areas of your life are more stressful and less stressful? Who or what are the major causes of stress for you?

PRACTICE

Knowing When to Get Help with Stress

If you ever feel as though you cannot cope with the amount of work and responsibility that you have—despite attempts to reduce your stress—seek professional help. Excessive crying, difficulty breathing, inability to get out of bed, and suicidal thoughts are severe reactions to stress. Knowing when to reach out to other people will be crucial in your recovery.

When asking for help, find someone you trust and who will be objective about your experiences. Sometimes, close friends and family members can be your best allies to combat stress, but other times an outside party, who will listen to what you have to say without judging, can be extremely helpful. When you talk to someone, be honest about what you are feeling. Don't try to minimize any fear or anxiety. The more the person knows about what you are experiencing, the better able he or she will be to help.

What's Good for You

Think about this scenario: You have just bought a brand-new car and you are about to drive it off the lot. Before you do, the salesperson provides you with an owner's manual and begins to tell you how often you will need to fill the tank, replace the oil, check the brakes, and rotate the tires. You tell the salesperson you don't need to know any of that stuff, and you drive the car off the lot. Besides, you know that the car needs to be filled up whenever the light on the dashboard comes on. What else is there to know?

For those who own and drive cars, you can imagine what will happen next. One day, maybe in a few months or a few years, you will find the car stops working regularly or stops working at all. In some cases, the repairs are minimal; in other cases, major repairs must be made to get the car into shape. The costs could be astronomical, so much so that you find yourself without a car and without hope for getting another one any time soon.

Now, consider that the car is your body. You know when you are hungry and when you are tired, when you feel happy and when you are stressed, but do you know how to take care of yourself? Maybe you do know that exercising will improve your health and help you manage your stress, but you won't make the time to include fitness as a part of your weekly routine. Just as a car may drive well for a while without regularly scheduled maintenance, there will come a day that the neglect will keep it from running properly or at all.

Learning to take care of your physical and mental health is crucial to getting where you want to go. To continue the car analogy, you won't be arriving at your destination if the vehicle is not in proper working order. One of the benefits of higher education, as stated earlier in this book, is that you learn to make better choices, and that includes making better choices about your health. You can do that by understanding what you can control and how to get information to stay physically and mentally healthy.

Healthy Eating

One key to living a healthy life is making it a priority to eat nutritious food. Getting the recommended daily allowances of fruits, vegetables, whole grains, proteins, and fats is a commonsense approach to healthy eating, but as a society, we are choosing less healthy foods that are quick and easy—and loaded with calories, fat, salt, and sugar. Some of the reasons for poor nutritional choices include lack of time, information, and access to healthy alternatives. Increased stress is another reason that students make poor food choices; they may choose comfort food over nutritious alternatives.

To make healthier choices, arm yourself with information. As with any aspect of your health, the more you know, the better choices you can make. Learn what healthy foods are and seek them out. Read about and pay attention to serving sizes; too much of even a healthy food can add unneeded calories and contribute to weight gain. Read and learn to interpret food labels and ingredient lists that provide information about what is in the food and how much of it represents recommended daily values. The U.S. Food and Drug Administration (2004) provides detailed information on their Web page "How to Understand and Use the Nutrition Facts Label," which can be accessed at http://www.cfsan.fda.gov/~dms/foodlab.html.

Another way of getting nutritional information is to talk with a physician or a nutritionist to get a better idea of what kinds of food will be best for you to consume. Regular doctor visits will determine if you have any potential health risks, such as high blood pressure or diabetes, which will make your food decisions even more crucial to good health. Keeping chronic illnesses in check with monitoring and medication will not only help you feel better, but it will also keep you healthy for the long term.

Eating healthy means eating regularly. Most experts recommend eating smaller meals more frequently rather than heavy meals 5–7 hours apart. At the very least, as nutritionists recommend, start the day with a healthy breakfast, even if you don't have enough time to sit down and eat a full meal. You will feel more alert and energized throughout the early morning. However, what you eat for breakfast is just as important as eating something. Powdered doughnuts and a sugary, caffeinated soda will not provide you with the nutrients you need to be at your best. A piece of fruit and a cup of yogurt, for example, would be a better choice if you have to eat on the run. In addition to smaller, frequent nutritious meals, drinking plenty of water throughout the day has numerous health benefits, including regulating body temperature and assisting digestion.

Avoiding fad diets is another strategy for staying healthy. Although they may promise increased energy and weight loss, the results may be short lived and potentially harmful. A better approach to eating healthy is to stick to the recommended guidelines from the Food and Drug Administration or a health expert. Be aware, too, of the potential for eating disorders such as anorexia and bulimia. Anorexia, a condition in which people strictly control how much food they eat, and bulimia, a condition in which people cycle between overeating (binge-eating) in a short amount of time and then purging (through vomiting or abusing laxatives), are two eating disorders that can cause serious physical and psychological harm. Students who suffer from anorexia or bulimia, or believe they do, should see a health professional as soon as possible.

Why should you be concerned about what you eat and how much? One benefit of eating healthy is that it improves your body's functions. You may find that eating better improves your ability to sleep or reduces the fatigue you feel by the end of the day. Eating well also improves your mental abilities. Studies have shown that eating certain foods, such as fish, can improve your test-taking abilities. Finally, healthy eating and avoiding overeating helps keep stress under control, which in turn keeps stress-related illnesses at a minimum.

TIPS FOR HEALTHY EATING IN COLLEGE

- Find and read reliable information about health issues.
- Eat consciously and take time to appreciate the nourishment you are receiving from healthy foods.
- Plan your meals *and* snacks ahead of time so that you are not susceptible to last-minute, poor choices.
- Take bottled water in your backpack and drink it throughout the day.
- Take healthy snacks with you to eat between classes to avoid making unhealthy choices at the vending machines or at the student union.
- Pay attention to serving sizes and eat what you need to stay healthy, not the amount that you want to eat.
- Make wise choices at vending machines by avoiding food that is high in fat, caffeine, sugar, or salt content.
- Make any changes gradually. Think long-term health, not short-term results.

Exercise

We all know that making good choices about nutrition and exercise are part of a healthy lifestyle, but busy students often find it difficult to squeeze in time to work out. Take into consideration that as a student, you will spend many hours sitting down studying or working on the computer. Even if you have had a regular exercise routine, you may find that you have to make studying a higher priority.

Because you may have less time for exercise, it will be even more important that you find time to include some exercise in your busy schedule because of the numerous health benefits. At the very least, getting regular exercise will help you relieve stress.

Regular exercise can lower blood pressure, increase your metabolism, improve muscle tone, and lessen your chances of suffering diseases that are directly related to a sedentary lifestyle. It can also improve your mood and your self-confidence. Experts vary on how much exercise is ideal, but most agree 30 minutes of sustained activity three or four times a week will provide you with health benefits.

If you have trouble getting started or staying in an exercise routine, consider setting fitness goals that are reasonable and achievable. Reward yourself whenever you meet your goals, and don't get discouraged if you fall short now and then. Exercising regularly should be a lifestyle, not a short-term activity, so think of your progress as part of a long-term plan to live better. As with any exercise program, see a doctor before you begin and start gradually if you are not usually physically active.

TIPS FOR EXERCISING IN COLLEGE

- Take a physical education class at your college.
- Use the exercise facilities and equipment on your campus.
- Take advantage of walking trails or paved walkways on your campus.
- Park farther away from the buildings and get extra steps in.
- Join a gym and go regularly.
- Ask a friend to exercise with you.
- Incorporate short sessions of exercise into your studying routine by taking walking or stretching breaks in between reading or writing papers.
- Learn how to play a new sport or investigate a new form of exercise.

Getting Enough Sleep

Getting an adequate amount of sleep each night is as important to maintaining good health as what you eat and how often you exercise, but most Americans, especially college students, do not get enough sleep to maintain their health. Experts say that adults should get 7–9 hours of sleep a night to function normally throughout the day, but millions regularly get 6 hours or less. While you are in college, you may believe that 6 hours a night sounds like a luxury as you juggle your multiple responsibilities. For sure, there will be times that, because of circumstances, you will not be able to get enough sleep, but those times should be few and far between. Maintaining a regular schedule of going to bed and getting up will help you get the amount of sleep you need. Despite the myth of what college life is like, pulling "all-nighters" to study for tests or complete assignments is strongly discouraged, because it will make you less likely to perform well the next day.

For some students, the idea of keeping a regular sleeping and waking schedule seems impossible because of other factors that limit their ability to sleep. The reasons for many students' sleep deprivation are varied, but include health problems such as breathing obstructions and stress. If you believe your lack of sleep is the result of medical problems, consider seeing a health care professional. For stress-related sleep problems, practicing the stress-relieving strategies in Chapter 3 will help alleviate the symptoms; however, if you find that relaxation techniques do not improve your ability to sleep well, then consider seeing a general practitioner or mental health professional for issues regarding stress.

What you put into your body can affect your sleeping habits. Eating high-fat and high-sugar foods near bedtime can slow you down, even if they seem to speed you up at first. Good sleep can also elude you if you consume alcohol and caffeine—even in small amounts—close to the time that you go to bed. Drugs, including medications for common illnesses, can deprive you of sleep or make you feel sluggish after you take them. Avoid consuming food, drink, or medications that overstimulate or make you drowsy right before bedtime. Never abuse prescription, over-the-counter medication, or illegal drugs to stay awake.

In addition to what you put into your body, what you do to it will affect your ability to get a good night's rest. Exercising too close to your bedtime will make it harder to fall asleep. However, too little physical exertion during the day can also contribute to difficulty falling and staying asleep. Experts suggest exercising early in the day—an activity as easy as walking for 30 minutes will suffice—in order to sleep more productively at night. Regular exercise will also help you alleviate the negative effects of stress. If you find, though, that you cannot "shut off" your mind because thoughts overwhelm you, consider writing down your worries—anything you may stay up thinking about after the light is off—in a journal, which will help you unwind and put away your day's thoughts.

Because sleep deprivation can contribute to irritability, depression, and physical health problems, it is important to make getting enough sleep a priority throughout the semester. If you have difficulty sticking to a regular sleep schedule, treat it like any other goal and write down what you want to do. Make it easier to achieve your goal by keeping your bed and bedroom free of clutter and by avoiding using your bed as a place to do homework or watch television. In other words, creating a sanctuary in your bedroom, a place where you can truly relax, may alleviate stress and anxiety that contribute to sleeplessness. Finally, avoid taking naps during the day, even on weekends, because they can throw off your sleep schedule. If you have an irregular schedule because of working different hours each day of the week, find a system that is relatively regular and that works for you. You may have to be creative about how you get enough sleep each evening or day.

The bottom line is that sleep deprivation can be dangerous and deadly. How little sleep you get should not be a medal of honor that demonstrates how much you work or how dedicated you are to meeting your goals. Getting enough sleep is a necessary part of living well, enjoying what you *do* accomplish, and being enjoyable to be around when you are awake.

Collaboration

Working with a group, share your sleep habits and patterns, especially how much sleep you get each night. Then, determine what realistic strategies you can use to get more sleep.

EXERCISE 5.2

Stress-Related Illnesses

Stress can cause a variety of health-related problems, and as you read above, sleep deprivation is one of those issues. Stress-related illnesses can vary from person to person, but there is one common denominator: With information and techniques for reducing stress, you can decrease the negative health effects. Although some of the following illnesses can be caused by other factors such as heredity and environment, they can be signs that stress is making you ill:

- Digestive problems including upset stomach, heartburn, constipation, diarrhea, and ulcers
- Severe headaches and migraines
- High blood pressure, heart attack, and stroke
- Muscle and joint pain
- Cold, flu, respiratory, and sinus infections

Staying healthy by eating well, exercising, and getting adequate sleep are all ways to help prevent stress-related illnesses. Be careful, especially at stressful times such as the beginning and end of the semester, that you do not neglect both your physical and mental health, for you will be more susceptible to stress-related illnesses that could keep you from doing well in college.

Drugs and Alcohol

There are some habits that we know are potentially hazardous to our health, and yet some people still do them. Smoking and using tobacco products, taking drugs, and consuming too much alcohol are known risks, but college students sometimes pick up these poor health habits because of peer pressure, a desire to fit in, and a need to find a way to relax or escape.

According to the American Heart Association (2008), about a quarter of Americans smoke, and people with the least education (9–11 years in school) are more likely to smoke than people with more education (more than 16 years in school). Smoking or chewing tobacco carries with it increased risks of heart disease, stroke, high blood pressure, cancer, and emphysema. The more educated you become about the health risks that are associated with smoking and using smokeless tobacco, the more it will be obvious that using tobacco products can cause serious health consequences. There are a variety of methods for quitting. It is worth investigating what your college and community offers if you are a smoker or a user of smokeless tobacco. Your college may provide information, support groups, or physician referrals for students who want to quit.

Alcohol and drugs are two other health issues that affect college students—sometimes even before they get to college. Having parents, partners, or friends who have abused drugs or alcohol is one way students can be affected. They may feel that they have to take care of others who drink too much or take drugs, which can take a toll on their time and emotional well-being. Students may also suffer from abusing drugs and alcohol while in college—and the effects can be far reaching. According to Facts on Tap (2008), a website that offers drug and alcohol education and prevention information, 159,000 first-year college students will drop out of college because of issues related to drug and alcohol abuse.

Being drunk or high can have grave consequences, the least of which is that you will do something you later regret. You increase your risk of having an unwanted sexual experience and causing physical harm to yourself and others. Death from overdosing on drugs and alcohol can happen even for those who are first-time users. Whether they are consumed for recreational purposes or because of other, more serious health reasons, abusing drugs and alcohol should not be a part of your college career because you will find it more difficult to reach your educational and personal goals.

In addition to abusing alcohol and illegal substances, using medications for purposes other than for what they were prescribed can have grave consequences, including death. Excessive use of medications that contain amphetamines and narcotics may seem like a good idea at first if you have trouble staying awake or going to sleep, but using them for a longer period than they have been prescribed can lead to dependency.

TIPS FOR AVOIDING DRUGS AND ALCOHOL IN COLLEGE

- Educate yourself about the effects of abusing drugs and alcohol.
- Cultivate relationships with people who have healthy habits.
- Avoid situations in which you know drugs and alcohol will be present.
- Take walking breaks instead of smoking breaks.
- Find other ways to relax that are healthy, free, and legal.
- Talk with a counselor or health care professional if you feel you are about to make a poor decision regarding the use of drugs and alcohol.
- Appeal to your vanity, if all else fails: Drugs, alcohol and tobacco make you look and smell bad.

Depression and Suicide

The pressures to succeed and juggle multiple priorities can lead to negative stress and feelings of being overwhelmed. Many times, feeling a little stressed during the semester is normal, but there are times that students can feel as though they are in over their heads, with no hope of getting out. It is no wonder that one of the most common mental health issues on college campus is depression.

In an online article about college students and depression, Neil Schoenherr (2004) reports that Alan Glass, M.D., the director of student health and counseling at Washington University–St. Louis, claims problems students face often start before they enroll in college: "Students arrive already having started various medications for depression, anxiety and attention deficit disorders." Signs of depression include loss of pleasure in activities, feelings of hopelessness, inability to get out of bed, increased use of alcohol or drugs, changes in appetite or weight gain or loss, changes in sleep patterns (sleeping too little or too much), extreme sensitivity, excessive crying, lack of energy or interest in participating in activities, and lack of interest in taking care of oneself.

Suicide is another mental health issue that is associated with depression. With the startling statistic that 25% of college students have contemplated suicide, it is no wonder that college health and counseling centers strive to educate students about the signs of severe depression and potential suicide attempts. Thoughts of ending your life should always be taken seriously and you should seek help immediately. Call a college counselor, an advisor, a hospital emergency room, or 911 if you are thinking about committing suicide.

Sexual Health Issues

A discussion of health issues would not be complete without talking about sexual health. Most colleges and universities strive to educate their students, especially those who are recently out of high school, about sexual responsibility and common sexually transmitted diseases (STDs).

Collaboration

A study of community college students recently reported that they are more likely to suffer from depression and mental health issues. Working within a group, discuss what factors may contribute to higher rates of depression and mental health issues in community college students.

EXERCISE 5.3

Gary Gately (2003) reports that many experts and college officials have been alarmed at the recent statistics that show 73% of students report having unprotected sex while they are in college. More disturbing is that 68% of those having unprotected sex do not consider themselves at risk (Gately, 2003). This last statistic points to a major reason why students, despite sex education in high school or elsewhere, continue to engage in risky sexual behavior: Students, especially those 18–24 years of age, believe they are immortal and that nothing they do will have negative consequences. Because most STDs lack immediate visible or physiological symptoms, students who are at risk for contracting a sexually transmitted disease rarely ask to be screened for signs of infection.

Risky behavior, which includes having sex with multiple partners and having unprotected sex, opens the door to possible infections and illnesses such as chlamydia, gonorrhea, genital herpes, HIV, and AIDS (see Table 5.2). Some diseases can be transmitted in ways other than sexual intercourse. Hepatitis B and C are both diseases that can be contracted through shared razors, toothbrushes, body piercing, and tattooing.

TABLE 5.2 Common Sexually Transmitted Diseases

STD	Symptoms	Treatment
HIV and AIDS	May have no symptoms; extreme fatigue, rapid weight loss	No cure, but prescribed medication can keep the virus from replicating
Chlamydia	May have no symptoms; abnormal discharge, burning during urination	Antibiotics
Genital herpes	May have no symptoms; itching, burning, bumps in the genital area	No cure, but prescribed medication can help treat outbreaks
Gonorrhea	Pain or burning during urination; yellowish or bloody discharge; men may have no symptoms	Antibiotics
Hepatitis B	Headache, muscle ache, fatigue, low-grade fever, skin and whites of eyes with yellowish tint	No cure, but prescribed medication can help guard against liver damage

If you are sexually active, it is important to be screened regularly for STDs even if you do not have symptoms. Your long-term health and the health of those you come in contact with are at risk if you do not. As with any health issue, educate yourself with the facts about risk factors and symptoms. Then, monitor your behavior, practice safe sex, and see a doctor regularly to maintain good health.

Healthy Relationships

Maintaining healthy relationships are as much a part of your good health as eating nutritious foods and exercising. Chapter 3 discussed the different types of relationships you will have in college as well as how to relate better with others, but there are some issues that are signs of unhealthy, even dangerous, relationships. One type of unhealthy relationship issue is abuse: physical, mental, verbal, and sexual. Being in a relationship with someone who is abusive is not healthy. Although the previous statement seems like common sense, take time to think about it. No one deserves to be hit, controlled, or humiliated, *ever*.

Although we know that someone who makes us feel bad physically or emotionally can prevent us from being our best, studies find that abused men and women find it difficult to get out of abusive relationships. One reason people stay with abusive partners is that the abusers are—at first—charming, attentive, and loving. Usually, abusers begin to show subtle signs that something is not right; they may be extremely jealous, verbally insulting, and focused on your every move. Victims may also be dependent financially or emotionally on their abusers, which makes eliminating their influence difficult at best.

One particular type of unhealthy relationship that occurs most frequently among traditional college students is date or acquaintance rape. Simply defined, date rape is a forced sexual act in which one party does not actively consent; often, the two people involved are not complete strangers—hence the terms "date rape" and "acquaintance rape." Both men and women can be victims of date rape, although women are more often victims. Alcohol or a "date rape" drug such as Rohypnol may be involved in the incident. Many experts warn college-age women and men about the risk factors for date rape and encourage them to get to know whom they are going out with, not getting intoxicated, making sure their food or drinks are not handled by others, and communicating loud and clear if they find themselves in an uncomfortable situation.

Maintaining a healthy relationship takes time and energy, but there are many ways to make sure your relationships are positive experiences. For example, get to know people well before spending time alone with them. Learn to communicate your wants and needs effectively. Say "no" loud and clear when you do not want something to happen. Watch for signs of abusive and controlling people; sometimes, people show you signs of their true selves in smaller, subtler ways early in a relationship. If a situation makes you uncomfortable, get out of it immediately. Last but not least, do not abuse alcohol and drugs, which can impair your ability to judge situations. If you feel as though you have no options in removing yourself from an abusive relationship, seek professional help.

Communication Challenges

Sometimes one of the most important activities that promote good mental health is communication. Keeping feelings bottled up inside can lead to unhealthy thoughts and expectations. Learning to express fear, anger, and disappointment can have the effect of lessening the negative stress from carrying those feelings bottled up inside. If you do not feel comfortable saying what is on your mind to family and friends, you may start by talking with a counselor or therapist who can help you learn to communicate more openly with others. You can also learn effective communication techniques as well as conflict management methods that will help you deal more successfully with strong feelings by reading books and articles and watching others who model effective behavior.

Reflection

EXERCISE 5.4

In what ways have you experienced changes in your family or work relationships since you have been in college? How much does your communication with friends and family affect your overall stress levels and health?

PRACTICE

Living a Balanced Life

Living a balanced life means paying attention to and improving all areas of your life—from relationships to cardiovascular health to your inner peace. If one area is overdeveloped, then the other areas will suffer from the lack of balance. There will be times that you will need to put in more hours at work and school, throwing the balance off slightly, but be careful that you make some time for the other areas that have been neglected.

A great way to stay balanced is to strive to create relationships with people on campus. Having healthy relationships with professors, advisors, and classmates will not only enable you to stay connected with your college work, but it will also provide you a personal support network in case you feel as though you need help with the stresses of being in college.

Balancing your life to eliminate stress also entails evaluating your values and priorities whenever you begin to feel stressed. You can then identify areas in your life that are getting out of balance and put those areas higher up on your list of priorities. For example, if you value exercise and are stressed because you realize that you have been spending most of your time at work or at school, you can make working out a higher priority, creating better balance in your life.

Getting Help When You Need It

An important part of making good choices and staying healthy is to get regular checkups and to see a health professional whenever you experience pain, difficulty, or even uncertainty about a health issue. Your college may provide access to a health clinic or health fairs. Free screenings, health seminars, and dispensing of over-the-counter medications are possible services that your college clinic may offer. Take advantage of these types of services, such as blood pressure checks or information about handling diabetes, because they may provide you with life-improving or life-saving information. If your college provides only limited access to health services, then you will need to find other ways to monitor your health. Regular checkups are part of taking care of yourself both in the short term and the long term.

Part of staying healthy is staying informed about health issues. Use what you have learned about finding reliable sources and determining their credibility when searching for information about your physical, mental, and psychological health.

Having healthy relationships provides a personal support network for you should you need help.

Never use information from the Internet to diagnose and treat yourself. Instead, if you find information that seems to pertain to your health issue, consider making an appointment with a doctor and provide him or her with your findings. Your doctor or health professional can help determine what the best course of action will be for you.

PLUS

EXERCISE 5.5

(Personality + Learning Style = Understanding Situations)

Let's revisit Evan's situation. He is a kinesthetic learner and extroverted; getting regular exercise and working out with others helps him stay healthy and release stress. However, his dedication to this sport has been taking away time and energy from college, and his coach doesn't seem very supportive of his competing activities. What advice can you give him that would help him be successful in college? Can he devote enough time to both parts of his life and expect to do well?

Now, considering your own learning style, personality type, and special circumstances, what would you do to stay focused on college when you find yourself challenged by competing priorities?

PROFILE

MY STORY
Learning Plan

Directions: Using what you have learned in this chapter and what you know about your learning preferences, choose a task or assignment that needs to be completed soon and create a learning plan that will help you accomplish this task. Then, write your *My Story* Summary, a one-sentence synopsis that crystallizes your newly created plan.

LEARNING TASK	
Time of Day	
Intake Preference	
Social Preference	
Task Management Preference	

MY STORY SUMMARY:

Path of Discovery

What are your top five health and stress issues?
What strategies will you use to address them?

HOMEWORK

From College to University

*How Your Stress Will Change and How to Handle
the New Pressures*

There are many possible stressors awaiting you when you make that move from your community college to university. Increased tuition, higher expectations, more difficult workload, impending graduation, and goal realization are all reasons to feel anxious about the transition, but remember that you have already succeeded in college by getting this far.

To meet the challenges that await you, be honest about them. For example, your professors will be asking more from you academically. In addition, recognize the fact that you will be graduating in just a few semesters and that you should plan for life after school. These realities, while daunting, do not have to be defeating if you are honest about them. With some work—and the good habits you form at your community college—you can overcome them with the same success.

Regardless of the new challenges, once you transfer, it will be even more important to have a solid support structure at work and at home. In addition, you will be making connections with people whom you hope will help you get a job after college. All of these relationships can provide you with a system for handling the demands of a four-year university. You will also need to be mindful of the stress-reducing strategies that work best for you. Practice them regularly and seek assistance in achieving your goals; you will then be more relaxed and more confident in your abilities.

From College to Career

Making Health Lifestyle Changes Is a Good Long-Term Strategy

Making healthy choices in college certainly has short-term results in that you will feel better and handle the negative effects of stress more effectively. However, the purpose of making better choices should be a long-term strategy to create a better life for you and your family. Therefore, when you complete your certificate or degree and enter into or back into the workforce, you may need to revise or reinforce your health goals. For example, you may have had time after classes to work out or play a sport as part of your exercise routine, but after graduation, you may have to change the time or place that you work out.

In addition to finding time to continue your positive health choices from college, you may also need to consider making your mental health part of your overall health plan. Maintaining healthy relationships with those who have positive influences on your life is one way to keep stress levels at a minimum and to create a safety net of friends and family when you may need them. Avoiding drugs, alcohol, and other poor health choices will be crucial to performing your best on the job. Some employers have strict policies about the use of drugs and alcohol on or off the job.

Because of the importance of good health, some employers have made keeping their employees healthy a top priority—it saves time and money in the long run when employees do not miss work because of illnesses. Talk with the human resources department about what your company offers its employees to support healthy habits. They may offer free screening, free or reduced-cost vaccinations, time off for doctors' appointments, health insurance, discounted gym memberships, and planned physical activities such as softball or basketball games.

Chapter Review Questions

1. What are the different ways students can incorporate exercise into their busy schedules?

2. What are the major health issues that college students face?

3. What can students do if they find themselves in an unhealthy relationship?

4. Predict what the effects will be for a student who makes poor health choices during a semester.

5. According to the categories listed in the chapter, evaluate how well you are improving or maintaining healthy habits.

Chapter 5 Case Scenarios

1. Vin-Singh has been having trouble sleeping since he started college. He shares an apartment with another student who likes to stay up late and play loud music. Vin-Singh eats well and avoids caffeinated drinks, but he does not exercise regularly and often feels anxious when he tries to sleep. What advice can you give him for improving his sleep?

2. Wanda has not exercised since she was in high school, and now, 20 years later, she sees the importance of improving her health. In fact, she wonders if the 30 pounds she has gained since high school is keeping her from feeling her best when she juggles the demands of college. She is about to start her last year in college, one that will be stressful for her as she takes classes that will help her pass a licensing exam and get a good job. She also wants to lose the weight and start an aggressive exercise program. In light of what she is about to face, what advice can you give her?

3. Ever since D. J. started college, he has focused on his studies and has cut out all activities that do not help him achieve his educational goals. He has told his friends that he won't be able to hang out with them; he has cut back on his hours at work; he has stopped playing basketball and running; he has even stopped attending religious services so that he can have time to take as many class hours as possible each semester. He wants to graduate with a degree as fast as he can and start working, and his grades are good. However, after a few semesters, he has felt depressed and isolated, but he is not sure why. What advice can you give him?

Research It Further

1. Interview three people about their health habits. Find out what they do to maintain good health. Write down your findings and present them to your class.

2. Search the Internet for national statistics regarding violence against college students. Determine what groups are more likely to experience physical and sexual abuse. Inform your class of your findings.

3. What does your college offer in terms of health care for its students? Create a list of services and events along with contact numbers for community services that students may need. Present your list to your classmates.

References

American Heart Association. (2008). Cigarette smoking statistics. Retrieved May 16, 2008, from http://www.americanheart.org/presenter.jhtml?identifier=4559

Facts on Tap. Alcohol and student life. Retrieved May 16, 2008, from http://www.factsontap.org/factsontap/alcohol_and_student_life/index.htm

Gately, G. (2003, August 23). College students ignoring risks of unprotected sex. *Health Day News*. Retrieved August 29, 2005, from http://www.hon.ch/News/HSN/514968.html

Schoenherr, N. (2004). Depression, suicide are the major health issues facing college students, says student health director. *News & Information*. Washington University–St. Louis. Retrieved May 16, 2008, from http://news-info.wustl.edu/tips/page/normal/4198.html

U.S. Food and Drug Administration. (2004). How to understand and use the nutrition facts label. Retrieved May 16, 2008, from http://www.cfsan.fda.gov/~dms/foodlab.html

6 Learning, Memory, and Thinking

Michael's Story

Michael can shoot the cap off a bottle of beer at 100 yards; he can hike 12 miles in a hot sandstorm with 30 pounds of equipment on his back; and he can build a jungle gym out of scrap wood for his two nieces. What Michael can't do, he thinks as he rubs his head, is understand algebra. He shifts his backpack to his other shoulder and looks at the sign on the door. He is in the right place—the tutoring center—but he doesn't know if he really belongs here.

Inside the student center, Michael sits back down on a chair outside the large window that overlooks the lot where his truck is parked, and he opens his math notebook where he has scrawled a few notes from the last class.

"The order of operations is F-O-I-L: first, outer, inner, last. But after that, I don't know what to do," he thinks to himself.

He writes on the red cover of his notebook, "F-O-I-L. F-O-O-L. F-A-I-L." He just knows that he will fail the class because he can't keep factoring polynomials and solving absolute value equations straight. If his professor would just slow down and allow students to "get it" before moving on to the next unit, he wouldn't feel so stressed. It doesn't help his nerves to know that when another student asked the professor to slow down, he told the class that they needed to get a tutor if they couldn't keep up.

"Isn't teaching me algebra *his* job, not a tutor's?" Michael asks the bulletin board that lists the tutoring center's hours. He notices that in 30 minutes, the tutor for algebra will be leaving and his hope of getting any help will be over. Before he decides to leave, his girlfriend Michelle calls him.

"Will you be home by the time I get off work?" she asks. "I need you to pick up something for dinner."

"Unless I can understand my algebra homework, I don't know when I will be home," he jokes.

"Did you do what I told you? Did you see Tamara in the tutoring center?" she asks.

"I'm standing right in front of it. But I can't make myself go in. It reminds me of being put in the 'dummy class' in junior high school because I couldn't get fractions," he tells her.

Michael's teenage difficulty in learning coupled with his military background makes it difficult for him to seek help on his own. By the time he got to high school, he was able to slide by, and in the military his superiors ordered everything he did. It is strange for him to complete homework that is not turned in or to get help from a peer who has only recently completed the class and who is 20 years younger than he. Plus, he has accomplished so much in his life on his own that he feels awkward asking someone for help. If he can't do it on his own, he thinks, maybe he can't do it at all. His girlfriend's voice shatters the silence.

"Michael, do you remember when I struggled through biology? I wanted to be a nurse so much, but I didn't think I had what it took if I couldn't pass one of the first classes," she says.

"Yeah, I do. I remember helping you study before tests."

"Do you remember how much better I did after I went to the tutoring center? I found someone who helped me take better notes and organize my studying time. Plus, she helped me figure out a study strategy that helped me deal with the huge amount of written material I had to remember for the tests."

Michael doesn't say anything in response, but remembers how she struggled. He feels a little guilty that he can remember that he tried to get her to quit school once because she seemed so stressed out all the time and never wanted to do fun things with him. Glad that she stuck it out, Michael suddenly feels competitive. If she can make it through biology and become a nurse, he can surely get through algebra—and with a better grade.

Michael pulls out a square of gum, a habit he developed after quitting smoking two years ago, and responds to Michelle.

"This may be the only time I will say this," he jokes, "but you are right. I need to see what kind of help I can get. I'll call you before I leave."

With a little more confidence, Michael digs around in his dusty backpack, grabs his calculator and a mechanical pencil, and walks through the double swinging doors into the tutoring center.

In This Chapter

Michael's story illustrates a typical situation in which a student struggles with learning on his own. For Michael, remembering the order of operations in algebra is part of his challenge. He is also unsure of reaching out for help to supplement what he can do on his own. Many other new students ask the same questions: "Isn't my professor supposed to make sure I master the material in class?" and "If I have trouble keeping up with the work, does this mean I will never be successful?" Experienced students know that most of the required work and learning expected of them will occur *outside* the classroom, and that often means working with others, either in a study group or at a tutoring center, to be successful *inside* the classroom.

To help you improve your learning, no matter where it happens, this chapter focuses on the latest brain research as it relates to learning and memory. It also explains the importance of active learning. Finally, the different types of thinking that will be required of you are explored at the end of the chapter. By the time you finish reading this chapter, you will be able to:

- Describe the stages of learning.

- Identify the importance of active learning.

- Explain how memory is created and what that means for learners.

- Define different types of thinking.

- Describe the processes of creative and analytical thinking.

- Follow the critical thinking steps to problem solving.

This Is Your Brain . . . in College

Seems like there are dozens of bumper stickers and T-shirts that broadcast what people are born to do. "Born to Run," "Born to Shop," and "Born to Boogie" are just a few that you may see. But could you add "Born to Learn" to the list? All of us, researchers say, are indeed born to learn. Babies do it without giving the process any thought. The process is simple: The more you do something, say Angus Gunn, Dr. Robert W. Richburg, and Dr. Rita Smilkstein (2007), the more you create connections in the brain that not only help you remember how to do something, but also help you get better at whatever it is you are learning to do. These brain researchers call this process "growing dendrites." Dendrites are the "tree-like" structures on the ends of neurons, or nerve cells in the brain. The more you practice something, the more those dendrites grow, improving the connections between the neurons in your brain (Figure 6.1).

In their book, *Igniting Student Potential*, Gunn, Richburg, and Smilkstein divide learning into six stages that begin with being curious and motivated to learn something new, move to practicing and refining the new skill, and then end with mastery of the skill (Table 6.1). If you think about anything that you are good at, you should recognize the same process that you went through to get better and better at it. We often recognize the need to practice sports and musical instruments, but sometimes we don't make the same connections with other skills such as writing, reading, and math. Michael would feel more confident about seeing a tutor if he realized that learning algebra is a process that involves time for practice. How much time is

FIGURE 6.1   Dendrites

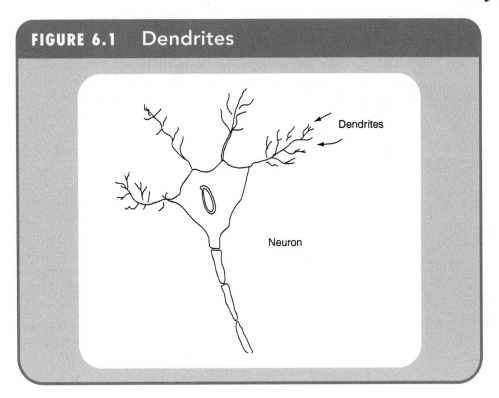

needed will be different for different people, but, brain researchers contend, your skills will increase just as your dendrites will grow.

What happens when you can't get motivated to learn a new skill and make it past the first stage in learning? Dr. Carol Dweck (2006) refers to people who lose interest when learning "get[s] too challenging—when they are not feeling smart or talented" as having a "fixed mindset" (p. 22). People who "thrive when stretching themselves" have a "growth mindset" (p. 22). In her book *Mindset: The New*

TABLE 6.1   Six Stages of Learning a New Skill

Stage 1	**Motivation:** Responding to stimulus. Not knowing how to do it or how it works, just trying it.
Stage 2	**Beginning practice:** Doing it ("practice, practice, practice"), learning from one's own mistakes. Starting to get the feel for it.
Stage 3	**Advanced practice:** Increase of skill and confidence through more practice, more trial and error, getting comfortable.
Stage 4	**Skillfulness:** More practice, doing it one's own way, deviating from the norm, taking risks, creativity, branching out. Building understanding, skill, and confidence.
Stage 5	**Refinement:** Activity becoming second nature, creativity, learning new methods, strong satisfaction.
Stage 6	**Mastery:** Increased creativity, broader application, teaching it, continuing improvement, expert.

Source: Adapted from Smilkstein, R. (2003). *We're born to learn: Using the brain's natural learning process to create today's curriculum.* Thousand Oaks, CA: Corwin Press. Used with permission.

Psychology of Success, Dweck asserts that people with a fixed mindset believe that they are either born smart or not, that there is no changing their "fixed" state of intelligence. People with a growth mindset, on the other hand, believe they can develop talents and skills; even if they fail at a task, they see it as an opportunity to learn more and improve on what they know about the task.

Reflection

EXERCISE 6.1

Think of something you know how to do well. Describe the process by which you mastered the skill. Follow the six steps that are outlined in Table 6.1 and detail what you did at each step. Then, identify a skill or task at which you don't think you could get better. Considering Dweck's theory of the growth mindset, write down a plan for practicing and learning more about how to master the skill or task.

PRACTICE

In the story at the beginning of the chapter, you learn that Michael knows how to do many things, which no doubt came from a belief that he could improve on his skills; however, he seems to have a fixed mindset about algebra. Sometimes one bad experience or several in a row can influence how we see ourselves as learners and masters of a skill. Dweck wants us to know that believing in our ability to learn will result in learning and mastery of whatever task we set our "growth" minds to.

Learning in College

How does the information about brain research and learning translate to what you are doing in college? It may be helpful first to identify where, how, and with whom learning can take place. If you think about a clock face in which the big hand is pointing to the 12 and the little hand is pointing to the 3, you can see that for a 3-credit-hour class you will be spending 3 hours learning in the classroom (Exhibit 6.1). As stated in Chapter 4, this means that you will need to spend 3 times more time learning outside of class.

You could easily spend those 9 hours a week per class reading the textbook and studying your notes. However, you may have to engage in a variety of activities that

EXHIBIT 6.1

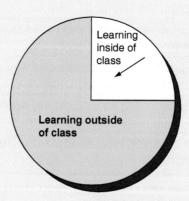

contribute to learning. Researching and writing papers, completing homework, visiting with your professor outside of class, studying with a classmate or in a group, working with a tutor, or tutoring someone else are activities from which you will benefit. Why do you need to do all of that to learn when listening in class, taking notes, and reviewing them before the test worked before? The answer is because in college, you will be responsible for more than just memorizing material and restating it on a test or in a paper. Instead, you will be asked to apply (use information in a new situation), analyze (break information down into its parts and examine it), synthesize (create new information based on what you have learned), and evaluate (judge the information), and you will be graded on your ability to do all of those activities well.

To see an illustration, look at the Learning Pyramid in Figure 6.2. Notice that listening to a lecture results in only 5% retention of the material. In other words, what you hear will be forgotten over time at an enormous rate! What does that mean for students who have an aural learning preference, like Laura, or students whose instructors rely on lecture to convey information in class? It means that whether you are an aural learner or a student in a lecture class, you will need to do more than just listen passively. You may need to record the lecture and listen to it again later; discuss the lecture with classmates; and help others understand it once you have mastered the material. Of course, you may need to read, take notes, and rewrite them as well. The goal for you, regardless of your learning style preference, is to move from learning passively—merely taking in the information through listening or reading—to learning actively—applying, discussing, evaluating, and making new information.

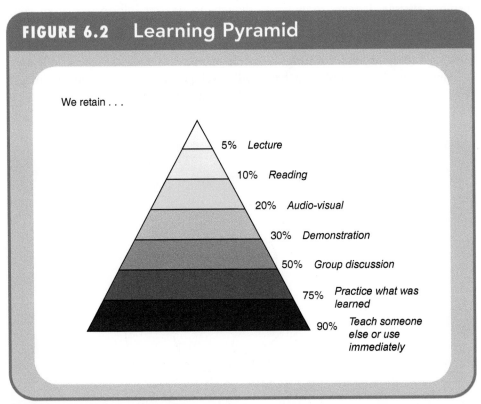

FIGURE 6.2   Learning Pyramid

We retain . . .

5%   Lecture
10%   Reading
20%   Audio-visual
30%   Demonstration
50%   Group discussion
75%   Practice what was learned
90%   Teach someone else or use immediately

Source: NTL Institute for Applied Behavioral Science, 1901 S. Bell Street, Suite 300, Arlington, VA 22202. 1-800-777-5227.

The Memory Game

The good news about brain research is that spending more time actively learning a subject can translate into deeper learning, and a positive attitude toward challenging learning environments will enable you to learn more. Thus, you will be more likely to remember what you have learned because you have moved it from your short-term memory to your long-term memory. Memory is divided into two types—short-term memory and long-term memory. When you meet someone for the first time, you will keep that person's name and face in your short-term memory; in fact, according to Harvard psychologist George Miller (2008), you can only store 5–9 items in your short-term memory. If you try to put too many items in there, you will find that some of them slip away. Try this by glancing at the following list for 30 seconds. Then, cover up the list and write down the words you remember in the space provided; the words do not have to be in the order that you see them.

cup	paper	pencil	magnet	ruler	scissors
spoon	towel	tape	apple	knife	straw

_____

_____

How well did you do? If you remembered 5–9 items, then you can consider your memory average. It takes some work, though, to transfer information from your short-term memory to your long-term memory.

Figure 6.3 shows what areas of the brain are used in memory. Your long-term memory is responsible for storing things like names and dates as well as skills such as tying your shoe. People can have well-developed memory storage for images (visual), sounds (aural), words (read/write), and processes (kinesthetic).

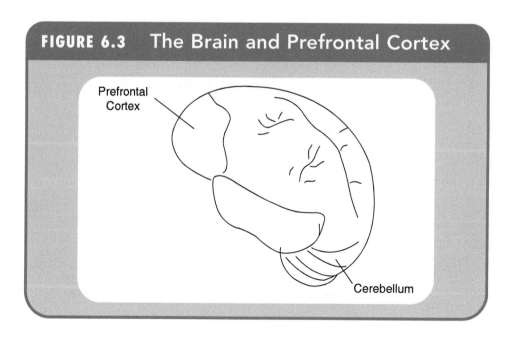

FIGURE 6.3   The Brain and Prefrontal Cortex

Prefrontal Cortex

Cerebellum

In the article "Remember This," Joshua Foer (2007) states, "It's hard for us to imagine what it must have been like to live in a culture before the advent of printed books or before you could carry around a ballpoint pen and paper to jot notes" (p. 49). We could add cell phones that take pictures and record video and voice to the list of technologies that keep us from having to remember every single detail of an event. All of these options for creating artificial memory are what Mary Carruthers, author of *The Book of Memory*, refers to when she states that "[a]ncient and medieval people reserved their awe for memory. Their greatest geniuses [are the people] they describe as people of superior memories" (in Foer, p. 49).

Today the information is at our fingertips and we don't have to memorize the ever-increasing amount of information that is generated daily. But memory played a significant role in ancient and not-so-distant history. Those who could remember significant events, poetry, and songs were revered for their gifts of memory. In many cultures, remembering was essential to surviving and thriving. People remembered the stories of celebrated heroes and the markings of poisonous plants. They couldn't just type key terms into a search engine and learn about them at their convenience!

Mnemonic Devices

Mnemonic devices are memory aids or strategies that help you remember items, concepts, or a series of events. Usually, mnemonic devices are *not* used for deep learning, but there will be times during college that remembering the names, for example, of all the bones in the body or all the constitutional amendments must be conquered before deeper learning can happen. Thus, you may find yourself using mnemonic devices as part of your learning process.

Let's go back to the list above and figure out how you could remember all of the items. Ancient Romans are credited with being able to remember significant amounts of information by using the Roman Room or loci method. This visualization technique can be useful when trying to remember a string of seemingly unrelated items or complex material that needs to be pulled together.

To create a Roman Room, visualize a familiar place, such as a room in your house. If your room is connected to other rooms, then you will have more "places" to put ideas. When you visualize your room, pay particular attention to the items that are already in the room, such as furniture or favorite pictures, and unique details, such as peeling paint. The more vivid the visualization, the better able you will be to remember the items you place there.

To see the Roman Room or loci method in action, take another look at the list.

cup	paper	pencil	magnet	ruler	scissors
spoon	towel	tape	apple	knife	straw

Can you place these items in your kitchen? Put the straw in the cup and place it in the cabinet. Tape the paper on the front of the cabinet. Place the towel on the counter next to the apple, spoon, and knife. Then, put the pencil, ruler, magnet, and scissors in the drawer.

Take 30 seconds to review the room above or visualize your own Roman Room with the items listed. Then, cover up both the list and the description of the room and see how many you can remember. Write the words in the space provided here.

_____

_____

_____

Did you remember more words this time? If not, then visualization strategies may not be the only type of mnemonic device you need to help you remember lots of information. There are other mnemonic strategies that may benefit different learning style preferences. Acrostic sentences and acronyms are just two methods that may help students with a read/write learning style preference.

Take the first letter of items in a series to form sentences that help you remember the items and their order—acrostic sentences. For example, music students remember the order of the treble clef staff, E, G, B, D, F, with the sentence "Every Good Boy Does Fine." To recall the order of biological groupings used in taxonomy, just remember "Kids Prefer Cheese Over Fried Green Spinach" (Kingdom, Phyllum, Class, Order, Family, Genus, Species).

Take the first letter of items in a series and spell another word to create acronyms. Here are a few examples of acronyms that we use every day: AIDS (acquired immune deficiency syndrome), SADD (Students Against Drunk Driving), REM (rapid eye movement), and SCUBA (self-contained underwater breathing apparatus).

Although there are too many words in the list above to create an acronym, you can create an acrostic sentence (or two) with the letters of each word. Because the order of the items is not important, feel free to rearrange the letters to make your sentence(s).

C	P	P	M	R	S
S	T	T	A	K	S

While a little more difficult to compose than acronyms and acrostics, rhymes and songs, which often appeal to aural learners, are another type of mnemonic device. Who doesn't remember, "Thirty days hath September . . . " and "In 1492, Columbus sailed the ocean blue"? Again, simple information works best for these memory strategies. It will take more work to remember the economic effects of Columbus' discovery of the New World.

When you have the time to explore the variety of memory strategies, try them out until you find the one that works best for the subject matter and your learning style. However, many students who need a memory strategy need it to work quickly as they are cramming before a test. Those students may be successful in remembering it when they get to the test the next day, but the possibility of their remembering it weeks, months, or even a year later is slim. That is why professors and tutors discourage students from cramming—it may work some of the time, and it is better than not studying at all for a test, but it often produces more anxiety and stress, and the material less likely to be in your long-term memory when you need it later.

With that warning, there will be times, nonetheless, when despite your best intentions, you will need a fail-safe memory technique to help you remember key concepts in a short period of time. One method, called *chunking*, was developed by

Dr. George Miller, the same person who discovered that the human brain can only hold "seven, plus or minus two" items in short-term memory. Chunking is similar to the Roman Room or loci method in that items are grouped together to allow the brain to make connections with the items. This will make it easier to recall the information later.

To see chunking in action, consider the following 10-digit number:

5114796210

It may be easier to chunk the numbers the way a phone number is divided:

511–479–6210

You probably don't realize that you chunk any time you memorize a phone number or Social Security number. In other words, you are taking the seemingly random numbers and putting them together in groups. The goal in chunking is to reduce a large number of items into only 5–9 items. To practice this mnemonic technique, use the following list of key terms: acrostic, acronym, chunking, cramming, loci method, long-term memory, mnemonic device, rhyme, Roman Room, short-term memory, teaching others.

First, make sure that you know the definitions of each term. Record your definition next to each term below:

Acrostic
Acronym
Chunking
Cramming
Loci method
Long-term memory
Mnemonic device
Rhyme
Roman Room
Short-term memory
Teaching others

Critical Thinking

EXERCISE 6.2

After reviewing the mnemonic devices, determine which ones would work best for you. Use them to create a memory strategy study sheet to help you remember the major ideas in this chapter.

PRACTICE

Next, group the items together logically. Then complete the chunking with the remaining terms.

For example, one way to group some of the terms could be:

Mnemonic devices are strategies for remembering items and they include **acrostics, acronyms, rhymes,** and **Roman Rooms.**

How else could the terms be grouped together? Use the spaces below to group them.

- _____
- _____
- _____

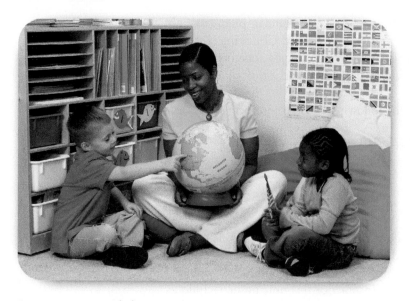

Participating in creative thinking, no matter what your age or what the situation, is a great way to stretch your mind and improve your thinking overall.

Think About It

Think about it. Those are three simple words that you have been asked to do before, but have you ever thought about how you are thinking? The term for thinking about thinking is *metacognition,* or the act of being aware of your own thought processes. So far in this book, you have thought about what you value, how you spend your time, what college culture is, and how you relate to others. You have also been asked to think about what you are reading and learning, whether it has been through the reflection and critical thinking exercises or the end-of-chapter questions and ideas for further research. In fact, this book has been designed so that instead of passively taking in the information, you are actively engaged in thinking it through and creating knowledge.

The same activities that have brought you to this point in the book are the ones you are currently practicing in your classes as well. You are moving beyond only taking information in to send it back out in the same form for a test or paper. Instead, you are building creative, analytical, and critical thinking skills with each course. Strong critical thinking skills will set you apart in the classroom and the workplace: You will be better informed, because you will know to seek out the information you need; you will make better choices, because you have thought through all the possibilities; and you will continue to improve upon your chosen solutions, because you will understand that evaluating your solution is the key to making better future choices.

Creative Thinking

Creative thinking, or the act of creating ideas for solving problems, is an integral part of education. Without creative thinking, there would be no inventions, new formulas, breakthroughs in technology and science, new art movements, advances in design and architecture—the list is endless. Without creative thinking, there would be no electricity, no indoor plumbing, no automobiles, and no zippers in our clothes. Just getting to your classes would be a totally different experience.

In his book, *Creative Problem Solving,* Robert Harris (2002) contends that creative thinking is a skill, a process, and an attitude (pp. 1–2). In other words, creative thinkers are not born with special powers of the imagination; they just use their imaginations more regularly than others. The good news is that you can learn to think creatively by following some basic guidelines.

- *Improve your imagination.* Find ways to keep your mind sharp and your imagination flourishing. Turning off the TV and picking up a book is another easy way to stimulate your imagination. If you enjoy kinesthetic activities, create something to get your mind active.

- *Think in all directions.* Thinking in all directions means that you consider ideas that have worked before, have not worked before, have worked for other problems, and have not been paired with another idea. Some of the most creative ideas have taken ordinary solutions and have reapplied them to other problems. Creative thinking will demand that all angles be considered as you generate ideas.

- *Suspend judgment.* For creative thinking, evaluation is not necessary—save it for critical thinking and problem solving. The focus should be on getting ideas down, not on judging them for their practicality or judging yourself as not capable of being creative. "There is no wrong answer" is a common phrase at this point to keep you generating thoughts.
- *Keep it up.* One main difference between people who think creatively and those who choose not to is perseverance, or the determination to see ideas through—and to keep generating them when the ones you come up with don't work.

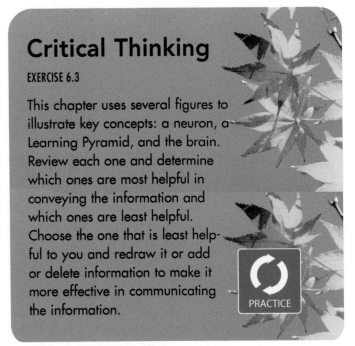

Critical Thinking

EXERCISE 6.3

This chapter uses several figures to illustrate key concepts: a neuron, a Learning Pyramid, and the brain. Review each one and determine which ones are most helpful in conveying the information and which ones are least helpful. Choose the one that is least helpful to you and redraw it or add or delete information to make it more effective in communicating the information.

PRACTICE

Robert Harris states, "Creative thinking creates the ideas with which critical thinking works" (p. 5). To improve your critical thinking and problem-solving abilities, you will need to consider the guidelines above, find ways to practice them, and maintain your curiosity and a positive attitude.

Critical Thinking

The term *critical thinking* is difficult to define, but it has a long tradition. Critical thinkers such as Socrates and Thomas Aquinas, to name only two, have had a tremendous effect on the way we think about the world. But what makes them critical thinkers? What is a critical thinker? Sherry Diestler (1998), in her book *Becoming a Critical Thinker,* defines a critical thinker as "someone who uses specific criteria to evaluate reasoning and make decisions" (p. 2). In other words, someone who thinks critically does not take information at its face value; instead, the information is reviewed for accuracy, authority, and logic before it is considered useable.

Chapter 7 discusses how to read critically, and that certainly is a start to making informed decisions about what you read, but you can also use critical thinking in other parts of your everyday life. Sometimes you will need to make an important decision, and you will need to use critical thinking in order to make the best choice.

To illustrate the importance of using critical thinking skills, consider this first scenario: Michael receives an email message from a friend who claims that she has sent him a virus unknowingly. Her email message instructs him to search for the offending file and delete it immediately. Unaware of any problems that are usually associated with viruses, he searches for the file and finds it, exactly where his friend said it would be on his computer. Michael's friend is a trustworthy person and he values her advice, so he deletes the file. He gets an email message the next day from her that says she is sorry that she sent him a hoax. Thus, he has deleted a perfectly normal file on his computer.

Now, consider this second scenario: Juanita sends Evan a link to a pop-up blocker because she knows that he hates those annoying intrusions while surfing the

Internet. Because Evan has been deceived by free software before, he decides to search several reputable sites that are devoted to reviewing new software. Evan finds that the pop-up blocker is a fraud; instead, if he were to click on the link that Juanita has sent, his computer would have been overrun with pop-up advertisements of questionable origins.

In the first scenario, two people, at least, have been deceived by what appears to be legitimate and helpful information. Who doesn't want to rid her computer of a potentially dangerous virus? Unfortunately, Michael and his friend did not question the information. In the second scenario, however, Evan has encountered false claims before and realizes that he must check out every piece of information that comes to him, regardless of the friendly source. Evan is a critical thinker. Thinking critically allowed him to review the information he was sent and to search for authoritative sources that provided reliable information so that he could make a decision about what action to take.

As the Information Age evolves, critical thinking skills are not just advantageous; they are essential to survival. Not only do you need to possess these skills, but you also need others to possess them as well so that you will not constantly have to evaluate every piece of information that you receive. Can you imagine a world in which everything that you read is suspect and there is no sure way of finding out what is true and accurate and what is not? For people who do not think critically, that imagined world is a reality.

Edward de Bono's Six Hats Thinking®

One method of critical thinking is Edward de Bono's Six Hats Thinking®. De Bono (2008) has identified six different ways you can approach a problem or situation; each way is color coded and represents a different view of the issue. Figure 6.4 shows what each hat means.

To put the Six Hats into practice, review the following issue. Then, use Figure 6.5 to determine how each "hat" would see or discuss the issue.

> Issue: The Student Government Association wants to offer and promote a money management workshop for students. They have had difficulty in the past getting students, who mostly drive to campus for classes and then leave immediately to go to work or to take care of children, to attend lectures, workshops, and special events.

Now it is your turn. Go back to Michael's dilemma regarding going to a tutor to help him with his algebra. How many different ways can he approach the decision to get help from a tutor? If Michael were to put on each hat, how would his view change? In Activity 6.1, fill in the blanks next to each hat according to each color's characteristics.

Critical Thinking/Problem-Solving Connection

Although not all critical thinking leads to solving a problem, problem solving relies on critical thinking as well as creative and analytical thinking. In order to think critically to solve a problem, you will need to go through a process within a group or as an individual. Remember that the more minds working on a problem, the more likely that all sides of the problem can be addressed, which may make the solution better.

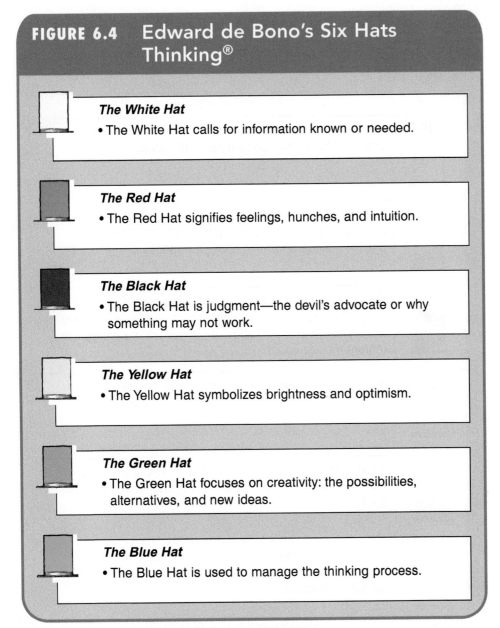

FIGURE 6.4   Edward de Bono's Six Hats Thinking®

The White Hat
- The White Hat calls for information known or needed.

The Red Hat
- The Red Hat signifies feelings, hunches, and intuition.

The Black Hat
- The Black Hat is judgment—the devil's advocate or why something may not work.

The Yellow Hat
- The Yellow Hat symbolizes brightness and optimism.

The Green Hat
- The Green Hat focuses on creativity: the possibilities, alternatives, and new ideas.

The Blue Hat
- The Blue Hat is used to manage the thinking process.

Source: http://www.debonothinkingsystems.com/tools/6hats.htm
Edward de Bono's "Six Thinking Hats" © 1985 reprinted with the permission of The McQuaig Group Inc. All rights reserved. No electronic reproduction or photocopying permitted without prior consent.

You may not always have an opportunity to work in a group on a problem, but you may be able to ask others for their advice during the process.

Here are the basic steps of using critical thinking to solve a problem:

- Clearly identify the problem.
- Brainstorm possible solutions to the problem.
- Analyze the possible solutions for their viability.
- Think through each solution and determine the benefits and drawbacks to each.
- Choose the solution that potentially works the best.
- Evaluate the solution after it is in place.

FIGURE 6.5 Six Hats® and Student Government Association Issue

Hat	View of Issue
WHITE	It is important to find out what we have offered in the past and how many people have attended.
RED	The money management workshop is a great idea because so many students talk about how hard it is to pay for college and work enough hours to pay their bills.
BLACK	Because students have so many other responsibilities and priorities, they are not going to stay after a long day to participate in a workshop about something boring like money management.
YELLOW	If we offer free pizza and a drawing for free textbooks, then we will easily have 200 students attend.
GREEN	What if we offer money makeovers to select students and give away copies of a popular money management book?
BLUE	Let's put all these ideas together and figure out which ideas will work and what we need to do to make this workshop successful.

Step 1: Identify the Problem

Sometimes we assume we know what the problem is, and we try to fix it only to find out that our solution doesn't work because we were fixing the wrong problem. Consider a crying baby who last ate two hours ago. If faced with the problem of the crying baby, you may assume that the baby is still hungry and wants more to eat. When you try to feed the baby, he rejects the food. Now what? Is the baby not hungry? Have you offered something the baby doesn't like? Is the baby sick, too hot, too cold, tired? You can imagine how much time and energy you will spend trying to find the solution to the problem.

Identifying the problem's cause is the first logical step before you can begin to solve it. If you do not identify the cause—or at least eliminate possible causes—before starting the next step, either you won't solve the problem or you might create a whole new problem to solve.

ACTIVITY 6.1 Using Six Hats®

HAT	VIEW OF ISSUE
WHITE	
RED	
BLACK	
YELLOW	
GREEN	
BLUE	

Step 2: Generate Ideas

This is the step where creative thinking will kick in. When you generate ideas, there are no rules except not to eliminate any ideas because they are too far-fetched or too odd. The goal for this step is to get the ideas recorded, and the more you can think "outside the box," the more likely you are considering all possibilities.

When generating ideas, consider using brainstorming, free writing, clustering, and role playing (if you are able to work with another person) to get ideas flowing. This is a good time to use your learning style strength to stretch your imagination.

Step 3: Assess the Possibilities

More creative and analytical thinking, or breaking down the different ideas, will help you at this stage. What are the different parts of the possibilities? Are there any that are impossible, impractical, and illogical? Determine what the least viable solutions are and eliminate them from the list.

Step 4: Think Through Solutions

Thinking through each solution will involve exploring their benefits and drawbacks. Consider the possibilities, but don't completely discard them after the next step. You may need them after you evaluate your final solution and find it to be ineffective.

Step 5: Choose the Best Solution

When choosing the best solution, consider the effects of the solution. Will it cause another problem? What kind of emotional, physical, and financial investment will it take? What will you need to do to implement the solution correctly? Creative thinking to consider all sides of the implementation of the solution will be needed before you make a final decision. Analytical thinking can help you put all the possibilities in a table so you can examine the consequences.

Collaboration

Working in a group, discuss some issues on your campus that need to be solved. Use the critical thinking process to develop a viable solution. Share your ideas with the class.

EXERCISE 6.4

Step 6: Evaluate the Solution

The final stage of problem solving is evaluation. The ability to evaluate allows you to use what you have learned in the process of solving the problem to solve other problems. Ask yourself if the problem was adequately resolved. Did the solution only partly solve the problem or was it a complete solution? What, if anything, would you do differently if you experience the same problem again?

Putting Critical Thinking into Practice

What do you do in the following situations?

- You have an exam at 9:00 a.m. and you get into your car at 8:20 to get to class on time. Your car won't start.
- You need a math tutor to help you get through elementary algebra successfully. The tutoring center's hours are not convenient for you because you work every evening that the center is open late.
- You are worried that you may not be able to purchase your textbooks for next semester because the bookstore's prices are higher than you had anticipated.

If your car won't start and you have to get to an exam, would you be likely to give up and go back into the house, hoping that you can make up the exam? If you cannot find a tutor for elementary algebra, would you plod through the course and pray that you make it? If you are not able to afford textbooks next semester, would you see how far you can get without buying them? What are the other possible solutions to these problems? If you use the critical thinking steps for problem solving, you may realize that there are other alternatives, or possible solutions, to your predicaments.

Here are one student's problem-solving steps for the first scenario:

1. **Clearly identify the problem.** I have two problems. The first is that my car won't start, and the second is that I need to get to school to take an exam.

2. **Brainstorm possible solutions to the problem.** To address my more immediate problem, getting to school to take my test, I can do one or more of the following:

   - Call a friend to pick me up.
   - Call a cab to take me to school.
   - Take a train, plane, or bus.
   - Call my instructor to ask about taking a makeup exam.
   - Run to school.
   - Walk to school.

3. **Evaluate the possible solutions for their viability.**

   - Call a friend—I can get Jessica to pick me up, but she will then be late for work.
   - Call a cab—It will cost $20 and I won't be able to get to school until 9:15 a.m.
   - Catch a train, plane, or bus—There are no trains or planes available. I don't know the bus schedule and will have to walk 1.2 miles to get to the bus stop.
   - Call my instructor—She may not allow me to make up the exam; I may not be able to get a message to her.
   - Run to school—I am not in shape to make it all the way.
   - Walk to school—The distance to school is 3.5 miles. It will take me at least an hour to get there, which will give me only 30 minutes to take my exam.

4. **Think through each solution and determine the benefits and drawbacks to each.** I have eliminated walking to school and catching the bus. I am left with three possible solutions: (1) Call my friend Jessica to pick me up; (2) call a cab; and (3) call my instructor about making up the exam.

   - *Option 1:* The benefit of calling Jessica is that she is a friend and would help me out. I would also be able to make it to the exam on time. Drawbacks to calling Jessica is that she would be late to work if she took me to school and I would still have trouble getting to work.
   - *Option 2:* The benefit of calling a cab is that I would definitely get to school. A drawback is that it would cost me $20, which I don't need to spend. Also, I wouldn't be able to get to school until 9:15. And how would I get to work after my classes?
   - *Option 3:* The benefit of calling my instructor is that I could explain why I could not make it to class, and she might be sympathetic to my dilemma.

Another benefit is that she might allow me to make up the exam.
A drawback is that I might not be able to get a message to her that I am
having car trouble, or she might not allow me to make up the exam.

5. **Choose the solution that potentially works the best.** My solution is to call
my friend Jessica because it is the easiest solution. I won't have to pay to get to
school, and I can get there on time. She may, though, be irritated at me for
asking for a favor at the last minute. Then again, she may be very glad to be
able to return a favor for me.

6. **Evaluate the solution after it is in place.** After I have Jessica take me to
school, I will be able to evaluate whether or not the solution worked. If Jessica
can get me to school on time without being late for work, then the solution
will be a success. If she has trouble picking me up or if she gets mad at me
because I have made her late, then I will have to consider other solutions if
I have car trouble again.

PLUS

EXERCISE 6.5

Let's revisit Michael's dilemma. He is a visual learner and extroverted with
friends, but introverted when he is around people he just met. Michael
prefers structured learning environments, ones in which he is told exactly
what he needs to do and what he needs to study. What learning and
thinking strategies can he use to improve his learning and retention both
in and out of the class?

Now, considering your own learning style, personality type,
and special circumstances, what would you do to feel comfortable
with keeping up with your classes and studying when you are
challenged by the material?

PROFILE

MY STORY
Learning Plan

Directions: Using what you have learned in this chapter and what you know about your learning preferences, choose a task or assignment that needs to be completed soon and create a learning plan that will help you accomplish this task. Then write your *My Story* Summary, a one-sentence synopsis that crystallizes your newly created plan.

PROFILE

LEARNING TASK	
Time of Day	
Intake Preference	
Social Preference	
Task Management Preference	

MY STORY SUMMARY:

Path of Discovery

How will practicing critical thinking steps affect future decisions? Do you think you will be better prepared to solve problems and make better choices, or do you think you will be more confused about the choices you have?

HOMEWORK

From College to University

Different Types of Thinking Will Be Needed to Continue Your Learning

When you transfer to a university, you will continue to use creative, analytical, and critical thinking skills in upper-level classes. In upper-level classes, your professors will move away from the knowledge and comprehension to synthesis and evaluation. You will spend more time doing research and determining if the sources you find are reliable and accurate. You will also use those sources to support your own new ideas, developed through creative thinking, about current issues in your major. All in all, you will be more responsible for the depth and breadth of your education, and strong thinking skills will help you deepen your learning.

From College to Career

How Critical Thinking Will Be Used on the Job

Critical thinking on the job is essential to a rewarding and successful career. Your employer, no matter what your position, will value your ability to think critically and solve problems, and you will value the work you do if you are allowed to use those skills to improve yourself and your environment.

How will you use critical thinking on the job? There will be, no doubt, countless opportunities to think critically at work. For example, you may realize that the office does not run efficiently and you have evaluated ways to improve the flow of work. You may be asked to think critically about a problem in order to solve it. No matter how you arrive at thinking critically on the job, keep the steps to problem solving handy.

As you have read in this chapter, critical thinking is a process, not an end. Once you have solved a problem, new ones will arise that will require critical thinking. To improve yourself and your progress on the job, you will have to be committed to thinking critically.

Chapter Review Questions

1. What has recent brain research told us about learning?
2. In what ways will you be expected to learn in college?
3. Define creative and critical thinking. Compare and contrast these ways of thinking.
4. Identify and describe the six steps of critical thinking/problem solving.

Chapter 6 Case Scenarios

1. Joan has been named a student ambassador for her college. One of her duties as an ambassador is to help prepare for fall orientation for new students. The advisors have told the student ambassadors that last year students rated orientation low because they had to wait in long lines to get registered and the information they received was too detailed and difficult to comprehend. Joan and her fellow ambassadors have been asked to create a new way of providing orientation to students. What process will Joan and her fellow ambassadors need to follow to create a successful program for new students?

2. Sidra wants to earn money for college tuition next year, but she doesn't have the time to work 40 hours a week. If Sidra's creative thinking process results in the following ideas, explain what steps she needs to follow in order to determine the most viable solution: sell blood, tutor classmates, tattoo herself with a local company's logo and charge them for advertising, sell items on the Internet, work as a telemarketer, house sit for friends and family members.

3. Kenya has decided to apply for a loan forgiveness program that will pay all her tuition as she completes a degree in computer networking. The loan forgiveness program requires that she find a job in networking within three months of graduation, or she will owe back the full amount of her loans. After she completes a year of her degree program, she learns that the job market for networking specialists does not look promising for the next five years, which may mean she will have great difficulty finding a job when she graduates in a year. What should Kenya do?

Research It Further

1. Using the key terms "critical thinking" and "creative thinking," search the Internet for tips for improving critical and creative thinking skills. Make a table of the different tips and present the information to your classmates.

2. Create a survey to distribute to fellow students that ask them what the top concerns on campus are. Report your results to the class and choose one to solve through the critical thinking process.

3. Interview faculty members in different programs on your campus and ask them to provide a critical thinking scenario that a graduate in their programs would encounter on the job. Ask them to work through the problem to a feasible solution. Share the different problem-solving scenarios with the class and ask them to compare and contrast the processes.

References

De Bono, E. (2008). Edward de Bono's web. Retrieved March 16, 2008, from http://www.edwdebono.com/index.html.

Diestler, S. (1998). *Becoming a critical thinker: A user friendly manual* (2nd ed.). Upper Saddle River, NJ: Prentice Hall.

Dweck, C. (2006). *Mindset: The new psychology of success*. New York: Random House.

Foer, J. (2007). Remember this. *National Geographic 212*(5), 32–55.

Gunn, A. M., Richburg, R. W., & Smilkstein, R. (2007). *Igniting student potential: Teaching with the brain's natural learning process*. Thousands Oak, CA: Corwin Press.

Harris, R. (2002). *Creative problem solving: A step-by-step approach*. Los Angeles: Pyrczak.

Miller, G. (2008). The magical number seven, plus or minus two: Some limits on our capacity for processing information. Retrieved March 10, 2008, from http://www.musanim.com/miller1956/.

7 Reading

Evan's Story

TO DO THIS WEEK

- 54 pages of genetics with pictures and boxes of stories about scientists and experiments on DNA from biology textbook.

- 72 pages of aviation mechanics with diagrams of interiors of airplanes, graphs, and dozens of drawings of different parts of the plane from aviation textbook.

- 213 pages of an autobiography that has to be read in addition to the textbook.

- 3 pages of an article that has be summarized and critiqued.

Even though he can bench press hundreds of pounds, Evan feels weak when he thinks about his "to do" list this week for his classes. When he was in high school, he didn't have to read much to get by—and he barely got by—but now his instructors not only expect it, they demand that he keep up with his reading. Between quizzes, required discussion, writing assignments, and tests, Evan is discovering that college without reading is like kickboxing without sore muscles.

All of his reading assignments swim in his head as he heads to the learning assistance lab to get help with the writing assignment for the article he has to read. When Michael heard Evan was having trouble with a reading and writing assignment, he told him about the center.

"Evan, I know exactly what you need to do. I just got help with my algebra homework, and the tutor explained it in a way that I could get it. It works. Just try it," Michael had said earlier in the week.

"It's not that I don't know what to do," Evan says to the tutor. "I just don't like to read. It's boring. I would rather run laps all day than sit down and read. And there is so much of it. It's insane," he says.

The tutor laughs at his last remark. "It does seem like a lot at first," she says, "but you will get better at reading the more you do."

"I don't think I want to get *that* good at it," Evan jokes. He pulls out his assignment from his freshman seminar class; the reading assignment is to find an article about community college students and write a summary and critique.

"Once you find the article you want, read the article first for meaning. Check out the title, the publication information, the date," the tutor says, "and once you begin reading, stop at every paragraph, at first, and see if you can summarize the author's ideas. When you can sum up what the article says, then you can read the article critically."

"I think I am getting this, but what am I going to do about the chapters and the book I need to read?" Evan asks.

"Just follow the same process. It works for other types of reading," says the tutor.

Evan knows that like sports, you only get better with practice and by challenging yourself with harder exercises.

In This Chapter

Whether you love to read or you find the activity to be a challenge, reading will be an integral part of your education in college. Can you imagine getting a degree and *not* reading a page? Technology may have changed the way we read and how we incorporate written information, but it has not changed the importance of reading in becoming an educated individual. This chapter addresses the different reading strategies for sharpening your reading skills, whether you are reading books, magazines, e-books, or Web articles.

More specifically, when you complete this chapter, you will be able to:

- Discuss the importance of reading effectively in college.
- Describe ways to break down a long reading assignment for better comprehension and understanding.
- Define active reading and critical reading.
- Identify different reading methods.

College Reading Expectations

If death and taxes are unavoidable parts of life, then reading is an inevitable part of college and lifelong learning; fortunately, reading is more enjoyable and more profitable than death and taxes. The bottom line is that you will not be a successful student if you do not read assigned and supplemental material regularly. Likewise, it will be difficult to practice lifelong learning after college without reading on a regular basis. As previous chapters have mentioned, reading class handouts and college publications as well as your textbooks are essential to success in college. The reasons that reading is important to your college education and lifelong learning are many, but here are just a few incentives for making reading an integral part of your daily college work:

- Reading provides you with basic information that you can use to create knowledge of a subject.
- Reading improves your understanding of others and the world around you by exposing you to new viewpoints, ideas, and cultures.
- Reading helps you understand yourself, which will assist you in making better life choices.

With this said, it must be acknowledged that some students just do not enjoy reading because of bad experiences in school or because of learning difficulties. Thus, for some college students, reading can be a challenge to academic fulfillment. Professors would be ecstatic if all their students read well and enjoyed all the assigned reading material. More realistically, students find some reading dull and difficult to comprehend, and they long to read something "exciting." The not-so-good news is that until you get into classes that pertain to your major or career choice, you may feel that the assigned reading is uninteresting, but the good news is that there are ways to improve your comprehension *and* enjoyment of the reading assignments.

In addition to the subject matter that you will encounter in college reading, you will also find the reading load to be more than it was in high school or more than it is for your job. If you are taking four three-credit-hour classes, you can expect to read more than 100 pages a week if each professor assigns a chapter from the textbook.

This number does not reflect full-length novels, supplementary articles, required periodical subscriptions, reserved library materials, online resources, and your own notes from class—all of which may be part of your weekly reading load. The truth about college reading is that there will be plenty for you to read and that you will also be held accountable for reading, comprehending, and thinking critically about the material.

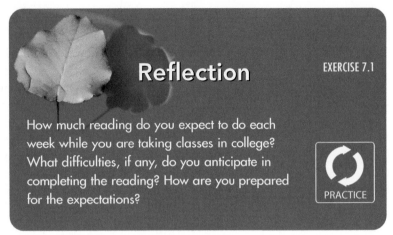

Reflection

EXERCISE 7.1

How much reading do you expect to do each week while you are taking classes in college? What difficulties, if any, do you anticipate in completing the reading? How are you prepared for the expectations?

PRACTICE

What to Do with a Reading Assignment

When you first get a reading assignment, you will need to spend a little time preparing to read, which will help you maximize the time that you have to complete it. No doubt, in the first week of classes, you will be given handouts, syllabi, and chapters to read in your textbook. How do you manage it all without getting behind and overwhelmed at the start of the semester? First, remember that all written material that your professors give you needs to be read. You will be held responsible for it immediately or at a later date; therefore, you will need to create a process for reading and remembering what you have read.

No matter how big or small the assignment, treat the reading assignment seriously. In other words, make a conscious effort to read and remember important information. A positive attitude about the reading assignment will help make the other steps easier to complete. Before you begin reading, you will also want to organize assignments according to size, importance, and date of completion; start with the most important documents first, and then work your way down the stack. A shorter assignment can be completed first unless its due date is far off.

To increase your chances of reading effectively, set a definite time and place to read. Just as you would set a time to study or go to work, you will need to schedule time to read, preferably at the same time each day. Finding a comfortable, quiet area to read is also important because it will put you in the mood to focus on what you are reading. Equally important to setting a definite time is to establish routine breaks from reading. Get up, walk around the room, get a drink of water, and get the circulation going in your

The reading load in college is heavier than in high school.

legs again. Taking breaks in which you physically move around the room will help your concentration and keep you from falling asleep.

In addition to finding the right place, consider setting a purpose for reading. Learning to understand and set purposes for reading will make the assignments easier to comprehend and complete. For example, if your reading purpose is to improve your understanding of networking, then when you sit down with the textbook for your computer networking administration class, you are in the right frame of mind. Conversely, if your reading purpose is to be entertained when you read a chapter in economics, you may be disappointed and less receptive to remembering what you have read.

As you have read in previous chapters, writing down goals is the first step to realizing them. The same holds true for reading. If you want to increase your reading speed, vocabulary, and understanding of the material, you should do more than give them passing consideration. Set specific, concrete goals for individual assignments or the whole semester. An example of a reading goal could be to increase the number of pages you can read in one sitting or to learn 5 new words a week and use them.

Finally, take care of yourself throughout the semester as you do your assigned work. You won't be able to read effectively if you are overtired, hungry, or sick. Don't try to force yourself to read if physical or psychological issues distract you. Too much sugar and caffeine and too little sleep can make reading more difficult; so can certain medications and emotional distractions. If you cannot concentrate, return to

FIGURE 7.1   Sample Reading Log

Title of text or chapter _____

Number of pages _____

Author _____

Class _____

Instructor _____

Date reading should be completed _____

Estimated time to complete _____

Reading goals _____

Actual time to complete _____

Reading goals achieved   YES   NO

Skimmed   YES   NO   PARTIALLY

1. What is the reading about?

2. What did I learn from the reading?

3. What questions do I still have about the reading?

4. What difficulties, if any, did I have while reading?

New vocabulary words and definitions:

the material when you are feeling better, but be sure to use this advice sparingly. Sometimes, you will just need to dig and get it done regardless of how you feel.

Another way to prepare to read effectively is to start a reading log that will help you focus your reading goals and prepare you to read actively. Figure 7.1 provides a method for reading effectively as well as critically. The first two questions at the bottom of the log support active reading while the last two ask you to think critically about what you have read.

Active Reading

Active reading, a term that you may hear often in college along with *active listening*, means that you are fully engaged in reading by focusing your mind and body on the activity. Many first-time students read passively rather than actively and do not fully concentrate on the material. Just reading the words is not enough for college classes. Instead, you must be a part of the process by participating in some or all of the following reading strategies: skimming, scanning, breaking down material, building your vocabulary, taking notes, checking your comprehension, and reviewing and recalling what you have read. The information that follows will help you become an active reader, and the reading log will help you reinforce these practices.

Skimming and Scanning

You may already be familiar with the terms *skimming* and *scanning* as they pertain to reading. Skimming is reading material quickly and superficially, paying particular attention to main ideas; use this method of reading when you first get a reading assignment because it can help you get a feel for what the material is, how long it is, and how difficult it will be to read. In order to skim a text effectively, you should read the first and last paragraphs, the main headings of each section, and the first and last sentences of each paragraph; of course, if time is a factor, you can delete some of the steps or add more in which you read the first and last paragraphs of each section. Ideally, skimming should be done before in-depth reading. However, sometimes skimming may be the only chance you have to read the material. If this is the case, be sure to pay attention to the major headings of each section and the first and last paragraphs of the material. Don't be surprised, though, if you miss major ideas that are sandwiched in the middle.

Although it now has a meaning similar to skimming, scanning is a method of reading that has traditionally meant "examining a text closely." Nonetheless, some reading experts define "scanning" as looking quickly for a specific item or topic as you would scan a phone book for someone's name or a dictionary for a particular word. Scanning also includes examining the table of contents and index of a book to narrow your focus and prepare you to find what you are looking for. Just as with skimming, scanning requires that your eyes move quickly over a page. However, the difference is that you know what you want to find and will slow down once you find it. Scanning is particularly useful when reviewing sources to use for a paper. You can determine rather quickly if the source pertains to your topic or not. Once you scan, you can then skim or read the text actively.

Breaking Down the Material

As stated earlier, part of scanning a text includes examining its parts. Certain pages of a book or article hold valuable information for deciphering its purpose. Students who want to "hurry up" and read the meat of the assignment often overlook some of the most important parts: The title, author, table of contents, chapter titles, introduction, section headings, headnotes, bibliography, and index are wonderful and revealing components of a piece of writing.

Title. The title of an article or book will give you a clue as to what it is about. For instance, the title of this book is *The Community College Experience* because the information within it reflects the unique needs of community college students, not students at other types of institutions of higher education. When reading any material, take time to think about the significance of the title of the work you are reading and go back to the title to look for additional meaning once you have completed the whole text.

Author. The author of a text can be just as important as what he or she has to say. Because of their reputations, some authors lend credibility to their words or they instantly make readers suspicious of their motives. If you recognize the author's name, then you should have a good idea of what the text is about. The more you read, the more you will encounter writings by certain people, and you will be able to expect certain viewpoints from them.

Table of Contents. Most books have a table of contents that shows how the book is organized. A table of contents lists the chapters as well as any subsections that appear in the chapters. Lastly, the table of contents contains the beginning page number for each chapter or section. Familiarizing yourself with the table of contents will make it easier to find information when you need it.

Introduction. Sometimes overlooked, the introduction can provide all the information you may need to determine if a particular book is what you want. When researching a topic, you can decide whether or not a book will be a good source for you by reading the introduction. Introductions typically tell the reader what the whole book is about, what unique features you will find, and what viewpoint is supported.

Chapter Titles. The titles of chapters are a good indication of what you can expect to read within the book. Chapter titles also help you locate information more quickly. Can you imagine trying to find information from this book about taking notes without any chapter titles? You would have to scan each chapter until you found it.

Section Headings. Section headings work in the same way as chapter titles. They indicate how the material is organized and they give you a sneak peek of what is to come.

Headnotes. The text that appears at the beginning of sections or before essays that explains or briefly summarizes what you are about to read is considered headnotes. Headnotes can provide biographical information about the author or can indicate the essay's main points.

Bibliography. A bibliography, or list of references or works cited, usually appears at the end of an article or a book, right before the index. Literally, a bibliography is a list of books that the author has read or used in preparing the text. This section of a book or article is often overlooked, but it actually contains a wealth of information for the reader. If you want to learn more about a topic that the author briefly mentions, you can look at the bibliography to see what other books are listed about the subject. Also, if you are doing research on a topic and need instant access to a list of more sources, an author's bibliography can supply you with potential sources.

Index. One of the last elements of a book is its index, which is an alphabetical list of major ideas or words that are keyed to the pages on which they appear. If you need to find that information on note-taking, for instance, you can use the index to pinpoint the exact page it is on. Indexes (or indices) are especially helpful in research when you are evaluating sources to see whether they contain material about your subject. For example, if you have located a book on African American playwrights and need some information on Lorraine Hansberry, you can look for her name in the index to see if she is mentioned in the book. If she is not listed in the "H's" (for Hansberry), then you know that the book is not a good resource for you.

You are probably thinking that this process seems time consuming and unnecessary, especially if you do not have much time to spend reading anyway. Yes, at first the process will take more time, but the more you do it, the less time it will take because you will know what to look for. Also, your reading speed and comprehension will improve, which will mean that you can complete your assignments more quickly.

Reading in the Disciplines

The following strategies for reading in the disciplines are just a sample of what you may encounter in college.

Math. Take your time to read both the written information and explanations as well as the visual representations of problems and steps for solving them. Reading assigned chapters *before* you get to class will help you check your reading comprehension.

Literature. You may find you have more reading in literature classes—novels, short stories, plays, and poetry. Start early with these long reading assignments and take notes along the way. Depending on the complexity of the literature, you may need to read the work a few times, especially poetry, and sound each word out. Although sounding out individual words, or subvocalization (see "Reading Difficulties" section), is often considered a reading difficulty, it may be necessary to slow down and read short pieces of literature aloud. Also, pay attention to details when reading fiction and poetry.

Languages. The goal in reading in a foreign language is to improve your comprehension first. Use a dictionary the first time you encounter new vocabulary and work on improving your speed.

Sciences. Reading in the sciences will take time and focus as you encounter new concepts and processes. Look for visual representations of the content in your textbook.

Social Sciences. Large amounts of assigned material will be part of any social science class. Start reading the chapters early and look for key ideas. People and their theories or their actions (in history) will be key components of the reading. Learning the who, what, when, and where of the material will make it easier to remember.

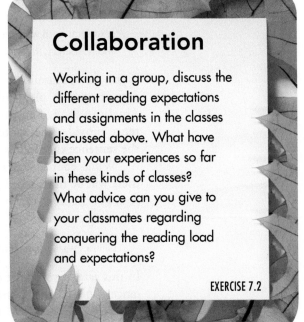

Collaboration

Working in a group, discuss the different reading expectations and assignments in the classes discussed above. What have been your experiences so far in these kinds of classes? What advice can you give to your classmates regarding conquering the reading load and expectations?

EXERCISE 7.2

INTEGRITY MATTERS

One definition of integrity is doing what you say you will do even in the face of adversity. Acting with integrity in college includes making a commitment to complete reading assignments in all your classes even if you face challenges to your commitment. Reading in college is not optional; rather, it is crucial to success. When you make the commitment to enroll in college, you must also follow through with that commitment by tackling the reading that is part of the experience.

Building Your Vocabulary

Increasing your vocabulary is another benefit to reading regularly. Some students get sidelined when they read because they encounter unfamiliar words; few students take the time to look up words that they don't know, and they subsequently miss out on learning new ideas or understanding the intent of the author. It is well worth your time to look up words when you read, but there are some methods you can use to decrease the time you spend flipping through your dictionary.

The first method of learning new vocabulary words is to look for context clues in the sentence. Many times you can figure out what the word means by how it is used in a sentence or by the words that surround it. Consider the following sentence:

Students often use context clues to *decipher* the meaning of unfamiliar words.

If you didn't know that *decipher* means to figure out, you could still understand the meaning of the sentence by the words around it and by considering that students are using something (context clues) in order to do something (decipher) the unfamiliar words. You could deduce, then, that students are making the unfamiliar words more familiar by using context clues. Now, try this sentence:

It was not until we traveled to Beijing that we realized how *ubiquitous* American fast food was. On every street corner we saw a McDonald's or a KFC restaurant.

If you are not familiar with modern-day Beijing, you may not know that American restaurants are plentiful; in fact, you may believe that China has very little American food. Thus, to understand the meaning of *ubiquitous,* the second sentence provides the context clues. With the phrase "On every street corner" from the sentence that follows you should realize that *ubiquitous* means "everywhere."

While context clues will allow you to make sense of most unfamiliar words, there will be times when you cannot rely on the other words in the sentence to help you. For example, can you tell what the words *amenable* and *obsequious* mean in the following sentence?

Charles was *amenable* to going out to eat with Sheila's *obsequious* mother.

In this case, if you don't know what the words mean, the sentence offers little assistance. Does Charles want to go out to eat or doesn't he? Is Sheila's mother someone who is enjoyable to be around or isn't she? To answer these questions, you may need to look up the words. Here is what you would see if you were to look up *amenable* in *Webster's New World Dictionary*:

> a·me·na·ble (ə me′ nə bəl) *adj.* [[<Ofr, L *minare*, to drive (animals)]] 1 responsible or answerable 2 able to be controlled; submissive—a·me′na·bil′i·ty *n.*—a·me′na·bly *adv.*

Now, look up *obsequious* for yourself and see if you can decipher the sentence.

Another way to figure out what words mean is to know some common Latin and Greek root words, prefixes, and suffixes. For example, if your professor calls astrology a "pseudoscience" and you know that the Greek root *pseudo* means "false," then you will be able to understand that your professor is claiming that astrology is not a true science. In order to learn the common roots of words that we use every day, you will need to study words' origins. A college reading class or looking up words in the dictionary regularly will help you learn to recognize the roots in other words. Table 7.1 provides a few common ones you will encounter.

TIPS ON BUILDING VOCABULARY

- Purchase or borrow discipline-specific dictionaries when you begin a class that contains a large amount of terminology (e.g., medical or scientific dictionaries, foreign language dictionaries, and glossaries for literary terms).
- Before asking your professor or classmate what a word means, look it up.
- Don't be afraid to look up words, even the same words multiple times. You will eventually be able to recall their meanings.
- Use new words in conversation to "try them out." Using them regularly will help you remember what they mean.

TABLE 7.1 Common Latin and Greek Root Words

Root	Meaning	Example Word	Definition
Ante	Before	*Antebellum*	Before the war, specifically referring to the American Civil War
Anti	Against	*Antibiotic*	Against life, specifically against microorganisms
Auto	Self	*Autobiography*	Writing about the self
Biblio/Bibl	Book	*Bibliography*	A list of books
Cede	Go, leave	*Secede*	Leave an organization or alliance
Chrono	Time	*Chronological*	Events ordered by time in which they occurred
Cogn	Know	*Recognize, cognizant*	To know from before; fully informed
Graph	Write	*Autograph*	Person's own signature
Inter	Within, between	*Intermission*	The period between performances
Phil	Love	*Philanthropy*	Love of humankind
Photo	Light	*Photography*	Producing images using light in the process
Pseudo	False	*Pseudonym*	False name

- Write new words on 3 × 5 index cards and jot down the book and page where they appear. Look up the definitions when you have time and write them on the cards. Take the cards with you and review your new words when waiting in line or stuck in traffic.
- Buy and browse a thesaurus, a book that contains synonyms for words. A thesaurus is handy when you are searching for a word that is similar to another.
- If you have an email account, subscribe to a word-a-day service that sends you a new vocabulary word each day, or buy a word-a-day calendar.
- Subscribe to magazines that challenge your reading skills: *The Atlantic Monthly, The New Yorker,* and *Harper's* are examples of print magazines that provide interesting and challenging material.

Taking Notes While You Read

Taking notes as you read, either in your textbook or in a notebook, is an excellent way to remember what you have read and to begin the process of critical reading. Writing down key ideas, terms to look up later, and questions that you have as you read helps you stay focused and improves comprehension. However, avoid highlighting large sections of text. Excessive highlighting defeats the purpose of noting only key or very important information. If you can write in your textbook, create one- or two-word summaries of each paragraph or section. If you need to keep the text clean, then use your reading log (above) exclusively. Otherwise, you may want to use it in conjunction with in-text notes.

Reading Speed

Knowing how quickly you read is helpful in planning time for reading and in marking your progress. The goal is to increase your speed *and* your comprehension. In order to calculate your reading speed, time yourself while you read the accompanying article from *The Chronicle of Higher Education.*

Community-College Students' Reasons for Dropping Out Are Familiar Ones, Study Finds

David Glenn

Community-college students drop out at much higher rates than do students in four-year colleges, but for similar reasons, according to an ambitious new study that was described here on Tuesday at the annual meeting of the American Sociological Association.

The study's central finding—that the dynamics of dropping out of community colleges and four-year colleges are essentially the same—might not sound like heart-stopping news. But the study's author said that her work should dispel any suspicions that community-college students are so different from their four-year counterparts—in age, ability, and life circumstances—that the traditional explanations for dropping out don't apply to them.

(continued)

Indeed, community colleges probably should follow some of the same dropout-combating advice that has been given to four-year colleges during the past decade, said the author, Regina Deil-Amen, an assistant professor of education at Pennsylvania State University at University Park. In particular, Ms. Deil-Amen said, community colleges should pay attention to their students' levels of academic integration (how frequently they interact outside of class with teachers, librarians, and other staff members) and social integration (their participation in campus clubs and friendship networks).

The terms "academic integration" and "social integration" derive from the work of Vincent Tinto, a professor of education at Syracuse University who during the 1970s developed a widely used model of how students decide to drop out. Students who face identical intellectual and financial obstacles can vary widely in their propensity to drop out, Mr. Tinto observed—and the difference often has to do with how well students believe that they fit at a particular college.

Many recent studies have empirically supported Mr. Tinto's basic insights, Ms. Deil-Amen said, but few of them have looked specifically at the community-college context.

In her project, Ms. Deil-Amen drew on a large-scale federal research project known as the Beginning Postsecondary Longitudinal Study, which followed students who first enrolled in college in 1995. From that study, Ms. Deil-Amen took data concerning 3,300 students who entered four-year institutions and 3,600 students who entered community colleges.

Ms. Deil-Amen's analysis found that, among community-college students, "participation in clubs or arts activities, study groups, and frequent interaction with faculty and advisers outside of class were all significantly negatively associated with dropout." This appeared to be true even for students who attended part-time, who had low grades, who had children, and who worked many hours outside of college.

Participating in study groups turned out to be one of the most powerful variables in Ms. Deil-Amen's analysis. All else being equal, joining study groups appeared to reduce a community-college student's odds of dropping out by approximately 28 percent.

Among four-year students, study groups had no statistically significant effect. That was one of the few strong differences Ms. Deil-Amen found between the two groups.

Along with her quantitative analysis, Ms. Deil-Amen conducted detailed interviews with community-college students and dropouts in the Chicago area. In her paper—titled "Do Traditional Models of College Dropout Apply to Non-Traditional Students at Non-Traditional Colleges?"—Ms. Deil-Amen quotes one of those students on the value of study groups and social networks: "When you doubt yourself, your intelligence, everything . . . you feel as though you can't make it, you're not going to make it, it's a horrible feeling. . . . When you find a student who says, 'Yes, I know what you're talking about. Yes, I have that same problem'—even if she's never solved it and you're still experiencing it, you're not alone anymore."

The article is 580 words in length. To calculate your reading speed, divide the number of minutes that it took you to read the passage into 580 to get your reading speed. For example, if it took you 2.5 minutes to complete the passage, then (580/2.5) you read at a rate of 175 WPM (words per minute).

Number of words $\underline{\quad 580 \quad}$

Number of minutes $\underline{\quad\quad}$

580/___ (number of minutes) = ___ WPM

Average readers read between 200 and 250 words per minute, but that does not reflect their comprehension of the material. Techniques for improving speed are worth learning and practicing. Your college may offer a speed reading class, or you may be able to read about the methods for improving speed through books or websites.

Checking Your Comprehension

The most important aspect of reading is comprehending and remembering what you have read. If your textbook has questions at the end of each chapter that will help you reinforce what you have learned, then get in the habit of answering them when you finish a reading assignment. Even mentally answering the questions will help you understand the material. If your textbook does not have questions, then create your own or write a short summary of the chapter. To reinforce what you have learned, trade summaries with a classmate.

A high WPM reading speed means very little if you do not remember anything that you have read. Your goal should be to improve your reading speed reasonably, to help you keep up with the reading demands of college, and to improve your retention and comprehension of the material.

Improving Your Reading Attention Span

Each semester will get more demanding in terms of reading because you will be advancing in your degree program and will be encountering new, more challenging content. Therefore, the more practice that you have in reading effectively, the easier it will be to complete larger reading assignments. If you find that your "reading attention span" is not long, then you can work on lengthening it.

First, you will need to figure out how many pages you can read comfortably without getting distracted or tired. Write down the number in your reading log, a notebook, or in a calendar. Each time that you sit down to read an assignment, notice how many pages it is. See if you can "beat" the number in the previous reading session. The more you read and the more you challenge yourself with reading, the better you will get. Just be patient.

Thinking Critically When Reading

In addition to all that you have learned about preparing to read and improving your reading skills, you will also need to consider reading critically. As stated earlier in this chapter and as you will see in other chapters, critical thinking is a requirement in college classes. Your instructors not only want to impart basic information to you through their lectures, class discussion, and assigned readings, but they also want you to think critically about that information in order to add to your understanding of yourself and the world around you. It will not be enough to know that Abraham Lincoln's

Emancipation Proclamation was delivered on September 22, 1862; instead, you will need to think critically about the reason the speech was made, the effect the speech had on its audience, and the far-reaching implications of its message long after it was made.

How can you begin to think more critically about your reading? First, you need to make sure that you understand what you are reading. Improving your vocabulary and reading comprehension will be essential in understanding the material. Second, you will need to get comfortable with taking notes whenever you read. Writing in the margins or in a designated notebook is the foundation for remembering what you have read so that you can think critically about the material.

Once you have checked your comprehension and started writing notes while you read, the next logical step is to question what you have read. Reading critically means that you question everything from the author's background and expertise to the information that she presents and how she organizes it. Since you may think that published authors must always be right—or they wouldn't be published—you may find questioning an authority on a subject to be uncomfortable at first. "Who am I to say this person is wrong?" may be a question that runs through your head as you begin to read and think critically. The answer is that you are the perfect person to question the author because you are his audience, the person to whom he is writing. If you have questions about his ideas, then others may as well.

Here are some standard questions that you can ask of every reading that you encounter:

- Who is the author? What is his or her background? What makes him or her knowledgeable of this subject? Does he or she have any bias toward the subject?
- What is the audience for this material? Are the length, vocabulary, and organization of the information appropriate for the audience?
- Are there any factual errors? Does the author misrepresent information or oversimplify it?
- Does the author say anything that seems confusing?
- Does the author's examples support the overall point? If not, which ones do not support the main point? Why don't they support it?
- Does the author leave anything out of the information?
- What else would you like to know about the subject?
- What questions do you have about the information that the author did not answer?
- Overall, how do you rate the reading?

When you first start thinking critically about your assigned readings, answer as many of these questions as you feel comfortable. You won't have to answer all of them each time that you read, but the more you read with a critical eye, the more questions you will have of the texts.

SQ3R Reading Strategy

One of the most popular reading strategies, SQ3R, was developed by Francis Pleasant Robinson in 1946 and published in *Effective Study*. Many books and websites since then have interpreted the strategy, but the overall strategy works this way.

(S) Survey: Before reading your text closely, start by examining the headings, subheadings, graphics, charts, and references if included.

(Q) Question: After you look for these major organizational signposts, you can either think or write questions that you have. One way to generate questions is

to turn headings and subheadings into questions. For example, the subheading "SQ3R Reading Strategy" can be turned into the question "What is the SQ3R reading strategy?"

(R1) Read: Read each section at a time, making sure you are concentrating on what you have read.

(R2) Recite: At the end of each section that you have read, say aloud what the section was about and answer the questions that you asked during the Question stage. You may also want to write your answers on note cards to review later.

(R3) Review: After you have completed the first four steps, you will be ready to review what you have read. Some experts suggest reviewing within 24 hours of reading; others recommend reviewing what you have read in short sessions over a period of time.

OK5R Reading Strategy

Many different reading strategies have been developed to help students read critically and effectively. What most methods share is a multiple-step process that involves spending time reading, writing, and thinking about the text.

Devised by Dr. Walter Pauk (1984), the OK5R method divides the process into 7 steps—notice that actually reading the text is in the middle of the steps.

(O) Overview: Chapter by chapter, you will be looking at the titles, headings within the chapters, and their subheadings. This sampling is an effort to get an idea of the book's overall emphasis. According to Pauk, there is no need to read whole paragraphs; instead, take a "taste" of the text.

(K) Key Ideas: To find the key ideas of a text, you will need to read the beginnings and endings of the chapter. You should have a good grasp of the key ideas from your overview.

(R1) Read: Now you can read your text more closely, stopping frequently to ask yourself how each paragraph, with its details, supports the main idea of the book.

(R2) Record: For each paragraph or page, write a one- or two-word summary of the key ideas. Mark any sentences or words that do not make sense, and write down any questions that you have about the reading.

(R3) Recite: In order to improve your ability to remember the material, stop to recite, or say aloud, what you have learned. Do not look at the book or your notes when reciting. When you are finished, check your notes and the book to see how well you have remembered what you have read.

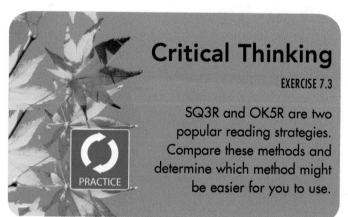

Critical Thinking

EXERCISE 7.3

SQ3R and OK5R are two popular reading strategies. Compare these methods and determine which method might be easier for you to use.

PRACTICE

(R4) Review: Look back over your notes and see if you can fit all the "jigsaw" pieces, as Pauk refers to them, of ideas together into one picture. Review your notes soon after you read and make a point of reviewing them later.

(R5) Reflect: Take some time after you read to think about how the ideas fit into your life. The more you understand how your life is affected by the main ideas of the reading, the more likely you will remember the reading and be able to create knowledge from it.

Putting the Pleasure Back into Reading

One of the most difficult reading obstacles that every college student faces, no matter how well he reads, is generating interest in the material. A common complaint of students is that the reading was "boring." True, some college reading material will be dry and dull, but you can change how the reading affects you by changing your attitude about the reading itself. Sometimes, you just need to trick yourself into enjoying what you read, and one way to do that is to tell yourself that you will learn something new and useful.

Another way to put pleasure back into reading is to seek out pleasurable reading yourself. If you have favorite authors or types of writing, go to a bookstore or library and get a copy of your favorite book, magazine, or something that may spark your interest. Make an effort to find reading (and browsing through aisles of books will help) that is interesting, stimulating, and even fun. Reading or browsing through a magazine or newspaper a week will help your reading skills. The habit of reading will also make it easier to stick to the schedule you have set for reading class material. If you have a good book on your table, it can serve as a reward for completing less exciting reading assignments. Once you create good reading habits, you will find yourself reading—and enjoying— even after classes are over. You will soon discover that you are curious to learn new things, and reading will satisfy your thirst for knowledge.

Reflection   EXERCISE 7.4

What do you enjoy about reading? What kinds of writing do you like to read and why?

PRACTICE

Reading Difficulties

For some students like Evan, no matter how much they want to read well, the activity is difficult. Dealing with reading difficulties can make a short reading assignment seem like climbing Mount Everest and can make it hard to stay motivated. The following paragraphs describe some common reading difficulties that students experience. It is not intended as a comprehensive list, nor is it intended as a diagnosis for problems that you may experience. If you think you may have a reading difficulty or a learning disability, you should see your college counselor for a proper diagnosis. Your college's counseling services should also provide you with resources that will help alleviate any problems you may experience because of a learning difficulty.

Some reading difficulties are more bad habits than disorders. Subvocalization, or pronouncing each word in your mind as you read, is one type of bad habit that some readers experience. Reading the same words or sentences over and over again, or regression, is another bad habit that some readers do. Improving your reading speed, or the rate at which your eyes move across the page, often eliminates the reading habits that slow you down. Moving a finger, pen, or pencil across the page as you read can also slow down your reading speed. Unless you are stopping to take notes along the way, eliminate the use of an instrument to keep your eyes moving. Finally, poor concentration can negatively affect how quickly you read. In some cases, poor concentration is part of a larger issue that may be diagnosed by a health professional. If poor concentration is just a bad habit, then you can work toward improving concentration by eliminating distractions and following the suggestions outlined in this chapter.

Dyslexia is a neurological disorder that makes it difficult for a person to comprehend and recognize written words; they may also have trouble writing and spelling. According to the International Dyslexia Association (2008), 15–20% of all students have dyslexia, and most people with dyslexia have average or above-average intelligence. The good news about dyslexia is that many students have learned to cope with the disorder and have succeeded in college and careers.

Attention Deficit Disorder (ADD) or Attention Deficit Hyperactivity Disorder (ADHD) is a behavioral disorder in which a person has difficulty paying attention. Reading can become just another obstacle that someone with ADD or ADHD must overcome. In order to work through any difficulties that ADD/ADHD may cause, you will need to contact your counseling center. As with dyslexia, ADD/ADHD can be managed so that your reading skills get sharper.

Some reading difficulties are actually the result of vision problems. A regular eye exam can determine if your difficulties are caused by the need for corrective glasses or contacts. If you think your eyes are the reason that you have difficulty reading words, get your eyes checked by a doctor. You may want to stop first at your college's health clinic, if one is available, for a screening. Also, take advantage of any health fairs that are offered on your campus where you can get a free screening that may pinpoint the problem.

PLUS

EXERCISE 7.5

(Personality + Learning Style = Understanding Situations)

Think about Evan's situation regarding how to tackle his reading for the week. The solitary activity of reading seems contradictory to Evan's kinesthetic, outgoing nature. He admits that usually he is not very interested in what he has to read, but not only does he need to read the assignments, he also needs to remember what he has read and respond to it. Using what you have learned from this chapter, what advice would you give him? Once he reads the article and writes his summary and critique of it, what strategies can he use to complete the rest of the reading?

Now, considering your own learning style, personality type, and special circumstances, what can you do to tackle the reading assignments you have for this week?

PROFILE

MY STORY
Learning Plan

Directions: Using what you have learned in this chapter and what you know about your learning preferences, choose a task or assignment that needs to be completed soon and create a learning plan that will help you accomplish this task. Then, write your *My Story* Summary, a one-sentence synopsis that crystallizes your newly created plan.

LEARNING TASK	
Time of Day	
Intake Preference	
Social Preference	
Task Management Preference	

MY STORY SUMMARY:

Path of Discovery

How do you plan to improve your reading skills in college? What do you hope reading well will do for you?

HOMEWORK

From College to University

How the Reading Load and Expectations May Change

You have probably noticed that with each chapter's discussion of moving from college to university, the demands are greater, and the reading expectations are no exception. Most definitely, the reading load will increase significantly—you may find that you have hundreds of pages a week to read and comprehend. You may also find that you are expected to do more than just recall the information. In addition, you will need to think critically about the reading by asking questions of the author (What does she mean? How does she know? What are the implications of her argument?) and of yourself (Do I agree? Does this argument make sense?). Professors in upper-level classes will also require you to discuss the readings in class. Most definitely, the discussion will move beyond the content of the reading to the formulation of new ideas and opinions about the topic of the reading. The more you are able to contribute, the more you will get out of the reading and the class.

From College to Career

How Reading Skills Will Help You Succeed

There are very few, if any, careers that do not require some level of reading. The jobs in computer programming and networking require constant reading to stay on top of new developments and trends in the field, as do industrial careers that require you to stay abreast of the latest regulations and laws. No matter how hard you try, there is just no escaping a career without reading.

The good news is that after completing your certificate or degree, you will be a better reader and you will understand the importance of reading regularly. A better vocabulary, improved reading comprehension, and faster reading speed will help you do your job better. An employee who reads well is an asset to a company because she is usually more attuned to the latest trends and ideas. An employee who reads effectively also knows what is happening in the company and can more easily handle challenges on the job.

Chapter Review Questions

1. Which reading skills are essential to success in college?
2. What are the differences between active and critical reading?
3. What strategies can you use to make reading more manageable?
4. What types of reading difficulties can a student encounter? What are the strategies for overcoming them?

Chapter 7 Case Scenarios

1. Gerry hates to read, and he will do anything to keep from reading in college. He does, though, like to read home improvement magazines. He is working on his associate of arts degree. What can he do to read well and enjoy reading?

2. Meghan thinks she may have a reading difficulty, but she has never been diagnosed. Instead, she has worked extra hard to keep up with and understand her reading assignments. However, as her classes have gotten more difficult, she is worried that she won't be able to keep up. What can she do to stay on top of her reading assignments?

3. Wilson can't remember anything he reads for class, even though he spends hours the night before reading the material. He also has difficulty remembering what words mean. While he is building his vocabulary slowly, he still finds himself looking up the same word several times before he can remember it. What should he do?

Research It Further

1. Interview three people about their reading habits and preferences. Find out what kinds of reading they do for their job and what kinds of reading strategies they use to complete the reading. Also, ask if they read for pleasure and what types of reading they enjoy most. Write down your findings and present them to your class.

2. The National Adult Literacy Survey (Kirsch et al. 2008) indicates that more than 40% of Americans are functionally illiterate, which means they can function in society but cannot perform complicated reading tasks. Most of these Americans are at a disadvantage socially and economically. Do your own research as to what challenges people who cannot read or cannot read well will face.

3. Create a survey that asks members of the campus community what can be done to encourage students to read more. For example, would they be willing to participate in a book club or to host a local author on campus?

References

Glenn, D. Community-college students' reasons for dropping out are familiar ones, study finds. *The Chronicle of Higher Education*. Retrieved May 15, 2008, from http://chronicle.com/daily/2005/08/2005081701n.htm.

International Dyslexia Association. (2008). Dyslexia basics. Retrieved May 15, 2008, from http://www.interdys.org.

Kirsch, I. S., et al. (2008). Executive summary of adult literacy in America: A first look at the results of the national adult literacy survey. National Center for Education Statistics. Retrieved May 15, 2008, from http://nces.ed.gov/naal/index.asp?file=OtherResources/ExecSumAdultLitFirstLook.asp&PageId=156.

Pauk, W. (1984). *How to study in college* (3rd ed.). Boston: Houghton Mifflin.

8 Listening and Taking Notes Effectively

Laura's Story

Laura settles in her usual seat in the front row of her world civilization class. After the lesson she learned about writing down important information when she is in class, Laura has gotten better about listening more closely even when distractions compete for her attention.

"The clip we are about to watch," her professor says as she pushes the play button on the television's DVD player, "discusses the ancient library in Timbuktu."

Laura laughs at herself as she tries to spell Timbuktu. She underlines the word so that she can remember to go back and check the spelling when she rewrites her notes. Having dyslexia is frustrating at times, but she has found that laughing about her challenges is a great way to relieve her stress in certain situations.

"I love it when she stops lecturing and shows us these videos," her classmate next to her whispers in her ear. Laura misses some of the information in the video because of the distraction, but makes another note to fill in the missing information later. She loves how engaging the films are, but her dyslexia makes it difficult for her to watch and take notes.

"Hey? Do you have an extra pen?" her classmate whispers again. She knows his name, Franco, because he is a friend of Juanita's, but she hasn't talked to him much. He seems more interested in socializing than paying attention in class.

She hands him a pen and makes another note to fill in any gaps she has from being distracted. Laura is not too worried about the missing information because she has been able to view a few of the clips on her own—the library has a copy of everything her professor uses in class—but even watching them over and over again is sometimes challenging despite her comfort with learning by listening.

As the lights come back on, her professor asks if there are any questions.

"Yeah, I have one. Will that be on the test? I mean, are we responsible for remembering everything that guy said?" asks someone from the back of the room.

"Sure. You have the material that was assigned for reading, the information I cover in the lecture, and then anything else that I bring in. All of this should be studied for the test," the professor says.

"And she's not lying," says Laura to herself. Even with help from her mentor and the tutor in the learning assistance center, Laura has her work cut out for her: The information in the book is arranged chronologically, but her professor lectures on causes and effects in history, constantly referencing other eras, people, and dates in the process. Then, there are the tests that cover major themes such as important reformers or federal policies. No one note-taking strategy seems to work for reading, listening, and studying.

"Any other questions?" her professor asks and pauses for a few seconds. "Okay, if you realize you do have questions after class, be sure to email me or come by my office early next week. You have only a week to study for this test. All essay questions. Be prepared to write." She smiles, straightens her papers, and heads for the door.

"I have another question," Franco says to Laura. "Are we going to pass this class?" She knows he is half serious, but Laura is worried about that, too.

Making sense of her notes may be only part of the challenge, but it is the first one she will have to overcome.

167

In This Chapter

Learning to listen and take notes effectively can give you the edge in college because you will be able to take in more information and remember it more easily. Laura can attest to the importance of developing a note-taking system, especially for those who have learning difficulties that prevent them from using just one style. This chapter discusses various note-taking strategies, including the method Laura developed, as well as improving your listening skills. When you complete this chapter, you will be able to:

* Describe ways to listen more effectively.
* Identify barriers to listening.
* Discuss different note-taking strategies.

The Listening and Note-Taking Connection

Listening, remembering, and note taking all have something in common: They are necessary in the process of learning. You will not be able to make it successfully through your classes without doing all three. Retaining and recalling information, however, is only part of the process. This chapter helps you with receiving the information, which will in turn help you with the process of turning the information into a knowledge base that you will build on for the rest of your life.

Preparing to Listen

Active listening is a term that you may hear in college classes; someone who listens actively is concentrating on what is being said and is taking steps to remember the information. The following tips are intended for those who want to listen actively and effectively. To be an active listener, you must decide that listening is a worthwhile activity and that important information will be shared.

The first step to effective listening is to prepare to listen before you get to class. In other words, you will need to read the assigned pages or chapters ahead of time so that you know what the lecture or discussion topic will be. If you have read the chapters ahead of time, you will be familiar with new words and concepts. Preparing to listen also includes reviewing your assigned readings before you get to the classroom. If you have a few minutes between classes or on the bus, pull out your book and skim the major headings, boldfaced terms, and text boxes that appear in the margins.

To listen effectively while in class, avoid distractions. First, you will need to sit up front, move away from a talkative person, and put away textbooks for other courses, cell phones, pagers, and other distracting items. Your best defense against interruptions is to clear your desk of anything except your textbook, a pen, and paper. Stow other items in your backpack or underneath your desk or table.

If you need to get anything out during class, such as a dictionary, minimize the disruption by being as quiet as possible. If you find yourself next to a chatty classmate or one who likes to write notes to you, simply move. Even if you are politely listening or reading her messages, you will be guilty of disrupting the class by association. Talkative classmates make it difficult for you and others to listen, and they distract you from taking good notes.

Another good way to listen effectively is by maintaining a positive attitude about the class. If you think the class is a waste of time or is boring, you will be less likely to pay attention. Even if your beliefs are true—and others bemoan the class as well—pretend that the class is the only one you have left before graduating and that if you don't pay attention and take good notes, then you will have to spend another semester in the course. In other words, do whatever you need to "psych" yourself up and invest in the class.

Minimizing outside distractions is another method of keeping a positive attitude. There will be times that you have to work late, stay up all night with a sick baby, or help a friend who has just had a crisis. If not handled well, these stressful experiences could affect your performance in class. As much as possible, leave your personal life at the door and concentrate on the class that you are sitting in. Even if the lecture for the day is overshadowed by a personal problem, remember that you *can* handle both your academic duties and your personal life.

Finally, prepare for class psychologically by preparing physically. Make sure you have eaten something before each class so that you won't be interrupted by a growling stomach. Moreover, dress in layers in case the room is an uncomfortable temperature. Nothing is more distracting than being too hot or too cold. Getting plenty of sleep the night before class will also help you pay attention and listen effectively. Although adequate sleep may be a luxury if you work a late shift or if you get up in the middle of the night to take care of a child, be sure you make an effort to get a good night's sleep often. You won't be able to maintain high concentration and retention or even good health without adequate rest.

Someone who listens actively is concentrating on what is being said and is taking steps to remember the information.

Listening Critically

As stated above, active listening, much like active reading, involves focusing on the task at hand and concentrating on what is being conveyed, whether it be words or sounds. Another part of listening effectively is listening critically, or the act of processing what you have heard and evaluating it. Listening critically will help you make decisions about what is important and what is not, what is objective and what is biased, and what should be stored for later and what should be discarded.

Listening critically is a skill, one that should be practiced regularly. Your college professors will invite you to think critically and challenge your assumptions (that is learning!). As you get more comfortable with listening actively and critically, you will move from merely listening and taking notes that reflect what your instructors have said to listening to evaluate and ask questions of the notes you have taken. Here are some questions to consider as you work on listening critically:

- *Speaker.* Is the speaker a credible source? How do I know? What possible biases does he or she have? What is his or her experience with the topic?

- *Message.* What is the speaker's purpose? What are the details he or she uses to convey the message?

- *Details.* Is the speaker using facts or opinions? How do I know? Which type of details work best for what the speaker is trying to convey?

- *Self-knowledge.* What do I already know about the topic? How does what the speaker is saying conflict or support my beliefs and opinions? Do I feel I have learned something new?

- *Larger picture.* How does what the speaker is saying fit into the larger picture? How can I relate the message to something I already know about life or the world at large? Are there any connections between what I have heard and what I have experienced?

Answering some of the questions above will get you started on the right path to listening critically. Even though you are listening critically and mentally asking questions of what you are hearing, you still need to "tune in" rather than "tune out" when you hear something that you don't agree with or don't understand.

Remember, too, that "critical" does not mean "negative." If you find that what you are hearing is not holding up to what you know about the subject or the speaker is not credible, you can still ask questions that are respectful and curious. Most people do not mind being politely challenged or debated.

Reflection

EXERCISE 8.1

Think about a time when you heard someone speak about a topic that you did not agree with. How did you listen? How did you react to what you were hearing?

PRACTICE

Listening Barriers

Despite your efforts to prepare for class, you may find barriers to listening effectively, barriers that you cannot avoid no matter how well prepared you are. For example, what should you do if your instructor talks too fast, uses technical jargon or an advanced vocabulary, is unorganized, digresses from the lecture material (tells stories, allows too many irrelevant questions), or does not explain key concepts? Although you cannot coach your instructor in the art of speaking, you can ask him or her to slow down or define terms. Most professors do not mind repeating information or defining specialized language on the board because they want students to understand the material during lecture or class discussion.

It may be a little harder to ask the instructor to be more organized or to stay on topic during a lecture. However, one way to get what you need without offending the professor is to ask if she would mind providing an outline before each class. Another method of getting the professor to stay on the subject is to ask a question about the topic or an upcoming exam or assignment. Your nudging may move the lecture back into focus.

Besides getting enough sleep and sitting comfortably in class as discussed in the paragraphs above, there may be other barriers to listening effectively. If you have an unaccommodated learning disability or a hearing problem, you may not be able to listen productively. Talking to a counselor about learning or hearing difficulties can help you listen more effectively. A more common hindrance to listening is students' insecurities about their ability to do well in the course. It is not uncommon for a new student to feel, at first, intimidated by the course, the instructor, or other students in the class. The reason for the discomfort could stem from a student's feelings that he or she is not good enough or smart enough to be in college. A student also may feel that everyone else, except him or her, knows what to do, what to say, and how to act. This fear is common, and usually it subsides after the first week or two.

Remembering What You Have Heard

Once you adequately prepare to listen in class and you remove any barriers that inhibit your ability to take in information, you will need to turn your attention to remembering what you hear in class. Taking notes, of course, is one way to retain information. However, there are some other methods that will help you recall information at a later date.

Participating in discussion and activities is an excellent way to remember key concepts. In fact, professors consider student participation as part of active, rather than passive, learning. You are more likely to remember a concept if you have incorporated it into your own thinking. There is a reason that the most talkative students are usually the most successful. They have made the material relevant to them, which makes remembering easier for them as well. However, participating in class discussion may be difficult if you are shy or feel out of place in the classroom. Some students refrain from asking questions because they don't want to look ignorant in front of their classmates.

Then, there is the other end of the spectrum from the silent student—the constant questioner. These students dominate the professor's time by asking questions that sideline the discussion or questions about material that has already been covered. Don't be intimidated by a predominantly quiet classroom or by a student who asks the professor excessive questions. If you have a question, ask it. Some instructors believe there are no "stupid questions." If you don't feel comfortable asking questions during class, visit with your professor after class or during his office hours. Some instructors ask students to write questions down and pass them up before class is over. Take advantage of such a practice; you will be able to ask questions without the fear of speaking up in front of classmates.

Another method for remembering, tape recording lectures, is popular with students who have the time to listen. Listening to a tape recording will work best if you have a long commute or if you go over your notes as you listen. Be sure to ask permission before you turn the tape recorder on, and make sure you have fresh batteries with you in case they run down.

Reflection

EXERCISE 8.2

What is your experience with listening effectively in college so far? What kinds of issues do you encounter in each class with regard to listening? What will you do differently if you experience listening barriers?

PRACTICE

INTEGRITY MATTERS

Listening with integrity means that you listen with an open mind and without judgment until the speaker is finished. Then, you can ask questions of the speaker if there are points that you don't understand. Listening with integrity also means that you avoid twisting the person's words to fit what you want to hear. Practicing active and critical listening will help you maintain integrity.

How Information Is Presented

Learning to listen effectively is the first step to taking good notes, but you will also benefit from understanding how information can be presented during a lecture. As you attend more classes, you will probably notice that professors have a certain way in which they present their material. Some will follow the textbook information in the same order. Others will lecture only on new material that cannot be found in the textbook or other course materials. Then, others will present a combination of the two methods. Reading assigned chapters and materials before you attend class will allow you to determine which information in the lecture is new and which has been covered in assigned reading materials.

As you will learn in Chapter 9, there are many different ways information can be organized. Recognizing the different ways material can be organized will help you stay organized in your notes and will provide you with strategies for revising and reviewing your notes when you begin studying.

- *Chronological*—details arranged in time (first this happened, then this happened, etc.).

   EXAMPLE OF CHRONOLOGICAL LECTURE NOTES

   > 1801: United Kingdom of Great Britain is created
   >
   > 1803: Louisiana Purchase is made by Thomas Jefferson
   >
   > 1815: Battle of Waterloo signals end of Napoleon's career

- *Cause/effect*—details arranged by presenting a cause and then its effects or an effect and its causes.

   EXAMPLE OF CAUSE/EFFECT LECTURE NOTES

   > Cause: Civil War
   >
   > Effects: slavery ended, industrialism began, the nation was brought back together, the federal government proved stronger than the states

- *Compare/contrast*—details arranged by similarities and differences.

   EXAMPLE OF COMPARISON/CONTRAST LECTURE NOTES

   > Similarities between Robert Frost and Walt Whitman: they were males; they used nature in their poetry; and they were considered "poets of the people." Differences between Frost and Whitman: Frost's poetry is more structured, while Whitman's is open and loose; Whitman's speakers are more positive and upbeat than Frost's; Whitman lived during the 19th century while Frost lived in both the 19th and 20th centuries.

- *Most important/least important*—details arranged in order of importance. The most important detail can come first with minor supporting details to follow, or the least important details can start a list that works to a major detail.

EXAMPLE OF MOST IMPORTANT/LEAST IMPORTANT LECTURE NOTES

Self-awareness (purpose of education)

Values

Goals

Mission

Personality type

Learning style

Note-Taking Strategies

There are numerous methods of taking notes for a class. Your goal should be to find the note-taking strategy that works best for you. Remember that you may have to adapt your note-taking style to each course, each teaching style, and each learning style strength. For example, outlining may work well in a history course in which the instructor writes key terms on the board and organizes her lecture around key ideas. If your professor prefers unstructured discussion, you will need to adapt your note-taking strategy to make the most of unorganized information.

Whatever you choose for the particular course, your learning style, and the specific situation, there are a few tips that you need to remember when taking notes.

- Listen for the main ideas.

Instructors will slow down and emphasize information, terms, and definitions. They may even use verbal signposts such as "The most important thing to remember is," "This may appear on an exam," or "Two crucial points about . . . ." If the instructor writes or hands out an outline, you can be sure that it contains the main points of the lecture.

- Leave plenty of "white space" (blank space on paper) when taking notes.

Don't try to fill your page with as much information as possible. You will need the white space to add more notes or to synthesize ideas once you have reviewed.

- Review your notes as soon as possible after class.

Waiting for two weeks to review your notes will ensure that you won't remember everything that you have written or how it all fits together. Most experts suggest that you review your notes within two days of the class.

Developing a Shorthand

As you take more notes in each class, you will find yourself using a few of the same words over and over again. These words are good candidates for abbreviating or denoting in symbols. You can then create your own shorthand. Shortened words such as "ex." for "example," "w/" for "with," and "b/c" for "because" are abbreviations you probably already use in notes and email messages. Symbols that you may already use include % for "percentage," + for "add" or "and," and # for "number." If you use a new abbreviation or symbol for a word, be sure to make a note of what it means; for example, "TR" could mean "Theory of Relativity" in a science course and "Teddy Roosevelt" in a history course.

Here is a list of other commonly abbreviated words and symbols:

At	@
Between	betw, b/w
Decrease	decr
Department	dept
Does not equal	$\neq$
Government	govt
Increase	incr
Equals	$=$
Example	eg, ex
Important	imp
Information	info
Regarding	re
Significant	sig

Developing a shorthand will allow you more time to concentrate on what is being said. As you get more practice, you will become better at judging what information is worth writing and what is not, and your shorthand will become more efficient. Just remember to read over your notes within a day or two so that your abbreviations are fresh in your mind. It is a good idea, then, to complete the words or concepts so that you won't struggle to remember what all the shortened words mean later in the semester. Plus, it will reinforce your learning the material.

Outlining

Using an outline is a good method for taking notes if the instructor is organized and offers information in a logical pattern. Some instructors encourage outlining by writing key words and concepts on the board or an overhead projecting device. If your instructor organizes lectures or class discussions in that manner, you will be able to write an outline for your notes quite easily. The key to making your outlines effective will be to provide plenty of space between the items so that you can fill in the blank spaces with extra information. An example of an outline for a lecture on effective listening could look like this:

I. Preparing to Listen Effectively

II. Listening Critically

III. Possible Listening Barriers

    A. External

        1. Hunger

        2. Climate discomfort

    B. Internal

        1. Feelings of self-worth

        2. Stress

IV. How Information Is Presented

    A. Chronological

    B. Cause/Effect

    C. Compare/Contrast

    D. Most Important/Least Important

Taking Notes within the Textbook

Writing in the margins of your textbook can be another effective way to take notes, especially if the reading assignment is lengthy. If you don't mind writing directly in your textbook, you can summarize main points that you have read. Writing brief summaries (two- or three-word summaries) or questions in the margins will help you make sense of and remember what you have read. Brief, marginal summaries will also help you review the material before class and after class when you start studying for an exam.

Annotating in your textbook and writing down critical questions are two methods of further reinforcing what you have read and will help you prepare for listening and note taking in class. To write critical questions about the reading, ask questions such as "How do I know this to be true?" and "What else should be considered?" Annotating your textbook with your own notes will help you not only reinforce main ideas, but will also help you synthesize the information in new ways that will produce connections between concepts, making the material more memorable and more relevant.

If you decide to write in the margins of your textbook, be sure that the book you are writing in is not one that you want to sell back to the bookstore. If you do not want to write in your book but still get the benefits of summarizing the material, you can write your summaries on a separate sheet of paper. Make sure that you label each piece of paper with the chapter title and page number of the book.

Highlighting in your textbook is another method that students use for taking notes on reading material. A highlighter pen can be used to mark important concepts for review, but be careful that you do not highlight too much information. Over-highlighting the text can have the opposite effect—instead of making it easier to understand key terms and information, too much highlighting can make everything seem of equal importance. If you do use a highlighter pen, use it sparingly. For example, don't highlight more than two sentences in a row. A better method would be to use highlighting and written summaries together for the greatest effect. See Chapter 7 to reinforce this idea.

The Cornell System

Cornell University professor Dr. Walter Pauk developed a system for note taking that has been popular with many students. The Cornell System, also known as the T System, is ideal for those who benefit from the visual impact of organized notes, and it can benefit other types of learners, such as Laura, because it is an organized way to take and review notes. The key to the Cornell System is dividing your notebook paper before you begin writing. To do so, you draw a horizontal line across your piece of paper two inches from the bottom of the page. Then, you draw a vertical line from the horizontal line to the top of the page about 2 inches from the lefthand margin. The page should look like Figure 8.1.

The largest area, the righthand column, is used for taking notes during class. The lefthand column is used for asking questions as you take notes if there is material you don't understand during the lecture or if there are possible exam questions that you think about as you are writing. At the bottom, the final section is reserved for summarizing your notes as you review them. The act of summarizing should help you understand and remember the information.

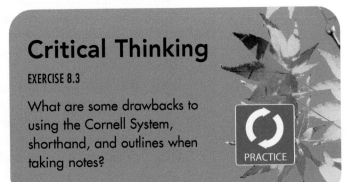

Critical Thinking

EXERCISE 8.3

What are some drawbacks to using the Cornell System, shorthand, and outlines when taking notes?

PRACTICE

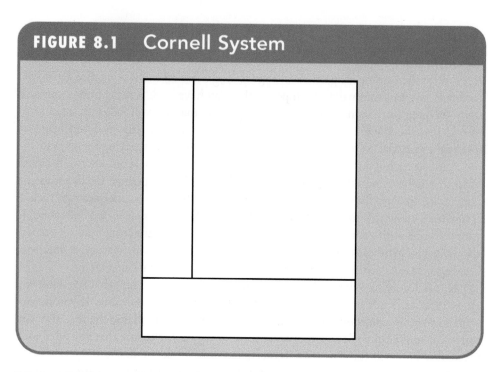

FIGURE 8.1   Cornell System

Note-Taking Strategies in the Disciplines

The following strategies for note taking in the disciplines are just a sample of what you may encounter in college. Chapter 10 will discuss specific study strategies within disciplines, but here we give some note-taking strategies, grouped by discipline, that will make reviewing your notes and studying easier.

Art. In an art appreciation class, you will need to identify eras (20th century), movements (Cubism), and artists (Picasso) as well as their characteristics, as seen in drawings, paintings, and sculpture. Quickly sketching the works in your notes and listing the characteristic details will help you record the information you are receiving through lectures. You may also notice that in the study of art there are times of intense change (usually coinciding with a world or cultural event) followed by artists who imitate or modify slightly the new style. As you review your notes, look for patterns within groups of artwork and for points of contrast.

Music. In a music appreciation class, the same suggestions for an art appreciation class will work when you take notes. Instead of recreating a painting or sculpture in your notes, you may need to write down descriptions of what you are hearing and what the sounds remind you of. Are the sounds fast or slow? Do you hear one instrument or many? Does it sound like a stampede or a trip down a lazy river? "Translating" music samples into written notes as well as reviewing music clips on your own will strengthen your understanding of the material. As with your art notes, upon review, look for patterns across movements and eras and denote contrasting ideas and elements.

Literature. Taking notes in a literature class will require that you have completed the assigned readings before class and that you have annotated and highlighted your text. Because literature classes, even survey classes, focus more on discussion than on lecture, you will want to be prepared to take notes on the analysis. As with music and art classes, being familiar with basic terminology before you get to class will help you take better notes. As you review your notes, look for ideas that pull the different readings together.

Languages. Foreign language classes center more on speaking and interacting than on listening to a lecture. Taking notes will not necessarily be advantageous, for you will need to focus all your attention on listening actively, processing what is heard, and interacting based on what you have heard. Daily preparation is essential to learning foreign languages; take notes as you encounter new material, and ask questions in class to get clarification on anything you do not understand. Any notes you do take should be reviewed soon after the class. As you review your notes, categorize material such as "irregular verbs" and include any tips for using or remembering the parts of language.

Science. Concepts and processes are key in science classes and your notes will reflect that. Prepare for class by reading assigned material, making note of new vocabulary words, and studying diagrams and figures in the text and handouts. As with any class, ask questions if you are having trouble following the steps of a process. As you review your notes, consider the different ways that you can represent these concepts and processes visually and physically.

History. History class lectures are usually presented in chronological order, so using the tips above for information that follows a time sequence will help you take notes in this class. However, you will also be required to move beyond specific dates and events by considering overall themes, ideas, and movements. In addition to chronological order, lectures may also use a cause/effect organization in which you list and elaborate on the effects of a cause or the causes of an effect. An example of a lecture topic in a history class is "The economic and social effects of the end of the Civil War." As you review your notes, look for major themes and be able to recall actions that have led to important events.

Collaboration

Working within a group of three or more, discuss your learning style strengths and weaknesses. Among your group, decide how you would take notes for an upcoming exam based on your learning styles and on note-taking strategies.

EXERCISE 8.4

Math. Taking good notes in your math classes will require that you prepare and attend each class meeting. As with foreign languages, studying for math should be an everyday occurrence because the skills you learn in each class build on the ones you learned in the class before. When reviewing your notes, you may want to recopy them and make sure that you understand, line by line of each problem, what you are copying. If you have any questions, you can write them in the margins of your notes and ask questions during the next class meeting.

Finding Your Own Note-Taking Style

Laura has developed a special note-taking system for herself because of a learning disability. After taking an introduction to college course, she discovered that the note-taking systems that were discussed in her textbook did not help her take good notes. Through trial and error, she developed a system that works for her.

To begin with, Laura writes in pencil on her notebook paper. Before class begins, she dates each page and leaves herself plenty of room to write. When taking notes, she writes on only one side of the page; in fact, most of her pages of notes contain less than fifty words. While she uses more pieces of paper, her notes are easier to read.

EXHIBIT 8.1 Laura's Notes

Ancient	Jewish Beliefs—Monotheism (1st)	Jehovah

Jews divided — all humanity

Strictly-segregated

We (Jews) — They (Gentiles) ✡

No outside conversion — non-Jewish

convenant with God — place on earth

↓ — ↓

chosen people — Tempters & obstacles

family-most important

↓ — Sacred text

society revolved around — Old Testament

Patriarchal male-dominant

↓ — Jehovah (Yahweh)

more rights — share—Christianity concepts (similar)

(+) marriage-lineage — ① Fall of man from grace

(−) bachelor-frowned — ② Day of judgment

male married by 24 — ③ Immortality

prefer 20 — ④ 1 God (worship)

Female-13 can marry

↓

more children

Next, she stars words that the instructor says are important. The most important part of her note-taking system is her use of arrows to make connections between ideas. By giving herself plenty of room, she can add connections that are revealed later in the lecture. If her instructor reviews the material before an exam, Laura highlights what she already has and adds notes in the spaces.

One strategy that Laura has developed to help her with her learning disability is that she doesn't worry about spelling. To make connections between ideas, she draws lines between words that relate to each other. She also makes charts for anything that is compared and contrasted (see Laura's notes in the accompanying figure). Finally, she keeps all of her notes in a binder that is divided for each class. Staying organized is an important part of her method. Although she uses only one binder during the semester, she keeps her notes easily organized by removing them after an exam. When she takes out notes she no longer needs, she places them in labeled folders at home. Then she carries with her only the notes she needs at that time.

A Note on Note-Takers

There may be a time that you will rely on someone to take notes for you while you are absent, or you may have a learning or physical disability that allows you to ask someone in the class to take notes for you all semester. Student or professional note-takers provide an important service for disabled students or unique learners so they can receive the same educational opportunities as other students. Whether or not you depend on someone every once in a while or for the duration of your education, there are still things you should consider:

- If possible, review the note-taker's notes with the note-taker or others in the class. Because the physical act of taking notes helps students remember the information, you will need to find other ways to reinforce the material.
- Stay focused when you are in class. Find ways to help you remember the material as well, such as creating visual maps or scenes in your mind.
- Prepare for class beforehand. Since you won't be taking notes, your preparation is critical.
- Don't take your note-taker for granted by missing class or not preparing. The note-taker is not a surrogate student, but a supplement.
- If your note-taker's notes are difficult to read, incomplete, or missing because he does not attend regularly, talk to the disability services counselor. She can arrange for a new note-taker.

Reviewing Your Notes

Notes are only as good as the extent to which that you review them. If you never looked at your notes after you took them, they would serve very little purpose. Therefore, to make the most of your notes, you will need to review them. As stated earlier in the chapter, reviewing should be done within two days from the time you took them. With this said, it is easy to be lulled into the sense of "studying" by merely reading over your notes again and again. When reviewing your notes, it is best to reorganize the material, make connections between concepts—even across disciplines—and ask questions about what you are learning.

If you use the Cornell System, then you have a built-in area for adding more information, summarizing, and asking yourself questions. However, if you do not use a particular method, you can still benefit from filling in any blanks or holes in your notes with information you have since learned. As stated earlier, you should also spell out any abbreviations you have that may cause confusion later. After you fill in any gaps, you should also include questions—either on the same page or a new page— that will help you think about the material on a deeper level. For example, asking "Why is it important to know this?" can help you move beyond demonstrating your comprehension of the material to making it relevant and useful for you.

Freewriting about the material that you learned is another way of remembering and learning the information that you have listened to. This technique is often used as a way to generate ideas for writing, but it can also be used to take advantage of all the thoughts you have in your head about the material. For optimum effectiveness, you will need to freewrite within a day or two of the class lecture. With or without your notes, write down (or type into a word processor) all the information that you remember from the class.

The key to freewriting is continuation; in other words, do not stop writing even if you can't spell a certain word or get stuck on a particular idea. Give yourself 5 or 10 minutes to freewrite; then, go through your freewriting material (some of it you will be able to use and some of it you will scratch out) and highlight or rewrite into complete sentences the information that pertains to the lecture. In essence, you will be learning the material in more depth as you write about it.

Finally, reciting notes with a friend can be a useful method for reviewing material. You can do this in person or on the phone. The benefits of reading your notes aloud and discussing them include filling in any gaps of information and reinforcing what you have learned. You can also engage in critical questioning of the material and take turns making connections between major concepts.

TIPS FOR SUCCESSFUL NOTE-TAKING

- Prepare for class by reading *all* the assigned material before arriving. If you cannot read all of it, then read as much as you can.
- Prepare to listen actively by removing distractions and bringing supplies.
- Listen actively; concentrate on what you are hearing, seeing, and experiencing.
- Listen critically by asking questions, either on paper or directly in class if your professor encourages questions during class.
- Use a note-taking strategy that takes into account both your learning style strength and the subject matter.
- Go beyond reviewing your notes by only rereading them; instead, focus on concepts and main ideas, make connections between the large ideas, and ask critical questions of processes and ideas.
- Continue the process regularly throughout the semester.

PLUS

EXERCISE 8.5

(Personality + Learning Style = Understanding Situations)

Think about Laura's note-taking situation in her history class. Because Laura is an introverted person, she finds it hard to ask questions in class or visit her professor one-on-one to get help; she is more comfortable with her mentor or the tutors on campus and is willing to get help from them. Because she has dyslexia, she is very motivated and works hard in her classes, often reviewing and rewriting her notes several times when she studies. However, the variety of ways she needs to arrange and remember information for this class is a challenge. Using what you have learned from this chapter, what advice would you give her? How can she make the most of her note-taking situation and learn the material with confidence?

Now, considering your own learning style, personality type, and special circumstances, what would you do to take notes in a class that requires a variety of ways to organize the material?

PROFILE

MY STORY
Learning Plan

Directions: Using what you have learned in this chapter and what you know about your learning preferences, choose a task or assignment that needs to be completed soon and create a learning plan that will help you accomplish this task. Then, write your *My Story* Summary, a one-sentence synopsis that crystallizes your newly created plan.

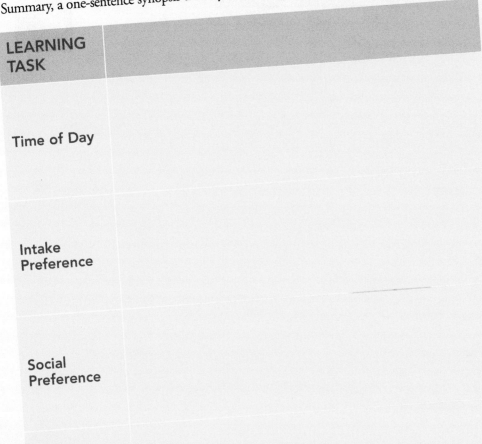

LEARNING TASK	
Time of Day	
Intake Preference	
Social Preference	
Task Management Preference	

MY STORY SUMMARY:

Path of Discovery

Have you ever experienced a time in which you did not listen? What happened and what did you learn from the experience?

HOMEWORK

From College to University

Improving Listening and Note-Taking Skills When There Are More Distractions

When you transfer to a four-year university, the good habits that you have practiced at your community college will help you succeed. However, you may find that you have more distractions. There may be more people on campus and in your classes, more organizations and associations to join, more activities to participate in, and more stress in deciding on a major and getting ready to graduate.

In addition to distractions, you may also find that professors at four-year universities lecture less and rely more on student discussion and presentations. Your ability to organize the material into coherent parts will be vitally important to your making sense of the course. If you find yourself at a loss for what to do to take good notes, talk to others who have been at the university longer than you. They may have their own tips. It may also be a good idea, now more than ever, to join a study group or at least find a "study buddy" to review your notes with. While you may have done well studying by yourself at the community college, you may now realize that group interaction and work is not only encouraged but also necessary for success.

From College to Career

Practicing Critical Listening Skills Will Give You an Edge on the Job

Most of the communication you will do on the job will involve listening: listening to clients' urgent needs, your employer's plans for the next six months, coworkers' explanations of how they would complete a project, and subordinates' questions about how to improve. Being a good listener will involve practicing the critical listening tips that are outlined in this chapter. Why do you need to listen critically on the job? The reason for cultivating this skill is that you will be bombarded with information at all levels: above you from your boss, at the same level as you from your coworkers, and below you from those who work for you. Critical listening skills will enable you to filter what you are hearing so that you can act appropriately and avoid making errors in action and judgment. Consider, for example, a coworker who comes to you to complain about a company policy. Without listening actively and critically, you may disregard what the speaker is saying because you don't have time to do anything about it. However, if you took the time to analyze the speaker (Is she a credible source?) and the message (Is the purpose to vent or to change something?) as well as what you know about the situation yourself (Is the policy flawed and in need of change?) and the larger picture (How will this proposed change affect others?), then you are more likely to act appropriately and confidently. On the job, as in life, you will not—and should not—respond the same to all messages you receive from speakers. Practicing critical listening skills will make it easier to determine which messages are critical and which can be acted upon later—which will make you a more efficient and effective employee.

Chapter Review Questions

1. What is the difference between active and critical listening?
2. What are the potential listening barriers in the classroom?
3. In what ways can information be presented in class?
4. List and describe the different note-taking strategies.
5. Name three disciplines and describe how note-taking differs in each.

Chapter 8 Case Scenarios

1. Juan is taking a visual arts class and is having trouble making sense of his notes each week because they are over information that pertains to specific artwork. The instructor does not hand out reproductions of the art, so the student must sketch the pieces during class, but that takes too long. Do you have any other suggestions for Juan besides trying to draw the actual artwork?

2. Theo has borrowed Jon's notes for his College Algebra class and has promised to return them before the next exam. However, Theo has lost them, and with only two days left before the next test, he is not sure what to do. Jon is a good student and probably doesn't need them as much as he, but he wants to be able to borrow future notes from Jon. What should he do?

3. Karla has a learning difficulty, and she struggles with taking notes. The counselor has assigned her a note-taker. Now that Karla is getting help with writing down notes, she has stopped preparing for class and has stopped listening closely. Sometimes, she doesn't get notes from her note-taker until a week later. If you were Karla's friend or counselor, what advice would you give her about using a note-taker?

Research It Further

1. Take a survey of the students in one of your other classes as to which of the discussed note-taking strategies they use the most. Create a table of your results and present them to your classmates.

2. Using the key words "note-taking strategies," search the Internet for websites that offer note-taking methods. Choose two or three and review the information to determine which site offers the most practical and complete tips. Present your findings to the class.

3. Create your own note-taking or listening strategy and present it to the class, highlighting the benefits of your method over another method.

9 Writing and Presenting College Assignments

Juanita's Story

"A 15-page research paper and 5-minute slide-show presentation. Due during the last week of class," Juanita repeats to her mother over the phone. She has grabbed a sandwich and is now heading out to a bench in front of the technology center that sits in the middle of campus.

"What do you have to write it on?" her mother asks.

"We get to pick from a list, but I don't even know what some of the topics are, like 'conflict theory,'" Juanita says as she looks over the list again. "I guess that is the point of research."

"Well, you better get started, Juanita. I know how you are about writing papers. Remember when you were taking freshmen composition last year?" her mother asks.

Juanita remembered, for sure, how many nights she stayed up writing papers at the last minute because she thought she worked better under the rush of adrenaline. She thought they were decent papers, but her composition instructor, a professor who taught dual enrollment classes, thought otherwise.

"I guess this is my chance to break those bad habits," Juanita says. "Michael told me that Dr. Kirsey grades hard."

"I thought this was sociology, not English," her mother says.

"It is, mom, but my instructors still expect me to write a good paper. They don't cut you any slack. If it is not written well and uses the right kind of resources, then you can kiss a good grade goodbye," Juanita says.

"You're a good writer, Juanita. You have always loved to write," her mother says. Juanita hears the sound of water in the background, a sign her mother is cleaning up the kitchen.

"I know, but that was when I could write creatively on a topic that interested me. This paper isn't something I can take lightly. I know I can write, but I don't know if I can write 15 pages of research on a topic I don't know anything about right now," she says as she crumples up her napkin and throws away her trash.

Juanita tells her mother she will call her later, and she heads toward the library where with all the information they have, there has to be answers for writing a 15-page paper and creating a presentation on a topic that she knows nothing about right now.

In This Chapter

Regardless of your major or final career destination, you will be asked to write in college and possibly in your job. As Juanita knows from college classes so far, writing well is an important skill, and you will have the chance to improve your writing while enrolled in college.

Although a discussion of all aspects of good writing is beyond the scope of this chapter, this chapter does give you an overview of the basics of writing well. It will also be a good reference to use when you have completed your composition class and need to refresh your memory about effective writing.

Specifically, after reading this chapter, you will be able to:

- Discuss why writing well is a necessary skill for success.
- Describe the kinds of college writing.
- List the expectations of college writing.
- Identify the steps in writing a paper.
- Define plagiarism and discuss ways to avoid it.
- Describe the steps for creating an effective presentation.

What to Expect for Assignments

Homework has a whole new meaning in college than it did in high school. These assignments are more than just reinforcements of what you learned in class, and they certainly are not the dreaded "busy work" that some high school students suffer; instead, the assignments you will be given in college will challenge you to think in ways that you may not be used to, and they will demand of you much more time than you may have taken to complete assignments in high school. For sure, you will encounter familiar assignments such as extra problem-solving questions in math classes and research papers in English classes, but you may also be required to complete a class multimedia project that involves using slide presentation software or even a community-based project that entails working with various agencies to develop a real-world solution to a problem and then presenting it to local politicians. Other types of writing and presentation assignments include

- Journals
- Portfolios
- Project proposals
- Essays
- Research papers
- Reports
- Demonstrations (lab work, procedures, etc.)
- In-class and out-of-class group assignments
- Formal and informal classroom presentations

Understanding the Assignment

Before you can gloat in the glory of a well-done project or essay, you will have to start with first things first. Understanding the assignment is the first, and sometimes the most crucial step, in succeeding. Too many students jump right in without fully understanding the directions, the requirements, and the time, equipment, and skills that are necessary to complete the assignment.

Due or Do? A colleague recently relayed the following story: An instructor was overheard telling her class that their papers were due on Friday. "There is a difference between D-U-E and D-O. When your paper is D-U-E on Friday, it doesn't mean that you D-O your paper on Friday." No truer words could be spoken to a new college student who learns that writing an essay the night before or even the day it is due can be an undertaking much larger than he originally anticipated. Most assignments in college will require hours of reading, understanding, thinking, and then completing. In some cases, you may need the entire semester to work on a large project. Say good-bye, then, to quickly jotting down answers or to writing an assignment the hour before class. When it is D-U-E, it will need to be D-O-N-E well before.

Following Directions. Giving yourself the time to complete an assignment will allow you to carefully read and follow the directions. Too often students rush through an assignment sheet only to omit a critical part of the requirements. If your assignment has multiple parts, it will be important that you complete each part and pay attention to how the parts will be presented. For example, will you need to submit your assignment via email? Will you need to prepare a list of resources you used to complete it? Does it need to be typed? Will you need to make visual aids? All of these are possible requirements, and if you are unsure of what is expected of you, despite the assignment details, be sure to ask for clarification. Consider the following assignment and see if you can determine what requirements you will need to consider when you complete it. Underline, circle, or highlight the important information.

EXAMPLE OF ASSIGNMENT DIRECTIONS

1. Topic Proposal   **Due: Wednesday, April 18**

Before you begin work on your research paper, you will submit a proposal to me for approval. This process is much like proposals that scholars submit to determine if they will be accepted for a conference.

Your proposal must be typed and must contain the following all on one or two pages:

- Your name
- Working title of your research paper
- Working thesis of your research paper
- A 75-word abstract (summary) of your topic
- A 100-word description of how you plan to research your topic

Assignment Integrity. One major consideration when beginning and completing your writing assignment is maintaining academic integrity. To maintain academic integrity when writing papers that require no research, follow one simple rule: Do the work yourself. Unless your instructor explicitly states that you can work together with a classmate *and* can share answers or help while completing the assignment, avoid collaboration when completing homework. At no time should you copy the answers that another student has written on your paper. Just as you would not share answers during a test, it is best not to share your answers on work that is assigned out of class. If you have taken a class in a previous semester, you will also want to keep your assignments from being shared. Instructors may use the same assignments from semester to semester, and you don't want to put a fellow student in an awkward or potentially bad situation.

Discussing the Grade. When you get your graded assignment back, be careful as to how you handle the feedback and grade. The only place and time to discuss grades on assignments is with your instructor either after class or during his or her office hours. If you want to compare your grades with fellow students, do so discreetly. Although you may be tempted to compare your work with someone else's, your instructor can only discuss your work and your grade, not how you compare with someone else in the class. Unlike high school, the Family Educational Rights and Privacy Act protects students' grades and personal information in college.

Speak Up Early. Whether it is understanding an assignment or making sense of the grade after you have completed it, talk to your instructor as soon as possible to get your questions answered. If you find, for example, that you have received a grade that is lower than you expected or if you have been given the opportunity to revise or redo an assignment, talk to your instructor immediately to find out why you did not do satisfactory work and what you can do to improve. Waiting until you complete another assignment or until you sit down to revise your work may be too late.

Writing in College

Whether you are just learning the basics of grammar and spelling or you are already comfortable writing 20-page research papers, writing is hard work. Students often ask, "What can I do to be a better writer?" And writers and professors often have the same response: "Read and write every day." To become a better writer, you must be a good reader and practice writing regularly, just as a concert pianist or a star athlete must practice frequently. Reading and writing regularly will help you recognize organizational patterns, the use of logic, and the grammatical construction of sentences. You will also build your vocabulary and improve your spelling.

Another tip for writing well in college is to buy a good dictionary and thesaurus and always keep them handy. The spell-checking function and www.websters.com are good sources for writing papers on the computer, but they just don't beat the convenience and portability of reference books. Be sure, though, that the books you buy are appropriate for college students; some reference books do not have words commonly used in college texts. *The American Heritage College Dictionary* and *Roget's Thesaurus* are excellent choices for college students. Surprisingly, some dictionaries that have the word "college" in the title are often not comprehensive enough for college classes.

Top Eight College Writing Expectations

Your writing should be clear and to the point while adhering to the assignment. The following paragraphs discuss the minimal requirements of college writing. The rest of the chapter elaborates on how to achieve them.

1. *Fulfillment of the Assignment* To receive full credit for writing assignments, read the directions carefully and make sure that you are fulfilling all requirements. Omitting one element, such as a reference page, could lower your grade significantly.

2. *Main Idea or Point* All good writing must have a point or a main idea. Make sure that your main idea is clear throughout the entire written response. One question you can ask yourself as you read your composition is, "How does this relate to my topic?"

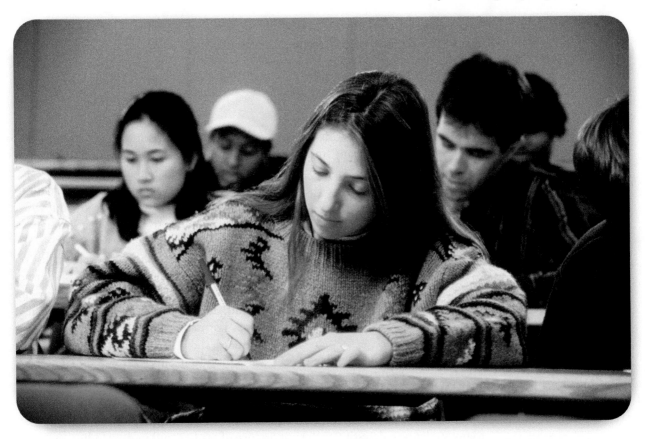

All good writing must have a clear point, a main idea.

3. *Clear Organization* Even if your ideas are insightful and enlightening, without clearly organized details, those ideas will not be communicated effectively.

4. *Focused Paragraphs* Paragraphs that handle one minor idea at a time are considered focused. This minor idea should support your overall point for the writing assignment. Paragraphs that try to say too many different things are considered unfocused.

5. *Concrete, Specific Details* Concrete details are the specific examples that you use to support your main idea. For example, if you were writing a review of a restaurant, you would need to provide concrete, specific details to recreate the experience. If you were to write "The main course was delicious," your readers would not be able to visualize or experience the meal. In other words, the detail is not specific or concrete. But if you were to write these sentences, the effect would be much stronger: "The main course of chicken parmesan was irresistible with the tangy tomato sauce that generously covered a bed of pasta. Although the breading was crunchy, it was not overwhelming, and the melted mozzarella cheese created a perfect complement to the juicy chicken." Besides appealing to the readers' senses, by providing specific details you will have demonstrated a thoughtful response.

6. *Neat Presentation* Although the presentation of your paper is not as important as clearly expressing your main idea, you still need to make sure that your paper is neatly printed on quality paper. If your paper looks messy or obviously does not follow format requirements, the first impression you have made is that you have hurried through the assignment.

7. *Grammatical Sentences* Good grammar is essential to effective writing. Some instructors demand perfect grammar, whereas others allow for a few errors in an otherwise well-written paper. If you find that you are making the same grammatical mistakes in each writing assignment, get help from your professor, the writing or tutoring center, or the resources in your library. Many websites also offer help with grammar.

8. *Correct Spelling* With the advent of the spell-checking function in word-processing programs, many students overlook correcting errors in spelling as an essential part of writing effectively. However, spell checkers cannot correct every misspelled word. For example, if you write "there" when you mean "their," the spell checker will not recognize the error because both words are in the spell checker's list of words. It is therefore important to reread your writing for spelling errors. Keep in mind, too, that although correct spelling does not necessarily indicate a good paper, it does show your readers that you pay attention to details.

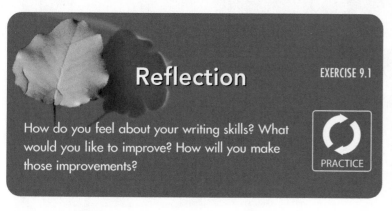

Reflection

EXERCISE 9.1

How do you feel about your writing skills? What would you like to improve? How will you make those improvements?

PRACTICE

Different Types of Writing Assignments

Many students underestimate the importance of reading and understanding the writing assignment before they begin writing. Carefully reading and taking note of what you are asked to do will save you time in the long run. One of the benefits of writing well is that you can easily move from one type of assignment to another. The key to fulfilling any assignment is to know what your instructor wants you to do. The following sections discuss different types of writing assignments and how to fulfill each one. Note how the verbs used relate to the type of assignment.

Summarize

A summary is a brief retelling of a subject. In a summary, you will cover the main points of an event or a text, but summaries do not contain your opinion on the subject.

EXAMPLE

Summarize Freud's contributions to psychology.

Evaluate, Review, Assess, State Your Opinion, Critique

An evaluation assignment asks for your opinion. You will need to consider the subject's strengths and weaknesses, and you will need to provide specific examples to support your ideas.

EXAMPLES

Evaluate a website's use of graphics.

Assess the effectiveness of the information you received from the financial aid office.

Synthesize

Although it may be more complex than reflecting on an experience you have had, a synthesis paper sounds scarier than it really is. If you have ever written a research paper in which you used two or more sources to argue an original point about a topic, then you have written a synthesis. The key here is that a synthesis moves beyond an essay that is only from one perspective—yours. Instead, a synthesis uses your perspective or argument as the foundation and provides the reader with ideas and support from other sources. When your instructor asks you to synthesize two articles' approaches to understanding the impact of immigration, you will read those two sources, form an opinion about the two sources' arguments, and then use information from those two sources to support your own perspective on the issue.

EXAMPLE

Read two articles on the importance of higher education and write a synthesis paper in which you contrast the points that are made in each article.

Describe, Define, Discuss, Explain

Discussion assignments are usually intended to assess how well you know a topic. The more specific details you can provide, the more likely you will adequately describe or define the subject.

EXAMPLES

Explain the major events that led up to the Civil War.

Define the terms *values*, *goals*, and *mission statement*.

Analyze

To analyze a subject is to break it apart and look at its components carefully. Once you have investigated the parts, you must put the subject back together again. When you analyze a poem, you may break it apart into rhyme scheme, language, images, and speaker. To examine each of these parts is to analyze the poem. Once you have completed your examination, you will bring the parts back together again with commentary on how the parts all work together.

EXAMPLE

Analyze the character of Willy Loman in *Death of a Salesman*.

Compare and Contrast

The purpose of a comparison and contrast essay is to examine two subjects more carefully to make a significant point about them. Before you describe their similarities and then their differences, you will set up the reason for the comparison and contrast. Take, for instance, the cliché, "It is like comparing apples to oranges." Well, you *can* compare and contrast them if you found something significant to express about their obvious differences and their not-so-obvious similarities. Is one more nutritious than the other or are they nearly identical in nutritional content? Is one more popular than the other or do they share the same status in the world of produce? Of course, as part of the comparison and contrast, you will also explore their similarities and differences as they relate to your overall point: Size, color, texture, nutritional composition, popularity, and taste may be details that you use to drive your point home.

EXAMPLE

Compare and contrast two types of welding techniques.

Persuade, Argue

Persuading an audience and arguing a point demand that you take a stand about a topic. Whether or not you are passionate about the topic you are assigned, you will need to argue avidly about it. An argument is most effective when specific, accurate details are presented. Effective persuasion requires that you treat your readers with respect and that you present your argument fairly. Overexaggeration and misrepresentation are not characteristics of a successful argument.

EXAMPLES

In an essay, persuade the college administration that students should have a study day before finals.

In an essay, argue that the American legal system needs to be reformed.

Reflect

When you are assigned to reflect on a topic, you are being asked for your thoughts about it. Reflections are usually informal and are a way that a professor gets to know more about you. If you are asked to reflect on your progress during the semester or how you have felt about writing a research paper, be sure to provide plenty of details that explain your ideas. By moving beyond "I have done well" or "I can't wait to get the paper written," the more thoughtful and helpful your response will be.

EXAMPLE

Reflect on what you have learned about the writing process so far this semester.

Length, Audience, and Purpose

Length, audience, and purpose are other key factors in understanding writing assignments. For many assignments, you will be assigned a length, such as a 2-page paper or a 1,500-word essay. Instructors assign lengths to help you gauge the development that you need in order to fulfill the assignment adequately. For instance, if your instructor assigns you a 1-page review of a website, then a 10-page paper will not be appropriate because too much information will be included. Conversely, if you have a 2,500-word research paper to write, a 750-word paper will not suffice because there will not be enough information and reflection to fulfill the assignment. If you worry that you cannot meet the length requirement of an assignment, talk with your instructor as soon as possible. He or she will be able to help you narrow or expand your topic so that you will have enough material.

The audience for your assignment is your immediate readers and potential readers of your paper. When creating a writing assignment, many instructors assume that the audience is your classmates or people who are interested in your subject, and many students assume that the only person who will read their paper is their instructor. If an audience is not specified for your assignment, imagine that you are writing to college students who have been studying the same subject—such as your classmates. How you present your ideas and the words you use should be appropriate for other college students.

There may be, however, times when you will be assigned a particular audience as part of the requirements for a writing project. The reason that instructors do this is to help you focus your ideas, language, and argument. Consider, for example, an assignment that may be part of a health class:

WRITING ASSIGNMENT

In a 3-page paper, discuss the latest information about sexually transmitted diseases.

This is a straightforward assignment that can be completed by anyone who has access to current information. However, how would the assignment change if your audience were 12-year-old public school students? What information would you add or eliminate? What kind of language would you use? Would you include diagrams and definitions or cartoons? How much detail would you provide? These are all new considerations you will have to make because your audience will have certain limitations. Unfamiliar vocabulary, technical terms, detailed information, and photographs may be inappropriate for these students. Simple terms, diagrams, and personal stories about kids their own age may be a better way to convey the more complicated information.

Now, consider the same topic with a different audience: 70- to 80-year-old men and women who live in a nursing home. Again, you will have the same questions: What information would you add or eliminate? What kind of language would you use? Would you include diagrams and definitions or cartoons? How much detail would you provide? Obviously, this audience will have different needs than the young students have. Because your audience is more mature, you will need to think about how to approach a topic that they have definite ideas about. Some may be resistant to hearing about the topic because they believe it is not appropriate to discuss, or others may feel they know enough to make their own decisions. Still others will not see the relevance for them. As our two examples show, these challenges are unique to your audience—changing *who* you are writing for changes *how* you present the information.

A final consideration for your assignment is your purpose. Your purpose for writing will be closely connected to your assignment (see the assignment types discussed in the previous section), but there are other purposes for writing. For example, in addition to evaluating a website, your purpose could also be to make your audience laugh. As you compare two popular diet plans in a paper, your purpose could be to persuade readers that one of the plans is a healthier choice. The purposes for writing are endless, but it is important to ask yourself why you are writing and what you want to accomplish besides completing an assignment or getting a good grade! The answers to those questions will be your purpose for writing, and knowing that purpose will help you complete your assignment effectively.

Prewriting Techniques

Once you have read and understood the writing assignment, it is time to use one or more prewriting techniques to get your ideas down on paper before you start organizing them and writing your rough draft. You probably have your own way of writing, but it is worth investigating some of these proven methods for generating ideas.

There are three common prewriting techniques that you can use to generate details for your paper. *Freewriting* is a simple way to get ideas down on paper. The only rules in freewriting are to start with an idea and stop only after you have filled a page or after a certain amount of time has passed. When freewriting, you can allow your mind to wander off the subject; you must, however, write down everything that comes to mind. Later, when you start organizing your details, you can eliminate anything that does not pertain to your subject. If you are a good typist, you can freewrite by typing into a blank document. Don't worry about spelling, grammar, or punctuation when you freewrite—the purpose is to free your mind of that little voice that censors everything you think.

The following example shows one student's freewriting. Notice that the student didn't worry about punctuation or even where she was going in the freewrite. Instead, she listed all her thoughts about a stressful experience when her financial aid was delayed.

FREEWRITING ON TOPIC OF FINANCIAL AID

Financial aid is a great way to help students go to college, but it is so hard to fill out all those forms and get all the information that I need I can't think of anything harder to do than fill out a financial aid form correctly when I applied I forgot to put my social security number and I can't believe I did that they called me to tell me that my application had been delayed because of the oversight I could have died because I needed to buy my books and get an apartment I don't think they understood that I didn't have time to waste I had bills to pay and I needed my financial aid to get into my classes and start school Now that I got everything straightened out I am glad I went through the process I know how to do it and know what to watch for and overall it hasn't been that bad but I was really stressed those first few weeks maybe the school needs to have workshops for new students that show them how to fill out forms and that stress the importance of filling them out correctly. That would be a good idea.

Clustering is another method of prewriting that works well for those who learn better by visualizing concepts. Clusters, or think links, are visual representations of ideas and their relationship to each other. The key to clustering is to start in the middle of a sheet of paper, write down your topic, and circle it. Draw a line from your subject and write down a related topic that is part of the subject. For instance, "types," "prevention," and "treatment" are all parts of the topic "sexually transmitted diseases." In addition, subtopics branch off "prevention": "abstinence" and "condoms." The words and phrases that surround a topic or subtopic must be connected to it, both logically, and literally, by drawing a line.

Critical Thinking

EXERCISE 9.2

Why is writing effectively an important life skill? In what other areas of your life will you use writing?

PRACTICE

Another effective method for generating ideas is *brainstorming*, a process that involves writing down ideas as they come to you. The goal in brainstorming is to get as many ideas as possible down on paper, no matter how ridiculous or off-topic they are. The more details you generate, the more you have to work with as you begin organizing your paper. To brainstorm, simply write your topic at the top of a sheet of paper, or type it into a new document on your computer, and then start listing any and all ideas that come to mind. Following is a list of brainstormed ideas for the topic of financial aid.

BRAINSTORMING LIST ON THE TOPIC OF FINANCIAL AID

Forms

Information

Financial Aid officer

Trouble with getting the information filled out properly

Fear that I won't get enough money to pay my college bills

Worried that I won't be able to pay it back

Feel good about how helpful the people at school are

Need to know more about when I start paying it back

Need to find out what I need to do to renew it each year

Wish there was a handbook for students that is easy to read and reassuring

Creating a Thesis and Organizing Details

Once you make a list of details that you would like to use in your paper, give some thought as to what your main point will be, a topic sentence if it is a paragraph or a thesis if it is an essay, before you decide how you would like to organize the details. Your main point will be at least one sentence that tells the reader what the whole writing will present or argue. For example, if you were to write a sentence that expresses a main point about the details generated above on financial aid, it could look something like this:

> My experience with applying for financial aid filled me with more questions than answers.

There are a variety of ways that you can organize a paper effectively. You can arrange them from most to least important detail or least to most important detail. Details can also be arranged chronologically, especially if you are writing about an event that needs to follow a specific time line. Moreover, details can be arranged from general ideas to specific or specific details to general. It is important to organize your details logically; how you arrange the supporting details will depend on your purpose and audience.

For example, suppose you are writing a paper on the greatest challenges to diversity on your campus, and your details include the lack of cultural appreciation activities, a recent racially motivated incident, the fact that there are few minorities in administrative roles, and the lack of African American literature classes offered.

The current order of the details provides no logical connections among them, so your reader will have a difficult time understanding the magnitude of the problem. Instead, you could order them according to importance. When Juanita chooses a topic and completes her research, she will want to consider the order in which to present her findings. Should she start with the most shocking? The most obvious? These will be questions that will start her on the process of organizing her paper for maximum impact.

Which of the aforementioned details do you think is the most important indication of the challenges to diversity on your campus? Certainly, the most striking is the racially motivated incident. You could use it as the first, most important detail in your paper, something that will grab your readers' attention and keep them interested and sympathetic to your thesis. On the other hand, you could start your essay with a least important detail and use the incident detail as your last, most important point. How you arrange your details, as long as each detail builds on the next and supports your thesis, depends on your purpose for writing.

Writing Paragraphs

Paragraphs, which are a group of sentences that are considered one complete unit, are the building blocks of an essay. Paragraphs begin with an indentation, known as a tab, on the left-hand side of the page. Well-developed paragraphs can be any length. However, if a paragraph is too short, the reader will think that something is missing; if they are too long, the reader may get lost in what you are trying to say. The key to writing a good paragraph—and you will write many in your college career—is to stay focused on one topic at a time and to let the reader know what that main idea is with a sentence called a *topic sentence*. A topic sentence can appear at the beginning of the paragraph, in the middle, or at the end.

Once you have determined what the paragraph will focus on, you can start putting your details in place. Just as you have considered the overall arrangement of the details in your paper, you will need to give some thought to arranging the details *within* the paragraphs. The same types of organization of details for an entire paper work for paragraphs as well: general to specific, specific to general, order of importance, and chronological. You can use a different method for each paragraph as long as all the paragraphs support your thesis. Following is an example of a chronologically ordered paragraph on the topic of a racially motivated incident that demonstrates a campus has challenges to diversity.

EXAMPLE PARAGRAPH

One of the most important reasons I believe that our campus needs to overcome its diversity problems is the recent racially motivated incident that occurred after a football game [*topic sentence*]. The incident began when a group of black and white students from our school started yelling insults at the predominantly white team members [*first detail in chronological order*]. Then, the taunting turned into bottle throwing at the white team members [*second detail in chronological order*]. While some of the team took cover, others fought back with rocks [*third detail in chronological order*]. The incident ended with three people in the emergency room, getting treated for cuts, scrapes, and a broken bone [*last detail in chronological order*]. If our campus did more to promote cultural sensitivity and racial diversity, outrageous behavior such as this would be a part of history rather than the present [*conclusive statement that restates the point of the paragraph*].

Incorporating Transitions

To make your sentences flow smoothly and your paragraphs relate clearly to one another, you will need to use transitions. Transitions are words or phrases that signal to the reader that you are moving from one thought to the next. Imagine describing over the phone how to get from the college to your house. If you didn't use transitions, your listener might be confused as to how to get there. Words such as "First," "Next," "Then," and "After" are transitional words that would help the listener see how the sentences of the directions relate to one another.

When you move from paragraph to paragraph in your paper, you will definitely need a strong transitional phrase or sentence to indicate that you are introducing a new idea or that a point is forthcoming. Phrases such as "In addition to," "Even though," and "Contrary to the point above" are strong enough to slow the reader down to pay attention to your next major point. The paragraph in the next example is taken from Chapter 8 and contains transitions set in boldface so that you can see how each transitional word or phrase is used. These words serve as signposts to indicate the beginning of each idea and how each idea connects to the others. The paragraph begins with the words "The first step," which tells you something important: This idea is the first in a series of steps that will follow. The phrase "In other words" indicates that the author is restating her first point in case you missed it. The phrase "If you have done your reading" ties the idea from the previous sentence. The transition "also" tells you that another point is being made in addition to the one at the beginning of the paragraph. Finally, the phrase "For example" provides an example for achieving the goal in the previous sentence.

SAMPLE PARAGRAPH WITH TRANSITIONS

The first step to effective listening is to prepare to listen before you get to class. **In other words,** read the assigned pages or chapters ahead of time so that you know what the lecture or discussion topic will be. **If you have done your reading,** you will be familiar with new words and concepts. Preparing to listen **also** includes reviewing your assigned readings before you get to the classroom. **For example,** take a few minutes between classes or on the way to school to pull out your book and skim the major headings, boldface terms, and text boxes that appear in the margins.

In addition to connecting ideas, transitions improve the readability of the paper. When you read your work out loud and it sounds "choppy" or repetitive in rhythm, you may need to add transitions. Adding transitions effectively takes practice. If you need help, see your instructor or someone in the writing center at your college. With a little work, the flow of your writing will improve.

Writing Essays

The word *essay* has its origins in French and means "an attempt" or "a trial." For college students, writing essays is an attempt, or a trial, in some sense, to meet the assignment without going crazy! In the context of college, an essay is a written composition on a particular subject that offers the author's view. If, for example, you are asked to write an essay on the death penalty or obesity in children, then you will need to present your viewpoint on the subject. Essays do not usually contain research; instead, they are built on your observations, details, and opinions. They are, in essence, an attempt by you to convey your viewpoint on a subject and perhaps to learn something more about what you think about that subject.

When you are assigned an essay for a class, you need to include some basic components. Without all of them, your essay is simply a piece of writing, just as a few bones do not make up an entire skeleton. At the least, you will need this basic format:

- *Title.* All essays must be titled, preferably something original and a reflection of the essay's topic.
- *Introduction.* This is a paragraph that introduces the topic and explains to the audience why you are writing the essay. It can also function as an attention grabber, luring the reader into the essay.
- *Thesis.* The thesis is a sentence or two that tells the reader what you will be discussing, or proving, in the essay. For example, your thesis could be, "The worst summer I have ever had was during the year 1993." Your readers, then, will expect you to prove to them why the summer of 1993 was the worst.
- *Body paragraphs* (three or more, depending on the assignment). Without body paragraphs, you won't have an essay, and you will need to make sure you have enough paragraphs to support your thesis. A general rule for a short essay is to have three body paragraphs that each makes its own point. If you were to follow the example of the aforementioned thesis, you would have three body paragraphs about the summer of 1993. One would focus on your first point (you broke up with your girlfriend); the second would present another point (you lost your job); and the third would offer your last point (you broke your leg in a water-skiing accident).
- *Conclusion.* The final paragraph of your essay is your concluding ideas about the whole subject. To extend our example topic, you could conclude your essay with reflections on what you learned from all the disasters. At the least, the reader should understand how all the points come together to support your thesis.

Writing Research Papers

Research papers differ from essays in that they require you to investigate and incorporate sources to support your ideas. You will need to consider length, audience, and purpose, and you will need to pay close attention to the requirements of the assignment. Instructors may require that you research certain journals or databases, or they may ask for survey results or literature reviews. As with any writing assignment, you should start early and break it up into manageable parts. For a research paper, you will need to invest a considerable amount of time and energy.

Preparing Portfolios

A writing portfolio is a collection of your writing throughout the semester. This type of project is popular with instructors because it allows students to work on their writing all semester. Instead of getting a grade on the first draft that is turned in, students can revise papers until they meet the minimal standards for the course. A benefit of the portfolio method is that students can focus on the process of writing instead of the final product—the polished paper.

The best way to handle a writing portfolio is to review the requirements for it, including due dates and policies on completing final drafts. If you have questions about the expectations, especially if you have never completed a portfolio before, ask your instructor and schedule periodic meetings to make sure that you are completing the components successfully. Finally, take advantage of the opportunity to submit multiple drafts and receive feedback on them. Revising essays for a portfolio takes time, but the rewards are that you will receive extensive feedback and help with improving your writing.

Avoiding Plagiarism

No word strikes fear and confusion in academic writers more than *plagiarism*. Simply defined, plagiarism is the use of another's words or ideas without proper acknowledgment. In other words, if the information or the expression of the information comes from another source, besides your own brain, then you must let the reader know what that source is. Proper acknowledgment can be as simple as naming the source (Martin Wilson said . . .), or it can be as complex as using a documentation system such as MLA (Modern Language Association) or APA (American Psychological Association). Penalties for plagiarism can range from redoing the assignment to facing expulsion from college. Because most colleges do not distinguish between intentional and unintentional plagiarism, it is in your best interest to learn how to avoid plagiarism.

INTEGRITY MATTERS

How to avoid plagiarism:

- *Do not buy or download a paper from the Web and turn it in as your own.*
- *Do not cut and paste any amount of material from a website without telling the reader who the original author is and without placing the material within quotation marks.*
- *Do not borrow a paper from someone else to turn in as your own.*
- *Do not allow someone else to write a paper for you.*
- *Ask questions if you are unsure how to avoid plagiarism.*

Collaboration

Working in a group, discuss the list above and determine why your group thinks students fail to follow the strategies above for avoiding plagiarism.

EXERCISE 9.3

You may ask yourself, "If I don't know what plagiarism is, can I still be penalized if I don't mean to do it?" The answer is that your professors will expect that you already know how to distinguish between your ideas and others' ideas. If you don't know how to do that, or if you are unsure how you can avoid plagiarism, you should talk with your professors or seek assistance from the writing center.

Writing Essay Exams

Writing essay exams always causes a little more anxiety than any other writing assignments because of the pressure of recalling information and writing with the clock ticking. Because you don't have the luxury of time to write an essay on an exam, you will have to prepare. Students who have trouble writing an essay in a timed environment should be comforted that they can improve their performance by practicing for the exam.

If you know the essay topic beforehand, you can practice writing your response to it by allowing yourself the same amount of time that you will have when you take the test. The key to writing well under pressure is to simulate the same circumstances when you practice. If you don't know what the topic is beforehand, you can still prepare for the essay exam by going back over your notes and checking to see if your professor talked about any major issues that would make a good essay topic. Then practice writing responses to questions you think might be on the exam.

How College Professors Evaluate Your Writing

Your college professors may vary widely in how they evaluate your written assignments. Some professors look for and reward key words and concepts in an essay exam, whereas others mark and count off for grammatical, mechanical, and organizational problems even if the key concepts are easily identifiable. You will soon learn, if you have not already, that each professor has his or her own criteria for grading written assignments, and the sooner you learn what the criteria are, the better able you will be to complete the assignment satisfactorily.

If your professor does not give you a list of grading criteria, you should ask for a sample assignment or a list of what the professor will be looking for. Talking with the professor before and after the assignment is graded is the best way to know what to expect. Asking other students who have taken classes with the professor is another way to get an idea of how you will be evaluated.

Remember that professors expect you to write at a college level and that your writing assignments should reflect the characteristics that are discussed at the beginning of this chapter. You may find that although you received good grades on papers in high school, you have to work much harder for those same grades on papers in college. In addition to higher standards, you should be aware that your professors' job is to make you a better thinker and writer, no matter what the subject. They will be correcting errors and making suggestions for improvement.

Knowing When to Get Help with Your Writing

There may be times when a writing assignment is confusing or overwhelming. If at any time you don't understand what you are supposed to do or you feel stressed about the assignment, contact your instructor as soon as you can. Stressing out about the assignment will only make it seem impossible to complete. Instructors know you have other responsibilities and classes and are often willing to work with you if you have planned ahead and asked for help early.

When getting help with an assignment, be sure to ask your instructor first—he or she is the one who will best know what needs to be done. If your college has a writing center, you should make an appointment with a tutor as soon as you realize you need some help. Writing center tutors will be able to explain what you need to do to complete the assignment.

Other students in the class and friends who are not in the class can be other sources of help, but use their help cautiously. Your classmates may not know much more about the expectations than you. Moreover, your instructor may prohibit any kind of collaboration, even if it is to better understand what you need to do. Getting help from anyone who is not in the class or not taking college courses should be your last resort because they are farther removed from your instructor's expectations.

No matter who helps you with the assignment, be sure that you are doing the assignment rather than someone else doing it for you. Some students, out of fear or frustration, have had other people complete part or all of their assignments. The most obvious reason that you should not allow someone else to help too much is that your instructor could penalize you for not doing the assignment yourself. More important, if you do not complete the assignment yourself, you are robbing yourself of an opportunity to learn more about the subject that you are studying and about yourself.

Knowing When You Have Received Too Much Help

How do you know when you have received too much help on a writing assignment? If someone else writes whole sentences, paragraphs, and pages for you or supplies you with many main ideas and examples that you use in your paper, then you have probably received too much assistance on your writing assignment. Some professors disapprove of editing and proofreading services as well. When in doubt, check with your professor and explain what kind of help you are getting.

Making Speeches and Presentations

Learning to speak and present on a topic effectively in college is a skill that will benefit you not only on the job but also in life. For example, you may need to speak on behalf of the parents at your children's school as president of the Parents and Teachers Association, or you may be asked to make weekly announcements at your church. In your college classes, you will more than likely get a specific assignment (Give a five-minute persuasive speech on a current event) or a specific topic (cloning). However, not all speaking experiences will begin with detailed directions. You may be asked to introduce someone or to "talk for about 10 minutes about whatever you think will interest the audience." Regardless of how you are assigned a speech, the process will be the same: You will need to plan, prepare, deliver, and assess.

Planning a Speech or Presentation

Choosing a topic is the first step to preparing to speak just as it is in the writing process. At times, you will be provided a topic, but in some of your classes—or for some occasions—you will be allowed to create your own. Topics for speeches can come from your personal experience, current events, or from in-depth research. If you are not sure which personal experience, current event, or research topic you want to explore, it is a good idea to use brainstorming or another method of generating ideas (see the section on writing) to determine which topic interests you the most.

Deciding what your purpose is will be your next step. You may need to inform, persuade, or entertain your audience. If you will be informing them of your topic, you will more than likely use details and language that present the information in an unbiased manner. If you will be persuading your audience, you will more than likely use examples and language to change their attitudes or beliefs. Entertaining your audience will also determine how you will present your topic because you will include information, details, and language that will get a laugh or amuse. Your speech can have more than one purpose—and sometimes all three—but one will be the most emphasized.

Just as writers need to decide who their audience is before they begin writing, speakers must also consider whom they will be addressing. Audience analysis is the process by which speakers determine who will be the receivers of the message.

Audience analysis questions include the following: How many people will be in the audience? What are the characteristics of the audience (gender, ages, race, culture, educational background, learning style, etc.)? What are their attitudes toward your topic? What do they know about the topic?

Occasion analysis questions include the following: When are you speaking? How long will you have to speak? What is the space like (if you can find out in advance)? What else will you need? Visual aids? Handouts? Time for questions or discussion?

Vocal Delivery

What if you crafted a fantastic speech and no one ever heard it because they couldn't understand what you were saying? Sound impossible? It has, unfortunately, happened before: A great speech is lost because the speaker didn't project his voice or mumbled through the words. Vocal delivery, then, is the most important aspect to getting the words out successfully. Consider the following suggestions when practicing and delivering a speech:

- Consider the tone and pitch, or vocal quality, of your voice. Is it soft or harsh? Do you sound angry or giddy? Audience members prefer voices that are easy to listen to.
- Speak slowly and deliberately, making sure that you are properly pronouncing words (check the dictionary) and using correct grammar (consult a writing handbook). Open your mouth and move your lips to ensure that you are enunciating. Speaker credibility is lost when words are not used properly or poorly pronounced.
- Use variety when speaking. Vary volume, pitch, and speed to create interest. Pause between points for effect. Do you remember the monotone teacher in the movie *Ferris Buehler's Day Off*? He didn't vary his volume, pitch, and speed, and his students were either asleep or were not paying attention.

Physical Delivery

Appropriate nonverbal communication while you are speaking can mean the difference between an effective and an ineffective speech. Paying attention to and practicing your body movements will help you develop good physical habits when speaking. Here are just a few to consider:

- Dress appropriately. If you look professional, you appear more credible. Unless you are making a point by dressing down or in a chicken outfit, dress up. A neat and clean appearance also suggests attention to detail and importance.
- Smile at your audience. It demonstrates a positive attitude and puts your audience at ease.
- Plant your feet. Place them firmly on the floor and stand up straight. Slouching or slumping lessens your effectiveness.
- Act naturally. The more you practice, the more comfortable you will be with your body movements and less likely to use unnatural, mechanical hand gestures and head movements.
- Move from the waist up only. Shuffling and pacing are distracting.
- Step out in front. Get in front of the podium when speaking to smaller groups of 30 or fewer because it helps create intimacy and connection.
- Use hand gestures appropriately. Keep arms and hands close to the body; avoid pointing your finger to emphasize an idea; instead, use a closed fist with thumb slightly up; open hands work well, but avoid banging on the podium or table.
- Maintain eye contact. Use the "Figure 8" method of scanning the room so that each area gets your attention throughout the presentation. Think of an 8 lying on its side and trace the curves and lines with your eyes, starting either on the right or the left of your audience.

PLUS

(Personality + Learning Style = Understanding Situations)

Think about Juanita's concern over writing a 15-page paper and making a slide-show presentation. Because Juanita has a read/write learning preference, she finds writing to be an easy task, although she has procrastinated in the past when it came to writing papers. However, now she is being asked to write on a topic with which she is not familiar and she is worried about creating a presentation that accompanies her research. Using what you have learned from this chapter, what advice would you give her? How can she divide her assignment into smaller tasks so that she does not wait until the last minute to complete it?

Now, considering your own learning style, personality type, and special circumstances, what would you do to tackle this major assignment?

PROFILE

MY STORY
Learning Plan

Directions: Using what you have learned in this chapter and what you know about your learning preferences, choose a task or assignment that needs to be completed soon and create a learning plan that will help you accomplish this task. Then, write your *My Story* Summary, a one-sentence synopsis that crystallizes your newly created plan.

PROFILE

LEARNING TASK	
Time of Day	
Intake Preference	
Social Preference	
Task Management Preference	

MY STORY SUMMARY:

Path of Discovery

Journal Entry

How have the writing and speaking expectations changed for you since high school? What do you expect writing and speaking expectations to be like on the job?

HOMEWORK

From College to University

How Writing Assignments and Expectations Will Change

Most definitely, when you take upper-level courses at the university, you will write more and the expectations will be higher. Your professors who teach at the junior and senior levels will definitely assume that any writing challenges that you had in your first two years of college have been overcome. Your professors will be more concerned with the strength and originality of your argument and with the depth and breadth of your research than with grammar, punctuation, spelling, and mechanics. Instead, they will expect that these lower-level issues will have been mastered, and they will want you to expand on the higher-level issues such as presenting a successful academic argument.

Certainly, you will be writing more to discover what you think about a particular topic. You will also find writing and research more enjoyable as you settle into a major course of study. Most students who transfer and take courses in their major learn that they enjoy writing about subjects that will help them in their careers. This kind of satisfaction comes over time, and although you may not enjoy every writing assignment that you must do in your first two years in college, realize that with each writing assignment you complete, you will become a better writer and thinker, which will help you make your transition to a four-year university that much easier. Clint Watson, a graduate student in social work, reflects on learning how to write during his first two years at a community college: "What I learned at my community college was to organize my thoughts. Writing is much easier for me now that I know how to arrange details logically."

From College to Career

Why Strong Speaking Skills Will Set You Apart at Work

Don't think of your speech communication class as the last occasion that you will speak in front of peers and superiors. No matter what career path you take, chances are likely that you will need to use those communication skills to work in groups, relate to your boss, and instruct or present information to your coworkers. Examples of when you will need to rely on what you learned in class include making a presentation to a client, summarizing the company's goals and projects to new employees, or presenting a new idea for efficiency to management. These will all be instances in which you will be able to use what you learned in class and what you learned by frequently practicing your speaking skills for other occasions besides Public Speaking 101. Just as good writing skills are essential to on-the-job success, solid public speaking skills will set you apart from your coworkers as someone who can communicate even the most complicated or mundane aspects of the company. That kind of ability will garner respect and admiration from those who work with you.

Chapter Review Questions

1. What are the different elements of writing effectively?
2. What should you consider after being assigned a speech?
3. How are speaking and writing different?
4. How do you evaluate a speech or a piece of writing?

Chapter 9 Case Scenarios

1. Renée is barely passing her literature class. She has not done well on the tests or the writing assignments, so she has asked someone to help her write her final literary analysis paper. A friend of her mother has offered to help her write her paper, and when she meets with Renée, her mother's friend has offered to write down all of Renée's ideas, organize them, and reword her sentences. The result is that Renée's paper is an A paper, something that she has not been able to achieve all semester. What do you think of the help that Renée has received? Is there some other way that she could improve her writing without the kind of help she received?

2. Paul is having a hard time understanding the research assignment that his government professor handed out to the class. He had two months to work on the paper, but he hasn't done anything yet, and now he has only two weeks. Where should he start and what should he do?

3. Pietra is afraid of public speaking and she has been postponing taking her speech class until her last semester in college. The professor has lectured about overcoming speaking anxiety and Pietra has read the material in her textbook, but she doesn't think that she will be able to pass the class. What can she do to overcome her intense fear and pass the class?

Research It Further

1. By searching the Internet, create a "hot list" of writing sites that would be beneficial to college students. You may want to focus on a particular aspect of writing such as grammar, or you can create a list for several topics that concern college writers.

2. Interview two people whose careers are in fields other than writing and ask them how writing is important to their jobs.

3. Interview two people whose careers are in fields other than professional speakers and ask them how speaking effectively is important to their jobs.

4. Create a survey of students' attitudes toward and concerns about public speaking. Poll your class and other students and compile your results. Present your findings to your class.

10 Studying and Taking Tests

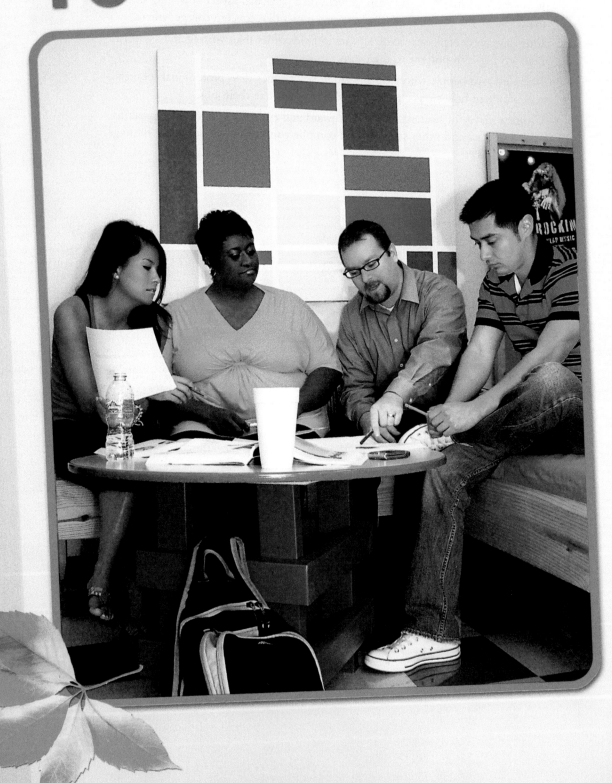

Four Students' Stories

Studying the origins of life in their Biology 101 class is becoming an exercise in their own survival. Juanita, Evan, Michael, and Laura formed a study group early in the semester, on the suggestion of their orientation leaders, and now it has become a precious lifeline. Their professor is great, they all agree, but the mountain of chapters, notes, extra readings, papers, and lab work is killing them.

"So much work for just one class," Michael says. "It's insane."

"Ha," Juanita replies, "I'm taking world literature and psychology. The reading alone takes me hours each night."

Both Michael and Juanita got to their study group early so that they could get a good booth in the food court before it gets crowded. Nervous about the first test, Michael thinks he has studied too much of the wrong things. Juanita has severe test anxiety anytime she takes a test, and studying with a group helps her relax before the big day.

"Are you starting without me?" Laura asks as she drops her heavy backpack on the booth seat by Michael.

"Of course not," Juanita says. "Michael was just crying about how much work this class is. I had to remind him of my schedule—nonstop reading that will make your eyes cross."

"My mother finished her degree right before I started school and I remember how much she studied. If she can do it, I think I can," Laura says. "But I am *not* ready for this test. Between a sick kid and a paper for history, I couldn't fit it in."

"Does anyone know what the test will cover? I think I have studied all the wrong material," Michael says.

"I have to study everything, even if I don't think it will be on the test," says Juanita. "If I'm not overprepared, I know I will lose it when I get the test. I've been studying since the first week of classes."

"Why am I not surprised?" Evan asks as he slides into a seat next to Michael. "Sorry, I'm late. I had to run by the gym. What have I missed besides Juanita reciting every biology fact from the first day of class?"

The study group laughs at Evan's comment, but they know he usually gets by with little studying. When he does meet with his group, he comes late or leaves early and rarely brings his notes or book.

"Can we get serious now? I have to pass this test," Laura says. Her single parent scholarship requires that she maintain a 3.0 GPA, and Laura works hard to keep it.

"I suggest we start going over everything that we have done since the first chapter," Juanita suggests. "If we work on this for the next four hours, then we can study four more tomorrow. I will probably stay up late tomorrow night to make sure I get it."

Evan, text-messaging while he talks, says, "If we just review our notes, we should be fine. When was the last time you failed a test? They have to give you something for just taking it."

"If I don't know it now, I won't know it in two days and that really scares me," says Laura.

Michael chews on the end of his pen and checks his watch. "I don't have much time to study tonight. My girlfriend needs a ride to work," he says.

"We need to start somewhere even if we can't all stay the whole time or agree on how to do this," says the youngest of the group who has stepped up as the leader.

In This Chapter

As they discuss in their study group, Juanita, Michael, Evan, and Laura have various levels of preparation for their upcoming biology test and different perspectives on how they should study over the next two days. Just as Laura admits to the group and Evan demonstrates by his late arrival, you may also have competing priorities and tasks that keep you from studying, or you may feel anxious about taking the test as Michael and Juanita reveal.

Whatever your experience with studying is until this point in your academic career, professors and experienced students alike agree that good preparation will make studying much easier. In fact, you may learn to look forward to studying, especially as you take classes that interest you and that apply to your career. This chapter's purpose is to help you improve your study skills, which will in turn help you improve your test-taking strategies. No matter what you have heard, successful students study frequently and effectively. If you have never been "good at" studying, you can improve your skills by following the steps that work best for you.

This chapter provides you with study strategies for preparing for tests effectively as well as tips for taking a test to maximize your success. Specifically, at the end of this chapter you will be able to:

- Determine the best study strategies.

- Identify strategies for effective study groups.

- Describe the kinds of test questions you will encounter and how best to answer them.

- List methods for reducing test anxiety.

Testing, 1, 2, 3

Although the terms are usually used interchangeably, a *test* is defined as a set of questions that are used to evaluate one's skills, aptitudes, and abilities on certain topics. Usually, tests assess your knowledge and abilities on a part of the course. An *exam*, however, by definition is an assessment of the material of an entire course. Final exams are sometimes called *comprehensive* or *cumulative* exams, which indicate that they will cover what you have studied all semester or term.

Unless your professor tells you directly what will be on the test, assume that anything that was assigned or covered in class may be there. Just about every college student has a story about taking a test that covered reading assignments and not what was discussed in class. These students were surprised to realize that studying the lecture notes was not enough. The following is a list of items that you may be tested on for any class:

- Material from the lecture, discussion, and in-class or out-of-class activity
- Information provided by a guest speaker
- Information from a workshop or field trip
- Multimedia productions such as video or audio
- Assigned readings, including chapters in the textbook
- Handouts including PowerPoint slides and outlines

You can be assured that you will encounter a variety of test types. Take clues from what you do in class to help determine what kind of test questions you may encounter. For example, if your professor spends time applying information from a chapter during class or as an assignment, then you will likely have test questions that will ask you to apply the information as well. Listen for clues that the professor gives you, such as "You should write this down" and "This is a really important point." Other cue phrases include "You may see this again on a test" and "If you saw this on a test, how would you answer it?" When you hear these phrases, write them down and review them when studying over your other notes. A professor who says these things is begging you to take notice!

The best advice to give college students is plain and simple: Study for all tests. No exceptions. Sometimes you will find that you do not need to study as much for some classes; however, remember that studying effectively is a habit. To form the long-term habit, you must do it even when you don't think you have to, which is fundamental to making an activity part of a routine, something Evan may need help establishing for himself.

A Place and Time for Studying

The best time to begin studying is as soon as the semester starts. Be careful of the mindset that because you are not in class every day you don't need to study every day. Some students begin studying the night or day before an exam, which may be too late to review and remember all the material that has been covered over the past several weeks. As stated in Chapter 8, start reviewing your notes within two days of taking them. If possible, you should start studying for future exams right now, today.

If you are a typical college student, then your time will be limited. You may not have the luxury of large blocks of time, so you will need to be creative about studying. Because it is more effective to study for short periods of time, consider studying in between classes, during breaks at work, and on the way to work and school (provided you are not driving). Another way to ensure that you study during the day is to get in the habit of always carrying your notes or books with you—this way you'll be able to take advantage of any unexpected "free" time. You can also get up earlier or stay up later so you can spend a few minutes studying before starting or ending your day.

If you have the luxury of choosing when to study, rather than sandwiching it in between work and family responsibilities, pay attention to what *time of day* you are most alert and receptive to learning. The best time of day for you to study is dependent on your schedule, your responsibilities, your age, and your personal preferences. Some people identify themselves as "night owls" whereas others claim to be "morning people." Whatever your peak performance time, as you discovered in Chapter 2, be sure to study your most difficult subjects at that time. If you have a predictable schedule all semester, plan to study at the same time each day.

The environment in which you study is just as important as the time of day and the length of time you spend studying. You will need to find the kind of environment that works well for you. Some people need complete silence with no visual distractions, whereas others need a little background noise to stay focused. At the least, create a place that is comfortable, has good lighting, and has space for your supplies and books. It is easier to make time to study when you have a place to do it. If you have nowhere at home that is quiet and roomy, then search for a place on campus or a local library that offers study space. Some people find that studying away from home is better because they are not distracted by the television, phone, or family members.

Small children can pose a particular difficulty in finding quiet time. If you have small children, make a concerted effort to find a quiet spot. You may need to hire a baby-sitter or find a classmate who can trade child care services with you when you want to study. For example, you could offer to baby-sit a classmate's kids when he needs to study in exchange for him watching yours when you have a paper to write. Some college students who are also parents find time to study only when their children are asleep. Therefore, their best studying takes place late at night or early in the morning at home. Do whatever works best for you.

How to Study Effectively

Setting Goals

Once you have determined when, where, and how much you need to study, set study and test-taking goals. Just as you set short-term and long-term goals in Chapter 2, write down goals that you want to achieve when studying and taking tests. Remember the title of Henriette Anne Klauser's book: *Write It Down, Make It Happen* (2001). This also applies to something as short term as studying for and taking a test. Your goals could be as simple as the following:

- *I will use my time wisely so that I am able to study all my notes.*
- *I will ask the instructor questions about any notes that I do not understand.*
- *I will remain calm before, during, and after the exam by practicing breathing techniques and by relaxing.*

Of course, your goals could also include studying with a group or making a high grade. If you have never written down goals for studying or taking tests, then start small. Once you have achieved your study and test-taking goals, create newer and more challenging ones with each test:

- *I will improve my writing skills by practicing the essay questions in a timed environment.*
- *I will improve my overall retention of the material after the test.*

Studying Actively

Goal setting is just one of the ways to prepare for exams, but one of the most important is how you approach studying. In order to build a body of knowledge, you will want to study to *learn*, not just to *remember*. In other words, you will want to transfer information from your short-term memory, which holds information for a short period of time, to your long-term memory, which can be retrieved long after it is "deposited" there.

One of the ways to improve your memory of the material you have learned is to actively take it in when you study. The goal of active studying is to make connections between concepts and theories so that you can more easily recall the information and write or speak knowledgeably about it. To achieve this kind of mastery, instead of simply rereading notes or passively reviewing the major headings in your textbook, your studying should include activities such as the following:

- Rewriting or summarizing your notes.
- Rearranging the order of the material from most important to least important detail; from least important to most important; or in chronological order.

- Making connections between what you have learned in one chapter, unit, or class with material you have learned in other places.
- Making connections between what you have learned in class and what you have experienced in the real world.
- Explaining concepts to someone else who is not familiar with the topic.
- Making visual representations of the material.

Creating a Study Log

After considering your study goals, you may also want to create a study log that will help you keep track of your tests and preparation steps. Figure 10.1 is an example of a study log.

Understanding Course Objectives

Another step in studying effectively is to understand the objectives of the course. You will find the course objectives in the syllabus or in other material that has been handed out to you in class. If one of your course objectives is to identify the processes of cell replication, then you can be sure that you will be tested on the processes of cell replication in some manner. Making sure that you study the material that appears in course objectives will help you focus your time and energy on the right course content.

Using Time Wisely

How much time you spend and how many sessions you have will depend on the type of learner you are. You could start with 45 minutes of studying three different times a day over the period of a week to see how well you retain and remember the material. Adjust your schedule as needed. Just remember to be conscious of how effective your study sessions are. If they are not helping you meet your study goals, then make changes in your schedule. In Evan's case, his biology study group may not be helping

FIGURE 10.1   Study Log

Class	Chemistry
Date	Tuesday, October 27
Material	Chapters 4–7, extra lecture material
Practice/Previous Tests	In library on reserve; answer key for practice test
Question Types	Multiple choice, problem solving
Study Methods	Review notes, work through extra problems, go through practice test, study with group
Time Needed	6 hours
Approved Materials for Test	Paper, pencil, calculator
Number of Points	150, 15% of overall grade

him study in the manner that is most effective for him. If that is the case, he may need to find a different group that fits his study goals better or consider that studying alone is his best option.

No matter how much time you spend studying, it won't be effective if you are unable to concentrate on the subject. Many times you will find yourself distracted by external and internal commotion. Externally, you may have a noisy or messy house, or you may have others who need or want your time and attention. Internally, you may be preoccupied by illness, stress, self-doubt, or fear. Both internal and external distractions make it difficult to study effectively, so you must take care of them or tune them out. If not, you will find that the time you spend studying is not productive.

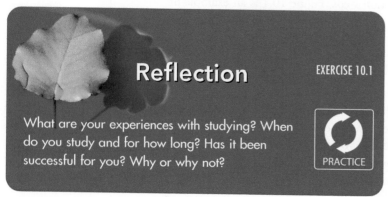

Reflection

EXERCISE 10.1

What are your experiences with studying? When do you study and for how long? Has it been successful for you? Why or why not?

PRACTICE

For some students, planning ahead to study effectively is not an option. Because of poor time management or procrastination, these students often try to study in one long session of cramming. Cramming and marathon sessions should be avoided when studying for an exam because they usually produce more anxiety than learning. If you do find yourself in a situation in which you must cram, try to maximize the effectiveness of the long hours and loads of material. Organize your time into short periods, no more than one hour at a time, and take many breaks. When you return from your break, review the material you had just been studying before you begin on new material. You may want to try a combination of writing down what you know, drawing pictures to represent the material, reciting key concepts aloud, creating songs with the material, or building a model of a key idea. The more learning preferences you use to understand the material, the better your chance of remembering it all for the test.

There is no reason that studying cannot include having fun. Some websites offer games and fun quizzes to help you study. One such site is www.quia.com. However, you don't have to look for games that are produced by others; you can create your own. Consider making flash cards to quiz yourself or others if you are in a study group. You can also tape-record questions and answers. Instead of playing the tape straight through, stop the tape after each question so you can answer the question aloud. Then, play the answer and see how well you have done. If you can push yourself to enjoy studying, you will be more likely to do it often.

"Cheat" Sheets

Creating "cheat" sheets was once considered an activity only for those who intended to cheat; however, many educators have seen the benefit that creating such sheets can have. You may have a professor who tells you that you can bring a three-by-five-inch index card to the exam with anything you want written on it. Students who may not have studied much beforehand usually jump at the chance to cram as much information as possible on that tiny, white space. The result is that students retain more of the information than they would if they had not created the cheat sheet. Many times, the cheat sheet is not needed because the student has, in effect, studied adequately in making the sheet.

To create an effective cheat sheet, organization is important. One way to organize the card is to divide it into thirds on both sides so that you have six sections (three on one side, three on the other) to work with. Then, use the top of each section to write a specific category such as "Formulas" or "Krebs Cycle." Underneath each heading, write the information that pertains to the category. If you are listing formulas, for example, be sure to write clearly and double check that all elements of the formula are correct.

Even if you are not allowed to bring a cheat sheet—only bring one if you are given permission—you can still reap the benefits of this technique by closing your books and notes and writing down as much information as you can remember about the subject. For example, if you have a test on genetics, take a blank card and write everything you know about DNA on the front and back. In this case, organization is not important; what is important is to see how much you have learned already. Once you have filled up the card, go back through your notes and books to see what you have missed.

Previous Exams and Practice Tests

If allowed by the instructor, study copies of old tests. Your instructor will put them on reserve in the library, post them online in an online learning system, or hand them out in class. Previous exams are an excellent source for what kinds of questions you will be asked. If someone offers to give you his old tests from the previous semester, ask your instructor first if you can study from them before taking them.

Equally beneficial to understanding how your professor will test you is to take advantage of practice exams if they are offered. Some instructors may provide opportunities for you to stop by during office hours to take a practice exam or to take an online practice test where you can get instant feedback.

Study Groups

Juanita, Michael, Laura, and Evan took the advice of their orientation leaders early in the semester to create a study group for one of their classes, and they have realized that there are several benefits of studying in groups. First, you have access to more notes and may find that you have missed important information. Second, you experience others' perspectives about the subject, and you may find that your classmates explain major concepts better than your professor. Third, you have a built-in support group while you take classes, because in the process of studying, you establish friendships.

A key to a successful study group is to limit the group to four or five participants or fewer. The more participants there are, the harder it will be to remain on track. It is also best to study with people who are not close friends so that you minimize distractions and off-topic conversations. When choosing members of your group, it is a good idea to discuss expectations for the group. If prospective members think that others will be helping them but they won't be contributing themselves, then they may not be right for your group. You will need members who will take on specific responsibilities that will benefit the whole group.

Once you have chosen your group participants, you should exchange contact information (phone and pager numbers and email addresses) and choose a leader.

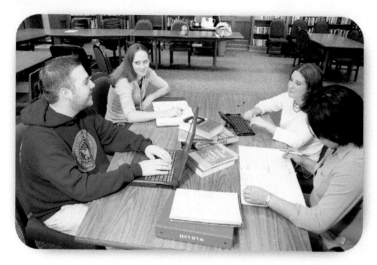

One key to a successful study group is to limit the group to four or five participants.

The leader can change from meeting to meeting, but one person should be in charge of contacting everyone to announce the meeting time and place for the first session. The leader should also be responsible for keeping everyone on task if the group gets off topic and for assigning roles to each person, just as Juanita does for her group when she leads a study session.

When you meet with your group, be sure that each person contributes to the study session and "teaches" his or her assigned part. Periodically, the group should take breaks to keep people focused. To make studying comfortable, try to meet in a quiet location that allows food and drink; this way there will be fewer breaks and fewer people will be distracted by hunger or thirst. Also consider taking turns bringing snacks and beverages or chipping in for a meal. Better yet, go out for a meal *after* you study so that everyone has a goal to look forward to.

The difficulty of forming study groups in college is that many students lead full lives and have very little time to schedule extra activities. They also may not have consistent free time since they work different shifts each week or have different family responsibilities from day to day. To make your study group work, you may need to be creative about how you meet and how you organize your time. For example, you may want to join a chat room or use email to create a sample exam and "quiz" each other about the concepts on the exam.

General Tips for Study Groups

- Start with a small group of three to five people.
- Choose a leader for each meeting.
- Keep a master list of contact information.
- Schedule a time and place that is convenient, comfortable, and conducive to studying.
- Be creative about meeting. Try doing some of the work, such as creating sample test questions, through chat rooms or email.
- Assign each person a role in the group and part of the material to "teach" to the group.
- Do your "homework" before meeting by preparing to "teach" your material.
- Review your notes with each other.
- Quiz each other on the material before you leave your meeting.
- Be respectful of others' commitments.
- Take frequent breaks.
- Stay on task.
- Meet often for short periods of time rather than "marathon" sessions.

Types of Test Questions

Learning how to take tests will be just as important as learning the material. Knowing how to answer each type of possible test question will make taking an exam that much easier; at least, you will have less anxiety because you will know what to expect.

There are two categories of question types: objective and subjective. Objective questions can require lower-level thinking because they ask you to recall facts and concepts and usually appear in the form of multiple choice, true/false, fill-in-the-blank, and short answer. Subjective questions ask for your opinion about the material or ask you to apply the material in a new way. Essay and problem-solving (critical thinking) questions are labeled subjective because there are a variety of ways the questions can be answered correctly.

Sometimes, objective questions are easier to answer because they provide a correct answer within the choices. However, objective questions can demand significant brainpower, especially when you must recall an answer with very few clues, which is often the case with fill-in-the-blank questions. Because objective questions usually suggest only one correct answer, some students believe that there are no "wrong" answers for subjective questions, and that may be true, but there *are* better ways to answer them. In the following sections we discuss typical test questions and how to answer them.

Multiple Choice

Multiple-choice questions can test your recall of information or they can assess your ability to apply information or analyze situations. Despite their reputation for being easier, expect more difficult and time-consuming multiple-choice questions for college exams, and don't be alarmed if the answers are not obvious.

When answering multiple-choice questions, the first step is to read the question or statement carefully. Then, mark any special words in the question or statement such as "not," "always," and "only." Before looking at the choices, see if you can answer the question yourself. For example, consider the following multiple-choice question:

1. **What should you NOT do to alleviate anxiety when taking a test?** [Notice the word "NOT" and think in terms of what is not an acceptable answer.]
   A. **Arrive early for the exam.** [This is something you SHOULD do, so it is not the correct answer.]
   B. **Skip over the directions.** [This is something you should NOT do, so it may be the right answer. Keep reading the rest of the choices and lightly mark this one.]
   C. **Pay attention to the time limit.** [This is something you SHOULD do, so it is not the correct answer.]
   D. **Read all the questions before answering.** [Again, this is something you SHOULD do, so it is not the correct answer.]

After you have read through all the choices, the only correct answer is B. Consider another multiple-choice question:

2. **When answering an essay question on a test, be sure to**
   A. **Answer each part of the question thoroughly**. [This is something you should do. Keep reading the rest of the choices.]

B. **Organize your essay before writing it by sketching out a quick outline.** [This is something you should do. Keep reading the rest of the choices.]

C. **Read the directions carefully.** [Again, this is something you should do. Keep reading the rest of the choices to see if All of the Above is a choice since all the choices so far are good choices.]

D. **All of the above.** [This seems the best choice because all the other choices are correct.]

After you have read all the choices, D is the correct answer because it allows for A through C being correct.

When you are ready to answer the multiple-choice question, read each choice carefully and eliminate any answer that is obviously wrong. If you have to guess, eliminate any answer that is misspelled (usually a sign that the instructor has hurriedly added false answers) or any answer that is shorter than the others. Also, pay attention to choices labeled "All of the above" and "None of the above." If you can determine that at least two of the choices are correct, then "All of the above" is probably the correct answer. Likewise, if at least two of the choices are not correct, then "None of the above" is probably the correct answer.

Matching

A matching section on an exam presents you with two columns: a list of words or phrases that are to be matched with a list of descriptors. Professors who use matching sections usually require basic recall of information, but you will need to read the directions carefully. There may be more than one match for an item in the list or there may be extra descriptors.

To complete matching questions, first read through the entire list and choices to match before beginning. Then, determine if there could be multiple matches to a word in the list. Make sure that you have chosen the correct letter to match with each word in the list.

EXAMPLE OF MATCHING QUESTIONS

Match the following descriptions of interests and strengths with the appropriate multiple intelligences category. The categories may be used more than once; some may not be used at all.

_____ 1. Enjoy outdoor activities

_____ 2. Know how and why they act

_____ 3. Good at design, architecture

_____ 4. Choose careers in science, computer technology, engineering

_____ 5. Use voice or instruments to express themselves

_____ 6. Enjoy reading and writing

_____ 7. Can read others' feelings well

_____ 8. Fascinated with pictures

A. Verbal/linguistic

B. Logical/mathematical

C. Visual/spatial

D. Bodily/kinesthetic

E. Musical/rhythmic

F. Interpersonal

G. Intrapersonal

H. Naturalistic

True/False

True/false questions can be tough even though there are only two possible answers: true or false. Guessing or randomly answering true/false questions should be done as a last resort. It is better to read the statements carefully, noting key words that could point to the correct answer such as "frequently," "sometimes," and "a few." These words usually indicate a true statement. Words such as "never," "only," and "always" usually indicate a false statement.

If you have any difficulty answering true/false test questions, try not to confuse yourself with how the statement is worded. Go with your gut instinct. If are not entirely sure of what the statement is expressing, write down a justification of your answer on the test. Sometimes, professors will give partial credit if the wrong answer is clearly justified.

EXAMPLES OF TRUE/FALSE QUESTIONS

Determine if the statements are true or false. Circle the appropriate choice.

1. Howard Gardner's theory of multiple intelligences includes the category Nutritional/Health.
   A. True
   B. False

2. OK5R is a test-taking strategy.
   A. True
   B. False

3. Priorities are beliefs that can be shaped by experience and are not the same for everyone.
   A. True
   B. False

4. A mission statement is important because it declares your beliefs and your goals.
   A. True
   B. False

5. A priority is something that keeps you from achieving your goals.
   A. True
   B. False

Fill-in-the-Blank/Short Answer

Fill-in-the-blank and short answer questions require that you recall definitions of key terms or items in a series. To complete these types of questions, first read the sentence or question carefully. Often, points will be lost if you don't answer exactly or misspell the correct term.

EXAMPLES OF FILL-IN-THE-BLANK/SHORT ANSWER QUESTIONS

1. The T System for taking notes is also known as the _____.
2. Abbreviating words and phrases is called _____.
3. An instructor who is difficult to understand is an example of a listening _____.

4. _____ listening includes making the decision to concentrate on what is being said.

5. _____ is a method of note taking that involves numbering items and organizing them.

Problem Solving

Problem-solving, or critical thinking, questions are used by instructors so that students can demonstrate or apply the concepts or ideas they have learned. When you answer problem-solving questions, read the question carefully, marking multiple steps or parts to the directions. Next, determine what information you will need to solve the problem. Then, break the problem into parts and write down what process or operation you will need to perform. Work through the problem, and once you arrive at an answer, check the question again to make sure you have adequately answered it.

Here is an example of a problem-solving question, and an explanation for solving the problem follows:

Beatrice has a scholarship that requires she maintain a 3.2 GPA while she is in college. During her first semester, she had 4 three-hour credit courses and made two A's and two B's. Now, she is taking one four-hour course and 4 three-hour courses. Can she make an A in her four-hour course and B's in her three-hour courses and keep her scholarship?

In order to answer this question correctly, you will need to know how to calculate GPA. If we break the steps down further, you will need to know the definition of grade points and quality points and how GPA is calculated when a student has taken classes for more than one semester. Then, you will need to know how to multiply, add, and divide. These sound like commonsense steps, but writing down every operation that you will need to perform will enable you to prepare to answer the question correctly and help you check the process by which you arrived at the answer.

EXAMPLE OF PROBLEM-SOLVING QUESTIONS

1. Lenise is taking a history class in which her grade is made up of four exams. So far she has made 65% and 74%. What are the lowest grades she can make to get a C in the course? Is it mathematically possible for her to earn a B?

2. In Carlos' biology class, the final grade is comprised of the following: homework (20%), midterm exam (30%), and final (50%). If Carlos makes 85% on his final, 71% on his midterm, and 68% for his homework grade, what is his final average?

3. Lester needs a 3.63 GPA to be inducted into the Phi Theta Kappa honor society. This semester, he has earned two C's, an A, and two B's in his courses (none of which have labs). Will he be inducted? Show your work below.

Essay

Instructors use essay questions to help them measure students' ability to analyze, synthesize, and evaluate the concepts they have learned; this type of question gauges more than students' recall of facts or terms. You can be assured that you will encounter more essay questions in college because they allow students to demonstrate a deeper understanding of the material.

One thing to remember about essay questions is that, although you won't have an enormous amount of time to complete an essay, your professor will still expect that you answer the essay question thoroughly and clearly. Always read the directions carefully. If the essay question has more than one part, be sure to mark each part and answer it in the body of the essay. If the directions specify a length, be sure to meet or exceed it. Before you begin writing, create a brief outline of what you will cover during the essay. Make a short list of transitions and details so that you can refer to the list if you get stuck during the exam.

Finally, because your professor will be reading and grading many essays, a clearly organized essay will stand out and make it easy for her to tell that you have discussed the key points. Just be sure to give yourself plenty of time to write the essay and use any remaining time you have to proofread and edit your work. Chapter 9 contains information about putting the finishing touches on writing that can help you with essay questions.

EXAMPLES OF ESSAY QUESTIONS

1. Do you think that colleges should strive, at whatever cost, to ensure that their campuses are diverse?
2. Do you think that colleges should prohibit personal and/or intimate relationships between professors and students? Explain your response and refer to the college's policy regarding student-professor relationships in your essay.
3. How have your relationships at home and at work changed since you have entered college?

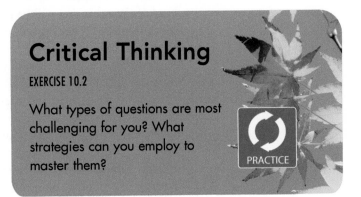

Critical Thinking

EXERCISE 10.2

What types of questions are most challenging for you? What strategies can you employ to master them?

PRACTICE

Types of Tests

Just as important as what types of questions you will encounter is what kind of test you can expect in different classes. For example, a math test will look quite different from a music test, and the strategies for studying for them and taking them will be different. Here we discuss a few different types of tests you may encounter in college. You may be able to apply the same tips to exams in other disciplines.

Math and Science Tests

For taking math and science tests, it is best to work through the problems you know first. Then, complete the problems that you do not know as well. If you complete your test early, consider reworking the test questions again on another sheet of paper and comparing your answers. If you discover two different answers for the same problem, figure out which answer contains the error. Always show your work and complete as many parts of a multiple-part problem as possible. You may receive partial credit for completing the process correctly even if you have not arrived at the right answer.

When answering questions on science tests that involve processes or major concepts, draw a picture to create a visual of the process and to help you answer questions about the steps. Regardless of what question types you will encounter, you will need to recall terms and definitions.

Fine Arts and Literature Tests

When taking exams in fine arts and literature classes, it is as important to explain the significance of the selected work, as it is to identify key passages, authors, terms, and eras. When taking exams in both disciplines, work through the easier questions first and save plenty of time for the writing portions. Think about the major themes and the historical importance of the works and look for those themes to be part of the questions on the test. While recall of facts about eras, dates, and creators of works will be part of the exam, there should be a significant emphasis on synthesizing the material.

Open-Book and Take-Home Tests

There will be occasions when you are given an open-book or take-home test. Although they sound as if they are the easiest kind of test to take, professors who hand out open-book tests make sure that you work hard to answer the questions correctly. In other words, these may be harder than in-class, closed-book exams. If you know ahead of time that you will be given an open-book exam, you will still need to study for it. Instead of spending too much time looking through your book and notes for the answers to the questions, you should be able to find the answers quickly. Chances are good that you will have many questions on an open-book exam to test how much you know about the subject. Likewise, take-home exams are often more difficult and time consuming than a regular test. At the least, your instructor will expect more from you if he allows you to take the test home to complete it. Because expectations are higher, you will need to give yourself plenty of time to formulate your answers and to check your work. Even though you will be unsupervised when writing the exam and probably expected to use a variety of resources for help, you will still need to maintain integrity. In other words, unless you receive permission from your instructor, do not accept or give help to other classmates.

Online Tests

Whether you take an online class or not, you may be required to take a quiz or test through an online learning system or through a website, such as a publisher's site that supports your textbook. Online tests are usually timed, which means you will need to keep an eye on how much time you have left after you answer each question. Instructors often place a time limit for online exams to discourage students from reviewing notes, going through the text, or surfing the Internet for answers. If your professor provides a practice test, consider taking it so that you can get a good feel for how much time you will have and what types of questions you will answer. Additional considerations include revisiting questions, if possible, to make sure you have not chosen the wrong answer for multiple-choice questions; ensuring that you have saved your answers before submitting your exam; and not sharing information about the exam to other students who have not taken it yet.

Comprehensive Exams

Comprehensive, or cumulative, exams are usually given during a week dedicated for "finals." Not all final tests are comprehensive—some professors choose to give their students shorter tests instead. However, most of the finals you will take in college will reflect the culmination of what you have learned all semester. Taking comprehensive exams at the end of the semester will seem like a daunting task if you have several classes, but there are some tips that will help you manage the task. First, it is important that you study for all your classes regularly. Reviewing notes daily will help you keep the information fresh. Second, make sure that you keep your notes and course materials organized so that you can easily find what you have covered throughout the semester. When you get closer to the date of your final exam, begin studying more intensely by reviewing the most current material and working backwards toward the material that was covered at the beginning of the semester.

Collaboration

Working within a group, brainstorm a list of tips that could help students study and take tests effectively. Divide your tips into categories that would help visual, aural, read/write, and kinesthetic learners.

EXERCISE 10.3

Test-Taking Strategies

Preparing for the Test

Before you begin to think about what is on a test and how you should study, you must make sure that you are taking care of yourself. Eating and sleeping are fundamental to doing well on tests. If you are not healthy, then you cannot perform at your highest level. Just as athletes prepare for performance days in advance by eating carbohydrates and resting, you should focus on getting regular sleep and eating well days before the exam. At the least, get a good night's rest the night before the test and avoid refined sugar (candy, cakes, and cookies) and caffeine. For more specific information on staying healthy, read Chapter 5.

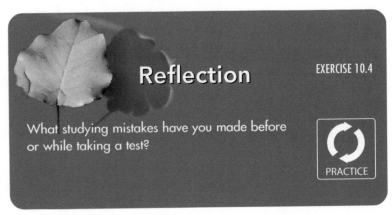

Reflection

EXERCISE 10.4

What studying mistakes have you made before or while taking a test?

PRACTICE

Maintaining a good attitude as you prepare for the exam is another effective strategy. Monitor and eliminate any negative self-talk about your ability to do well on exams. Instead, visualize yourself taking the test successfully and earning a good grade.

Taking the Test

Once you have prepared for the test, both physically and mentally, you should be ready to take it. Before you leave for class, be sure that you have the appropriate supplies: Will you need a watch, paper, pen, pencil, a calculator, or a dictionary and thesaurus? Are there any approved test-taking aids that you need to bring as well? Will you be able to use your textbook or a cheat sheet with formulas on it? Once you arrive in class, take a seat away from distractions and where you feel comfortable to spread out and get to work. If you are not wearing a watch, sit somewhere you will be able to see a clock. Cell phone access, which many students use to keep track of time, may be restricted during tests, so be sure to keep track of time some other way. When taking tests that use a Scantron or bubble form in which you have to pencil in your answers by filling in circles, be sure to bring at least two sharpened pencils.

When you first get the test, read through all the questions, noting which ones will take longer to answer than the others. Taking that time to read all the questions is actually a time saver, because you will know what to expect and how to pace yourself. Turn the paper over and check out the back. Your instructor may have made two-sided copies of the test, which means you will have questions on the back and front of the paper.

As you read through the test, make note of the types of questions and use the tips in this chapter to answer them. Read the directions for each section carefully and mark any special instructions. For example, in a matching section, there may be more than one match for an item in one of the columns; in an essay writing section, there may be a choice of topics. Also, be aware of how many points each section is worth. If one section is worth half the points for the entire exam, you will need to spend a majority of your time working that part.

Pacing yourself during the exam is very important. Before you begin the test, you should determine how much time you need to spend on each section based on the types of questions, your comfort level with the questions, and the amount of points it is worth. As a general rule, you should spend less than a minute per multiple choice and true/false questions and 15 minutes or more to answer essay questions. For the other types of questions, you will need to spend somewhere in between 1 and 5 minutes. If you get off track and spend too much time on one section, don't panic. You will just need to work quickly and carefully on the rest of the exam.

Working the easiest questions first, mark questions that you don't know the answer to or that you find confusing. Don't come back to them until you have completed all the questions that you can easily answer. If you are unsure of an answer, mark that question as well and plan to review it before turning in your exam. If the question or problem has multiple parts, work through as many of the parts that you can. Do not leave questions unanswered. Partial answers may receive partial credit unless you have been instructed otherwise.

Finally, leave yourself 5–10 minutes to check your work. If you finish an exam early, always go back through the questions and go over your answers by ensuring that all questions are answered and that all parts are completed. If you have written an essay, read through your response and check for grammatical, spelling, and punctuation errors. Initial each page and number the pages of your essay, if appropriate. Turn in your exam and any paper on which you worked problems or drafted an essay.

Maintaining Integrity During the Test

You may have recently read about the new lengths that students go to in order to cheat on exams or to plagiarize. Advances in technology have made cheating easier and have made it seem more widespread. Although there is no clear evidence that more students are cheating now than they were 30 years ago, there does seem to be more confusion about what constitutes cheating. For example, some professors require group presentations and collaboration on projects; however, very few offer guidelines on who should do what and how to document the part that each student does. In addition, collaboration on homework assignments, which was encouraged in high school, may now be prohibited in college. When in doubt about how you should complete homework or group projects, ask your instructor for specific guidelines.

The integrity rules are a little clearer when taking a test. Unless otherwise stated, do not use notes, books, or classmates as references for the exam. Most instructors will ask you to clear your desk of any material except paper and a pen or will ask you to move away from the nearest person. All of these actions are to ensure that there are no questions about the originality of the work. Other instructors are more trusting of students and may leave the classroom or give the class a take-home test. An instructor who allows such freedom is sending you a message about integrity: He trusts that his students will act maturely, responsibly, and honestly. Violating that trust can have grave consequences because not only does the cheating student create problems for herself, but she has also damaged the relationship of trust for the entire class.

To ensure that you act with integrity when taking an exam, whether supervised or not, do your own work and keep your work surface clear of books, papers, folders, cell phones, pagers, and even drink bottles. If possible, distance yourself from other students so that they are less likely to cheat off you. If you are ever in doubt, however, about your actions or the requirements for an exam, be sure to ask your professor.

Beating Test Anxiety

All of the information in this chapter is difficult to put into practice if you have overwhelming anxiety about taking tests. It is not unusual to experience nervousness, anxiety, and fear before or during a test, but extreme anxiety accompanied by excessive sweating, nausea, and crying is not normal. If you are experiencing conditions that make taking and completing tests impossible, you should see a college counselor or other professional. However, if you occasionally experience very mild conditions, there are some techniques that can help minimize your anxiety and fear. Remember that some degree of nervousness is normal and can actually give you an adrenaline boost, as Chapter 5 mentions.

In order to cope with mild anxiety, there are a variety of activities you can do to relieve tension. Basic relaxation techniques such as deep breathing and visualizations can take the edge off the tension of taking a test. Taking the time to breathe deeply whenever you feel overwhelmed will help you stay in control. Also, visualizing yourself relaxing or succeeding at a test can help you get beyond self-defeating doubt and stress.

INTEGRITY MATTERS

According to Dr. Donald McCabe at the Center for Academic Integrity, 75% of college students admit to some cheating. Almost 25% have admitted to serious cheating, and nearly 50% admitted to cheating in one or more instances.

Source: "CAI Research." Retrieved August 2, 2005, from www.academicintegrity.org/cai_research.asp.

PLUS

(Personality + Learning Style = Understanding Situations)

Let's revisit the study group's discussion. Juanita, the youngest, learns best by writing and has severe test anxiety, while Michael is visual and needs more direction in what to study. Evan, a kinesthetic learner, has gotten by with little studying in the past, and Laura learns best when she hears information, but she has been distracted with other obligations. What study strategies and test-taking tips can each use?

Now, considering your own learning style, personality type, and special circumstances, what would you do if you were studying with fellow students whose own learning styles and levels of preparation differ from your own?

PROFILE

MY STORY
Learning Plan

Directions: Using what you have learned in this chapter and what you know about your learning preferences, choose a task or assignment that needs to be completed soon and create a learning plan that will help you accomplish this task. Then, write your *My Story* Summary, a one-sentence synopsis that crystallizes your newly created plan.

PROFILE

LEARNING TASK	
Time of Day	
Intake Preference	
Social Preference	
Task Management Preference	

MY STORY SUMMARY:

Path of Discovery

Journal Entry

How do you study best for tests? How did you develop these study habits? What do you want to change, if anything, about how you prepare for an exam?

HOMEWORK

From College to University

How Studying and Testing May Differ after Transfer

As you take upper-level classes, you may find that tests and papers seem to get fewer and farther between, but their importance to the overall course is greater. Your reading load will increase and the subject matter will get more technical. You may also find yourself reading a variety of material: textbooks, journal articles, lab manuals, dissertations, novels, surveys, charts, graphs, and statistics.

Your critical thinking skills will be essential to making it through these courses. Your professors will also expect that you have strong study skills and solid test-taking strategies because they will provide few clues as to what you will be tested on and how you will be tested. This is not to say that university professors are cold and uncaring about your learning; instead, because they are concerned with pushing your abilities in terms of thinking and learning, they may have little time for helping you improve your study skills.

If you have a solid foundation of skills and strategies, then you will be successful. You will just need to monitor your progress and make adjustments as necessary. For instance, while you may not have studied with a group before, at the university, you may find that study groups are essential for covering the massive amounts of material. Your goal should be finding what works best for you and what continues to help you succeed.

From College to Career

Preparation Counts

Just as you will prepare for exams and presentations in college, you will use the same skills on the job. Time management, attention to detail, and careful preparation will be necessary to be successful in your career. Depending on your career choice, you may have to pass proficiency tests or certification exams at least once or even once a year. Failing an exam in college may not mean the end of your academic career, but failing a licensing exam or a certification test could very well be the end of your job. Thus, the stakes—and the stress—will be much higher on the job.

Although the pressure to pass will be greater, chances are good that since you have been to college and passed many tests, your test-taking skills will get you through exams on the job. In addition to reviewing the test-taking strategies that are outlined in this chapter, you should also take advantage of any test preparation seminars that your employer offers. Also, now is the time to demonstrate your ability to study with others. There is no better study group than your coworkers because they all have the same investment as you: They want to pass the exam in order to keep their jobs or advance to a higher position.

Chapter Review Questions

1. What kinds of study strategies will benefit visual, aural, read/write, and kinesthetic learners?

2. What kinds of questions can you expect to be asked on science tests? On literature tests?

3. Compare studying in a group with studying on your own. What are the benefits of both? What are the drawbacks?

4. In what ways can a student beat test anxiety?

Chapter 10 Case Scenarios

1. Sylvia's accounting professor has announced to his class that he allows students to study from old tests. In fact, he keeps a folder of previous exams in the library for students to access. One of Sylvia's classmates asks her if she wants to study for the test, and she agrees. When they meet, her classmate pulls out a copy of a test with the current semester's date on it. Sylvia questions her classmate, who says that the professor gave her a rough draft of a test that he decided not to use. When Sylvia gets to class, she recognizes every question because it is the same test that her classmate had. What should Sylvia do?

2. Ryan does not think he knows how to study well. He glided through high school without cracking open a book. Now, he is in college and taking five classes: Intermediate Algebra, Reading Improvement, Introduction to Sociology, Speech Communication, and Concepts of Health and Wellness. He is struggling through his health and math classes. What can you tell him about studying for those subjects that will help him get back on track?

3. Betty gets sweaty palms and wants to throw up each time she takes a test. She has failed classes before because she couldn't calm herself down enough to take a major test. This semester, though, Betty wants to do better because she cannot keep dropping or failing her classes. What advice can you give Betty that will help ease her fears? What can she do and what kind of help can she get so that she can be successful?

Research It Further

1. Investigate methods of cheating that have occurred with "high-stakes" testing such as licensure and college-entrance exams. Write a report about these methods and the effects that they have had on how organizations test.

2. What are the most popular ways that students study at your college? Create a questionnaire that asks students how, when, and where they study. Once you tally the results, determine whether the students at your college need a one-page reminder of how to study effectively. If you think they do, create one based on the shortcomings of their methods of studying.

3. Using the material in this chapter, create two or three games that can help students remember and understand the material.

References

Klauser, H. A. (2001). *Write it down, make it happen: Knowing what you want and getting it!* New York: Simon & Schuster.

11 Planning for Next Semester

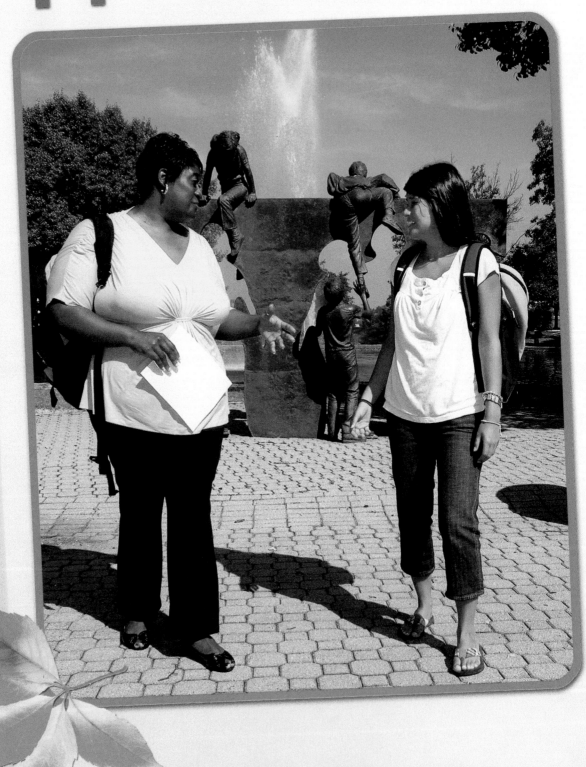

Juanita and Laura's Story

"Hey, Laura, who are you taking for world history?" asks Juanita as she squints in the bright sun outside the library. Laura pulls out a sheet of paper with her schedule for next semester. Her brightly painted nails catch the sunlight and look like twinkling stars.

"I have Dr. Franks," she says. "I interviewed him and Professor Martinsen last week to see which one would be a good fit for me." Laura takes a moment to take off her jacket and stuffs it in her backpack while Juanita checks her phone to see if her mother has called her, a daily ritual that she has been able to lessen as she has taken classes on the college campus. When Juanita was in high school, she talked to her mother four or five times a day.

"Really? I just checked out that website where you can write about your instructors. I think I want Mr. Bernstein's class. He makes you do a group project rather than take an exam—at least that is what they say about him," Juanita says.

"It's hard to get a good picture just from an Internet site, don't you think? I think you should go talk to him first. How do you know what he is like as a person?" asks Laura, frowning at her friend. Because of Laura's dyslexia, she spends much more time rewriting her notes and working on assignments than her fellow students. Getting professors that she feels comfortable with is important to her. She knows she is not as technologically savvy as the younger students, but sometimes she thinks finding things out the "old-fashioned way" is best.

"Maybe I need to find someone who can also help me with my degree plan. I am still unsure about what I want to major in. I know I am only 18, but I need to get this decided soon," Juanita says. Her phone vibrates. She has a new message, but it is from her cousin, not her mother.

"Are you still worried that your parents are going to be upset if you choose something other than engineering or medicine?" Laura asks. She feels lucky that even at her age, her mother encourages her to do what she wants.

"Probably, but now that I am 18, I guess I don't have to worry about my mom calling my advisor to tell him what I should major in," Juanita says, smiling at Laura and shading her eyes from the sun.

"I tell you what. Pick up your things and come with me. I need to go to counseling anyway. I am worried about my scholarship for next semester and I need to know, if I bomb our final in biology, what I should do," says Laura.

Juanita gathers her books and stuffs them in her backpack. She follows Laura to the campus center, hoping to get some answers to her questions about how she should plan not only her next semester, but also her life. As they walk across campus, Juanita's phone rings again, and she sees that it is her mother this time.

In This Chapter

The purpose of this chapter is to help you navigate the last few weeks of classes and to help you plan your semesters to come. As both Laura and Juanita remind us, these last weeks will be filled with decisions to make about finances and course work, but once you have successfully completed a certificate or degree program you will be able to say, "I did it!" This chapter provides information that will enable you to:

• Identify how to prepare for the end of the semester and what to expect.

• Recognize the steps for planning for next semester.

• Determine the steps to complete your education at this college or another.

• Identify methods for paying for college.

Endings and Beginnings

By the time you start reading this chapter, you should have completed most of your first semester and perhaps even have been thinking about next semester and beyond. The end of the semester is a good time to start assessing how you have done and where you want to go. Before you can begin planning for next semester, there will be some loose ends to tie up for your current semester. You should now know what to expect at the beginning of next semester, and with that additional information, you should be able to make better choices and prepare yourself for what lies ahead.

Course Evaluations

Course evaluations (sometimes called "student" evaluations because students evaluate the course and the instructor) by students are an integral part of taking a college class. Each semester you may be asked to complete an evaluation form for your instructor. The evaluations are anonymous and are not given to the instructor until grades have been posted; thus, you should feel comfortable being open and honest about the course when answering the form's questions.

The purpose of course evaluations is to provide the instructor as well as the administration with a description of how students feel about the instruction they received in the course. Some colleges look very closely at course evaluations and determine raises and promotions based in part on the scores that instructors receive. Other colleges merely use it as a discussion tool to improve the instructors' teaching. No matter how your college uses the information, you should try to be honest about your instructors' abilities. Providing constructive criticism, rather than general comments, is most helpful to the instructor.

Phrases such as "Professor Banks is not a good instructor" or "Dr. Wright is perfect" do not provide specific information that will help your instructor improve or help him or her to continue doing what you think works very well. Instead, you may want to offer comments such as "The instructor graded fairly and handed back exams in a timely manner" or "The professor rarely explained the assignments." These statements allow your instructors to pinpoint exactly what worked for you and what didn't.

Most student evaluation forms contain questions that you answer by checking a box or filling in a bubble as well as questions that you answer by writing a narrative response. Here are examples of two types of questions that you may see on a course evaluation form:

1. My instructor uses class time effectively.

   A. Strongly Agree   B. Agree   C. Strongly Disagree

2. My instructor grades fairly.

   A. Strongly Agree   B. Agree   C. Strongly Disagree

3. What can your instructor do to improve the course? _____

4. What does your instructor do well? _____

When answering questions such as these, take time to reflect on the instructor's performance during the semester. Create a list of activities that you did in class during the semester and think about them. Then, consider the overall performance of your instructor. Did he come to class on time? Was she easy to contact when you needed her? Did he act professionally? Did she seem to have a good knowledge of the subject matter? Remember that the objective of student evaluations is to provide feedback that will help instructors improve, so the more information you provide, the better.

Preparing for Final Examinations

Another traditional "ending" to the semester is final exams. Surviving "finals week" is often considered a well-earned badge of a college student. The reason that finals are so stressful for some college students is that they often carry more weight than any other tests during the semester, they contain questions about material from the entire semester, and they are all scheduled around the same time.

To help you survive finals, go back to Chapter 10 and review the material about taking tests. There are additional steps you can follow to get ready for them quickly in these final weeks of the semester. First, be sure to note the day, place, and time of each final and write it down on your calendar. Double-check this information a week before the exam. Be aware that where and when you take your finals may differ from where and when you took your classes during the semester.

A few weeks before the final, ask questions about the exam. What will you be allowed to use? What do you need to bring? What should you study? Is photo identification required? Get plenty of rest during the days that lead up to the exam. When you take the exam, use your time wisely. Final exams usually take longer to complete than regular tests, so be sure you use the entire time that you are allotted (one to three hours). Be prepared by bringing ample writing supplies and any approved items such as a calculator or dictionary.

Collaboration

Working within a group, make a list of reasons or circumstances that would prevent a student from doing well on a final exam. Then, present a list of solutions or preventive measures that would help the student complete the course successfully.

EXERCISE 11.1

Mapping a Plan for Your Educational Future

A Difference of Degrees

You probably discovered when you enrolled that community colleges offer a variety of certificate and degree options, but you may not be entirely clear about the differences between those programs. Certificate programs usually last a semester or two semesters (sometimes referred to as "one year" programs) and require about 15 to 30 credit hours. Students enroll in certificate programs either to gain skills to enter the workforce or to complete training requirements for a job. Most certificate programs are not transferable, which means they do not necessarily meet the requirements of an associate's or bachelor's degree. Instead, they usually serve a specific purpose of providing graduates with a set of skills that they can readily use on the job. If you plan to use a certificate program as a stepping-stone for an associate's or bachelor's degree, be sure that you check with the department or college (if it is not the same as the one in which you are currently enrolled) where you will complete your final degree plan. For example, if you want to complete a bachelor's degree in nursing, but you are thinking about completing a nursing certificate first, talk to an advisor in the bachelor's program to determine what, if any, courses they can take from your certificate program. Although you may choose, for personal or professional reasons, to earn a certificate first and then take additional classes to complete another degree, knowing what will be accepted and what will not can help you make the best educational decisions now.

In addition to certificate programs, community colleges offer associate of arts (A.A.), associate of science (A.S.), and associate of applied science (A.A.S.) degrees (see Table 11.1). Unlike certificate programs, an associate's degree usually requires that a student take twice as many credit hours, at least 60. Associate of arts and associate of science degrees more closely mirror the first two years of a bachelor's degree and are often transferable to a four-year university with little problem. Nonetheless, as with any degree program, always check with the institution from which you will graduate last to make sure that the classes you take for your associate's degree fulfill the requirements of the bachelor's program. Other associate degrees include associate of fine arts (A.F.A.) and associate of arts in teaching (A.A.T.).

The associate of applied science degree is different because it is a 60-hour (at least) program that is intended for students who plan on entering the workforce after graduation; it is not usually intended for students who want to transfer to complete a bachelor's degree, although some four-year universities are beginning to accept courses that are completed in this degree program. An associate of applied science in accounting degree, for example, is meant for students who want an entry-level job in bookkeeping. To earn a bachelor's degree in accounting, however, a student would earn an associate of arts degree that will fit into the bachelor of science in accounting degree at a university.

Choosing the right certificate or degree program will take some thought and discussion with college advisors, people in the career you want or already have, and your instructors. Ultimately, your career and life goals will determine which program to choose. Remember that no matter which certificate or degree you complete, you

TABLE 11.1   Program Types

Program Type	Length/Requirements	Purpose
Certificate	One semester or two; 15–30 credit hours	To obtain skills necessary for a job-related or personal goal or for direct entry into the workforce; not intended to fit into a higher degree
Associate of Applied Science	Four semesters; about 60 credit hours	To obtain knowledge and skills for direct entry into the workforce; usually not intended to fit into a higher degree
Associate of Arts/Sciences	Four semesters; about 60 credit hours	To obtain knowledge and skills for transfer to a higher degree program or for direct entry into the workforce

can always return to college at any time to continue your education. With the fluctuations in job requirements, changes in industry, and longer life spans, you may find yourself back in college again at some point in your life to learn a new skill, change your life's direction, or dabble in a hobby.

Exhibit 11.1 shows an example of a degree program that Laura may consider.

This degree plan is relatively simple to follow. However, Laura may be a little confused if she has to take prerequisites before she can take some of the courses. For example, when Laura entered college, her ACT test scores placed her below college entrance requirements; thus, she had to complete her developmental courses before she could take some of the college-level courses that are part of her degree program.

So, how does Laura plan for next semester? In her first semester, if Laura completes Introduction to College (a three-hour credit course), Developmental Reading

EXHIBIT 11.1   Degree Plan

EARLY CHILDHOOD DEVELOPMENT [THE DEPARTMENT]

Associate of Applied Science [*type of degree—usually completed in four semesters*]

Option: Early Childhood Education [*the emphasis within the degree*]

This option is for early childhood caregivers and paraprofessionals who wish to improve their skills and credentials. Early childhood curriculum is the focus. This option is also appropriate for supervisors, for curriculum coordinators, and for CDA renewal. [*description of how this degree will benefit you*]

[*Suggested schedule for each semester. It is usually not mandatory that you take the courses in the order that they suggest, unless one is a prerequisite for another.*]

FIRST SEMESTER		CREDIT HOURS
ECD 1003	Foundations of Early Childhood Education	3
ECD 1103	Child Development	3
ECD 1203	Healthy, Safe Learning Environment	3
ECD 1303	Practicum I	3
ENGL 1311	English Composition I	3
Total Credit Hours		15
SECOND SEMESTER		
ECD 2003	Child Behavior	3
ECD 2103	Preschool Curriculum, or	

(*continued*)

ECD 2403	Infant/Toddler Curriculum	3
ECD 2503	Nutrition for the Young Child	3
ECD 2303	Practicum II	3
MATH 1301	College Business Mathematics	3
Total Credit Hours		15

THIRD SEMESTER

ECD 2703	Language Arts	3
ECD 2803	Special Needs	3
ENGL 1312	English Composition II	3
PSYC 2300	Psychology and the Human Experience	3
HLSC 1304	Concepts of Lifetime Health and Wellness, or	
MUSC 2300	Introduction to Music, or	
ARTS 2300	Introduction to Visual Arts	3
Total Credit Hours		15

FOURTH SEMESTER

ECD 2903	Trends in Curriculum	3
BUS 1303	Introduction to Computers or higher-level computer course	3
SOCI 2300	Introduction to Sociology	3
SPCH 1300	Speech Communication	3
ANTH 2310	Cultural Anthropology, or	
PSYC 2300	Developmental Psychology	3
Total Credit Hours		15
Total Hours for A.A.S.		60

(receives no college-level credit), Developmental Writing (receives no college-level credit), Introduction to Sociology (a three-hour credit course), and Psychology and the Human Experience (a three-hour credit course), then she has already met two of the requirements for an associate of applied science degree in early childhood education. She would check those courses off her degree plan and start working toward the remaining courses as long as she has met the developmental requirements for them.

An example of Laura's schedule for next semester may look like the following:

ENGL 1311 English Composition I	3 hours
ECD 1103 Child Development	3 hours
ECD 1003 Foundations of Early Childhood Education	3 hours
PSYC 2300 Psychology and the Human Experience	3 hours
ECD 1203 Healthy, Safe Learning Environment	3 hours
	15 hours

If Laura takes 15 hours her second semester and 15 hours each semester after that, she still will need to take an extra semester, because in her first semester she earned only 6 hours toward her degree. Even though the early childhood associate's degree plan maps out four semesters, for some students it may take longer to complete because they need to take fewer hours per semester or they have to complete developmental classes. These are things you will need to consider as you map out your degree program.

Choosing Classes and Professors for Next Semester

Even if you have not completed your classes this semester, you can start planning for next semester. By now, you should be familiar with the college catalog and can identify the courses that you may want to take.

Just as important as what classes you take next semester is with whom you take those classes. By now, you should realize that choosing the right instructor could make the difference in how much you enjoy and learn in a class. If you have the option of choosing an instructor, then you should start talking with other students about them. Ask specific questions and ask a variety of people. Remember that each student has his or her own view of what makes a good instructor, a view that might not match your own. Questions you should ask need to move beyond the vague "Is she a good teacher?" Instead, you should ask about her teaching style, the types of assignments she gives, and how available she is during office hours. Be wary of Internet sites that rate professors. They are not reliable because anyone can post just about anything they want without regard to accuracy, or sometimes decency. There is no mechanism to keep the same people from posting multiple positive or negative comments, which can present only part of the picture.

An even better way to determine which instructors are the best for you is to talk with them before you enroll in their classes. Make an appointment with a potential instructor and ask pertinent questions: How much reading is involved? How do you teach the course? Do you require a research paper? What do you expect students to know when they complete the course? The benefits of interviewing your instructor before you sign up for the class are that you get to determine whether the instructor is a good fit with your learning style and you get to make a good impression by demonstrating your maturity and interest in your education.

Building Your Schedule

What worked this semester and what didn't? Why? What will change for you next semester? Did you have enough time in between classes? Did you waste time that could have been spent more productively? You will need to answer all of these questions before you set your schedule for next semester.

When planning your next semester (and beyond), consider four factors: how many hours you need to take, how many hours you need to work, what other obligations (planned trips for work or with family, for example) you have, and how much stress these three factors will cause.

- *Number of credit hours.* To determine how many credit hours you need to take, be sure to review your financial aid, scholarship, and degree plan information. If you are receiving financial aid, you may be required to take a full load, which often means at least 12 hours. As you can see in the previous example, Laura needed to take 15 hours each semester in order to finish her degree in four semesters. However, because she had to take developmental classes her first semester, she only met 6 hours of the required courses for her associate's degree.

- *Number of work hours.* If you will not be working next semester, you can skip this section. However, even if you are only working a few hours a week, you will need to schedule your work hours so that they do not overlap with the times you are in class. You also need to allow plenty of time to get to and from work and school. Be realistic when calculating this time and plan for delays. An accurately planned schedule will help keep your stress levels at a minimum.

- *Amount of learning support and learning opportunities.* If you know or anticipate a need for learning assistance or tutoring, be sure to build that time into your schedule. You may also need to see each of your professors on a regular basis, some more than others, which should also be a consideration when creating a schedule. If you leave little time for meeting with your instructors, it will be difficult to get the help and advice you need. Good time management and a flexible schedule will allow plenty of time for visits to the computer lab to get help with sending an attachment to an email, to the library for assistance in using the databases, and to the tutoring lab at the hours and locations that are most convenient to you.

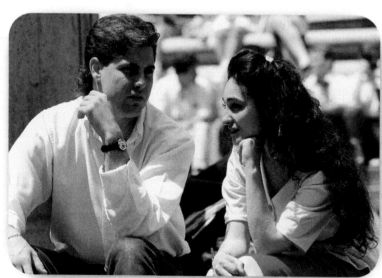

Letting others know what you plan to take next semester and how that will affect them will create less stress for you in the long run.

- *Other obligations.* Working, going to school, taking care of a family, and participating in social and community activities all require your time and energy. To balance all your activities, you will need to keep an eye on upcoming events and make sure you plan accordingly. For example, if you are thinking about registering for the fall semester and you know that you must take a weeklong trip for work in October, you should contact potential instructors to see what their policies are for missing class. Likewise, if you like to participate in your child's school activities, you will need to consider how much time you can give if you are also studying for classes.

You may find that you need to cut back on social and volunteer commitments or at least postpone them until after the semester.

- *Stress levels.* Your work schedule, course load, and other responsibilities can lead to high levels of stress. For example, if you have to take 15 hours of courses to maintain your financial aid and you have to work 40 hours to pay your bills, but you feel overwhelmed and anxious about balancing it all, then you are not likely to handle both well. If you find yourself in this situation, you will need to reconsider your plans before you get in over your head. Getting locked into a rigid schedule that doesn't allow you to drop a course that is too difficult or to decrease your hours at work will lead to frustration and high levels of negative stress.

On the other hand, you may thrive on such a schedule because you work better when you have to manage your time carefully. You may be the type of person who cannot study well if you have unlimited amounts of time to do it. If this is the case, you may feel excited about having so much activity in your schedule. Still, you could encounter a problem in which having flexibility (being able to drop a class or reducing your work hours) will help you cope. If you don't have this flexibility, then you need to pay extra attention to staying on top of your work. For example, if you find on the first day of the semester that one of your classes will be much more demanding than you had anticipated, you will need to be more careful about keeping up with assignments and managing your stress effectively. Planning ahead and managing your time will help you cope with a stressful schedule.

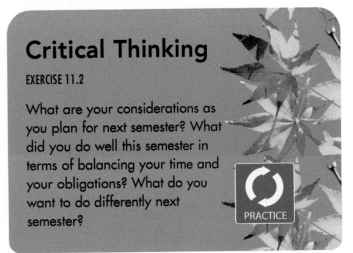

Critical Thinking
EXERCISE 11.2

What are your considerations as you plan for next semester? What did you do well this semester in terms of balancing your time and your obligations? What do you want to do differently next semester?

Troubleshooting Your Schedule

What should you do if you cannot work your schedule out despite your efforts to make it all fit together? There may be a semester in which a course you need is not offered or the class is filled before you can register. Should you throw up your hands and quit when faced with these problems? Of course not. Instead, you should take advantage of the relationships you have cultivated at college. Now is the time to talk with fellow students, instructors, and advisors. They may be able to offer solutions that you have not considered. If, however, there is an academic need for you to get into a class or rearrange your schedule, you should point that out. Some college officials are willing to bend the rules if you need one more class to complete your degree and transfer on time.

Deadlines and Dates

Once you decide on your schedule and the classes you want to take, you should take advantage of early registration periods and due dates. If there is even a small chance you will return next semester, consider registering for courses just in case. Depending on your college's policies, you should be able to drop courses by a certain date without penalty, and it will be easier to drop classes than build a schedule from classes that are still open. In addition to being aware of registration periods, take note of payment due dates. Some colleges require that you pay soon after you register, even if that means paying for tuition and fees a few months in advance. If you do not pay on time, your classes may be dropped, and you will have to start all over right before the new semester, which could mean that you don't get the classes for which you originally registered.

Mapping a Plan for Your Financial Future

Paying for College

When thinking about your financial future, most likely paying for college will be at the top of your list. Even if you have a solid plan for paying tuition, fees, and books, it will be worth your time to investigate other methods in case your current one falls through. Despite what many think about the costs of college, community college tuition is a real bargain and perhaps one of the reasons that you enrolled. Regardless of where you choose to go to school, it is likely that you will need to decide how you will pay for the costs you incur.

Scholarships

Winning a scholarship is by far the most rewarding way (financially and psychologically) to pay for college because it is literally free money—you don't have to pay it back. There are thousands of scholarships out there for needy and accomplished students. All you have to do is find them. To find the ones that match your profile, you will need to get the word out that you are looking. Talking with friends, family, employers, and college officials is a great way to start the process. They may know of obscure scholarships that will fit your needs perfectly.

Another way to get information about scholarships is to talk with the financial aid officers and counselors at your college. They have access to and knowledge of scholarships that fit the college's student profiles such as single-parent and transfer scholarships that will pay your tuition and fees at a four-year university. Other effective methods for finding scholarships are to investigate sources at your library and search the Internet. Searching print and Web-based databases will provide you with more than enough information; the only problem will be narrowing your focus.

Whatever information about scholarships you find—whether it's in books, in counselors' offices, or on the Internet—don't pay for it. Some services claim to match your qualifications with scholarship qualifications but charge a fee to do so. You can get free help from high school and college counselors as well as libraries and Internet searches. No reputable scholarship service will require that you pay a fee to apply, and very few scholarship services will require payment. The website FinAid! (www.finaid.org) provides information about different types of financial aid for college students as well as tips for avoiding scholarship services scams. According to this site, any service that guarantees to match you with a scholarship or that offers you an award that you did not apply for is likely to be a scam. Many colleges recommend www.fastweb.com as a great starting point for finding scholarships that match your accomplishments.

Grants

By definition, grants are financial assistance that does not need to be paid back. A common federal grant is the Pell grant, which can be awarded for full-time or part-time enrollment. To determine your eligibility, talk with your financial aid counselor or visit any of the various websites that provide government information about financial aid. When you research Pell grants, you will find that there is a limit to the amount of the award ($4,310 in 2007–2008) and that your college will receive the money and then disburse it to you once classes start. Because of recent federal requirements about grants and student loans, colleges may wait several weeks before paying students. If you are expecting to receive your grant the first day or week of classes, you should make alternative arrangements to pay bills (including your bookstore bill).

Another type of grant that a student can receive is the Federal Supplemental Educational Opportunity Grant (FSEOG), which is available to those who demonstrate an exceptional need. According to the U.S. Department of Education (2008), the difference between a Pell grant and an FSEOG is that "each participating school will receive enough money to pay the federal Pell grants of its eligible students. There's no guarantee every eligible student will be able to receive an FSEOG." The procedure for receiving an FSEOG is similar to that for receiving a Pell grant; your eligibility will determine the amount that you receive, and your college will disburse the money to you after the semester begins.

In addition to payment schedules, you will need to maintain good academic standing at your college to remain eligible to receive grant money. If you apply for a grant, be sure to make note of the minimum GPA that you must have in order to ensure your eligibility to receive future grant money. One last tip for continuing to receive grant funding: Make sure that you adhere to the college's attendance policy. As stated in Chapter 1, you may be penalized (and lose your grant funding or have to pay it back) for missing too many classes or for dropping a class. As always, check with your financial aid officer to make sure that you clearly understand the expectations for receiving grants.

Student Loans

In the event that you are not eligible for grants, you should investigate student loans. The idea of taking out a loan to attend college makes many students shudder with fear because they don't want the added pressure that they must pay back what they borrow. If you can avoid a student loan, then by all means do so. However, receiving a student loan sometimes makes more financial sense in the long run.

Federal student loans typically charge low interest and can be paid back over 10 years. For families that would otherwise have to deplete their savings or borrow against retirement or their mortgages to pay for college, a low-interest student loan is a good option. Most loan programs allow you to defer payment (but you may accumulate interest) until after you graduate, or you can sometimes defer payment if you remain unemployed after you graduate.

One type of federal loan is the Stafford loan, which comes in subsidized and unsubsidized versions. A subsidized loan is one in which the government pays the interest for you while you are in college. Once you graduate and start making payments on your loan, you will accrue interest as well. The government does not make interest payments for an unsubsidized loan; however, you may, instead, pay the interest while you are in college (usually a small amount), or you can wait until after you graduate to make any payments, but your interest will be capitalized. In other words, the interest will be added to the principal amount of the loan, which makes your monthly payments higher.

A federal Perkins loan is a loan between you and your college. The Perkins loan allows you to borrow $4,000 per year up to $20,000 for 5 years, and you don't have to repay it until 9 months after you graduate or drop below at least part-time status.

One benefit of a Perkins loan is that you may be able to cancel up to 100 percent of the debt if you meet certain criteria. For example, upon graduation, if you choose to teach in a "teacher shortage" area or if you serve as a full-time nurse, you may be eligible for cancellation of your loan.

PLUS, which stands for Parent Loan for Undergraduate Students, is another method of receiving money to help pay for college. If you are fortunate enough to have parents willing to take out a loan to help you pay for college, a PLUS is a possible option. To qualify, you must be a dependent student, which means your parents support you financially. A PLUS can be provided by the government or by private lenders. Parents who take out a PLUS are usually trying to make up the difference between the cost of tuition and the financial aid package that their children receive. Nonetheless, it is the parents who are ultimately responsible for repaying the loan, which can be as early as 60 days after they receive it.

Reflection

EXERCISE 11.3

What are your options for paying for college? Do you have a backup plan if your current plan falls through? If so, what is your backup plan? What other options are open to you?

PRACTICE

Military and Veterans Financial Aid

Being a member of the military can be especially helpful when you are paying for college. There are numerous benefits for active members and veterans as well as their dependents. To find out about military benefits, talk with a financial aid officer. If you have served in the military, you may want to contact a local service branch for more information as well.

Work-Study

Work-study is a program that allows students to earn money while they work on campus. The reason it is called "work-study" is that the job may allow for you to study when you work, but most work-study positions are similar to office assistants and will

INTEGRITY MATTERS

Student loans, because they charge low interest and have a long-term payment plan, are often a good way to pay for college if you do not have the financial means to do so otherwise. However, there are serious consequences if you do not pay them back when you are required to do so. Defaulting on student loans can make you ineligible for future federal aid and can have negative consequences on your credit rating. Before you sign to receive a student loan, be sure that you have a plan to pay it back after you graduate. And if you find yourself unable to make a payment after your loan payments become due, notify your lender immediately. Sometimes, the lender can work out a repayment plan for you if you have an unusual hardship.

keep you busy for the majority of the time you work. To work in such a program, you must be eligible for federal work-study money, and you will be limited to a certain number of hours you can work per week. Not everyone who is eligible for work-study will be able to find a position on campus, however. Each department and area of the college advertises, hires, and manages work-study positions; sometimes, hiring can be competitive. There may be specific requirements (such as computer skills) that a candidate must meet before being hired. Because some positions require working with students' personal information, work-study students must also abide by the college's privacy standards.

The benefits of participating in work-study are that you can earn some money that will help pay your expenses and you will be able to work closely with college employees. By getting to know professors and administrators better—and by working for them—you may have access to valuable advice and information. To investigate whether work-study is available for you, talk with your financial aid officer. He or she will review your eligibility and help you apply for on-campus employment.

Tuition Waivers for Employees

Another source of financial help is your employer. Large corporations sometimes offer financial assistance for employees, although there may be stipulations that you work for a certain amount of time after graduation. If your employer doesn't offer scholarships to employees, you should still ask if he or she is interested in doing so; employers will benefit from employees who further their education. Finally, your college may offer tuition waivers for its full-time employees. Some students take jobs offered at colleges so that they can take classes for free or at a reduced cost. If you need a part-time or full-time job while you are in school, you may want to check out the openings at your community college.

Applying for Financial Aid

Each college is different in how it handles the application process, but it is worth talking generally about what to expect when applying for financial aid. Even if you have applied and received financial aid for this academic year, there may be some information that you need to know before applying again. The first step in the process is obtaining a Free Application for Federal Student Aid (FAFSA), which can be picked up from the financial aid office of your college or can be accessed online (http://www.fafsa.ed.gov/). Financial aid applications must be renewed each academic year; the time line for receiving aid for a year starts in August and ends in July. Thus, if you applied for financial aid in November and received it for classes that started in January, you will have until July to use that aid; then you will need to reapply for aid for the fall semester.

As part of the FAFSA application process, you will need to determine whether you are considered "independent" or "dependent." The federal government defines a student as being independent if he or she meets certain criteria such as being married, being born before 1981, or having both parents deceased. Students who fit the definition for dependent status, but who have extenuating circumstances, may be able to request that their status be changed to independent. In addition to determining your ability to pay for college, you will also be asked to provide an Estimated

Family Contribution (EFC) amount; for example, if you receive child support payments or Social Security payments, you will have to report that income as part of your EFC. One other consideration when applying for financial aid is that each year a certain percentage of loan applications get identified for verification. This means that student financial aid applications may take longer to process because of the requirements of verification.

Renewing Financial Aid and Paying It Back

In order to continue to receive financial aid, you will need to make sure that you understand and follow the requirements of your college. Many colleges maintain a satisfactory academic policy that states you will need to stay enrolled in a certain number of credit hours and maintain a certain grade point average to continue to receive grants and loans. Sometimes, the required GPA is higher than the GPA to remain in college. For example, you may have to maintain a 2.7 GPA to continue to receive financial aid, whereas you have to maintain a 2.0 GPA to stay in college. If you do not meet the requirements for a semester, your college may place you on financial aid probation, which means you must meet the college's requirements for the next semester to be removed from probation. The next step after probation can be suspension from financial aid. This means that you may not be able to receive financial aid, but you may still be able to enroll in classes as long as you pay for them yourself. Just in case your suspension is the result of extenuating circumstances, some colleges have an appeals process for financial aid suspension. This means you may file an appeal and appear before a group of people who will determine if you can reapply for financial aid.

Whenever you apply for loans, you will need to consider how you will pay them back after you complete your degree or when you stop attending college. Student loan default is a common problem nationwide, and there are stiff penalties for failing to pay back the federal government. On the other hand, loan forgiveness programs are often available for students who major in fields that are in high demand in their community. To find out more about these types of programs, be sure to talk to someone in the financial aid office at your college.

Creating a Budget

Whether or not you rely on financial aid to pay your tuition bills, creating a budget will help you meet your financial and personal goals. A budget doesn't have to be a headache. In fact, it is relatively easy to create a budget. The hard part is following it. First, you need to create a customized budget sheet. Table 11.2 shows a sample budget form that you can start with. In the first column, you will estimate your income and your expenses. The middle column will be used to record your actual amounts of income and expenses. Record any differences in the marked column by subtracting the actual amount from the estimated amount. For example, if you estimate that you earn about $1,000.00 a month, but this month, you earn $1,092.56, your difference is $92.56. If you earned $997.36, then the difference is −$2.64.

Once you determine the categories that fit your lifestyle, you will need to gather all the bills and paystubs that you have and add up your expenses and income. It is a good idea to review at least three months' worth of bills to get an accurate picture

TABLE 11.2   Sample Budget Form

Category	Estimated Amount per Month	Actual Amount per Month	Difference
Income			
Source 1 (wages/salary)			
Source 2 (scholarship, financial aid, etc.)			
Source 3 (alimony, employee tuition reimbursement, child support)			
Total Income			
Expenses			
Mortgage/rent			
Utilities			
Car payment/transportation			
Insurance			
Groceries			
Household items			
Clothing			
Gas			
Car maintenance			
Cell phone/pager			
Eating out			
Entertainment			
Health care (medications, doctor's visits, etc.)			
Credit cards or loans			
Total Expenses			
Net Income (Total Income minus Total Expenses)			

of your expenditures. If you have any bills that are paid less frequently than once a month, then you will need to convert them to a monthly expense. For example, if you pay $240 for car insurance every six months, your monthly expense is $40 ($240 divided by six months).

One key to an accurate budget that helps you track your spending is to be honest about your expenses. That means you must write down everything you spend, even the money you spend on snacks or supplies. You may find that you spend $25 a week ($100 a month) on items that are unnecessary. The more you can track unnecessary items, the better you can control your spending.

After you get an accurate picture of your income and expenses, you can start setting short-term and long-term financial goals. Because you are in college and probably trying to keep expenses to a minimum, you may think that creating and working toward financial goals will be a difficult undertaking until you have a job with a steady income and secure future. However, you can start setting small, short-term goals now. For example, your first short-term goal could be keeping a monthly budget and making adjustments periodically. Another short-term goal could be to gather all the documents about your financial aid and keep them organized until after you graduate. Meeting these two goals will help you reach larger goals down the road.

You should also write down your long-term financial goals. One of these goals could be financial freedom and security. However, in order to reach that long-term goal, you will need to make a list of other goals and start working toward them. Be sure to include in your long-term goals ones that prepare you for retirement and the unlikely event of disability and unemployment.

Credit Cards

Credit cards can be very tempting when you are in college because they are so easy to use and the offers pour in just about every day. The reality of credit cards, however, is that they can cause big financial problems, ones that are sometimes difficult to pay off. Think about this: You don't want to start a new career after college that pays a good salary only to send a substantial portion of it to a credit card company. While it may seem easy, try to avoid paying your college tuition with a credit card. The interest rate will be more than double (possibly even five times higher) than you can get with a student loan. Additionally, avoid as many unnecessary expenses as you can. Use the rule that if it is not vital to your life, then it can wait until you have the cash—even if it is a one-of-a-kind, super-duper deal.

In case you are still enticed to use a credit card, think about this sobering information. If you were to charge $1,000 on a credit card that charges 17% interest and you only pay $100 a month, you will be accruing more in interest than you will be paying each month. And that is only if you do not charge anything else!

Table 11.3 shows that paying twice as much—$200—each month for six months only reduces the balance by $276.21—after paying $1,200. Unfortunately, some students have many more thousands of dollars of credit card debt, and with

TABLE 11.3 Credit Card Payments

Month	Previous Balance	Interest	Balance + Interest	Payment	Remaining Balance
Month 1	$1,000	$170	$1,170	$200	$970
Month 2	$970	$164.90	$1,134.90	$200	$934.90
Month 3	$934.90	$158.93	$1,093.83	$200	$893.83
Month 4	$893.83	$151.91	$1,045.78	$200	$845.78
Month 5	$845.78	$143.78	$ 989.56	$200	$789.56
Month 6	$789.56	$134.23	$ 923.79	$200	$723.79

the current interest rates, it is no wonder that students can find themselves in an endless cycle of charging and paying minimums. If it is at all possible, put the cards away until you are out of college, and then use them wisely.

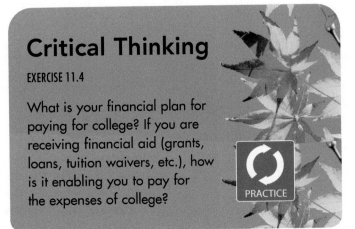

Critical Thinking

EXERCISE 11.4

What is your financial plan for paying for college? If you are receiving financial aid (grants, loans, tuition waivers, etc.), how is it enabling you to pay for the expenses of college?

PRACTICE

What if College Isn't for You?

There is tremendous pressure on those who do not have higher degrees to get them. Frequently high school students hear this pitch from parents, counselors, and teachers: Success in life depends on obtaining a college degree. People who have been in the workforce know, as well, that a college degree can be the difference between doing the same job until retirement and being promoted.

But does everyone need to go to college? College is a great place to continue your education and to make your career dreams a reality. There are also indirect benefits to pursuing higher education, such as improving your health and financial well-being because you know more about yourself and the world around you. Nonetheless, going to college is not the only key to success. There are many vibrant, intelligent, successful people who have not completed a college degree.

How will you know if college is not right for you? It may be difficult to tell, but you shouldn't quit going if you are unsure. The best way to discover how you feel about being in college is to ask yourself a series of questions. Then, talk about your responses with a college counselor, advisor, or trusted friend who can give you good advice.

- Who wants me to be in college?
- Do *I* want to be in college?
- How do I feel when I am in class?
- How do I feel when I am studying?
- How do I feel after I take an exam?
- What do I want to major in? Why?
- What do I want to do with my life? Do I need a college degree to do it?
- What do I value about higher education? What can it do for me?
- What is my passion?

Take your time answering these questions. You may find that your discomfort about being in college is really fear about a new beginning and the unknown. Being apprehensive about a new program or a new environment is perfectly normal and does not necessarily indicate that you are not right for college.

On the other hand, you may know very clearly that you do not want to be in college at this point in your life. College may not be right for you *right now,* which means that you should consider returning when you are certain it will be your top priority. Many people put off going or returning to college. One of the benefits of waiting is that when you return you will be more mature and more responsible, which means you will be more likely to complete your degree.

PLUS

(Personality + Learning Style = Understanding Situations)

Think about Juanita's dilemma regarding which instructor to take next semester and what degree plan to follow. Juanita is an independent learner and is usually shy. Because she still lives at home, although she is 18, she feels some obligation to consider her parents' opinions about her future. Using what you have learned from this chapter, what advice would you give her? How can she gain confidence in mapping her future for herself?

Now, considering your own learning style, personality type, and special circumstances, what would you do to choose the right classes, professors, and degree plan if you were unsure of what to take, from whom to take it, and how to choose the right major?

PROFILE

MY STORY
Learning Plan

Directions: Using what you have learned in this chapter and what you know about your learning preferences, choose a task or assignment that needs to be completed soon and create a learning plan that will help you accomplish this task. Then, write your *My Story* Summary, a one-sentence synopsis that crystallizes your newly created plan.

LEARNING TASK	
Time of Day	
Intake Preference	
Social Preference	
Task Management Preference	

MY STORY SUMMARY:

Path of Discovery

What degrees are you interested in pursuing?
Why do these degree plans appeal to you?

From College to University

Preparing for Unexpected Higher Costs

It is very likely that you will see a change in college costs when you transfer to a university. You may be paying twice as much for tuition at the four-year school as you did at your local community college. In addition to tuition, you may see added fees that you didn't have at your community college: fees for athletic facility use, sporting events, campus organizations, and labs are possible additional expenses. Be sure to read the college catalog carefully and add the fees to the cost per credit hour to get an accurate picture of what you will be spending per class.

Despite the increase in tuition and fees, you may notice that your bookstore expenses stay the same. Although the price of books can be a significant portion of your overall college expenses, it is unlikely that you will experience an increase in cost. However, upper-level science and computer classes require weighty textbooks and additional software. These books can cost as much as $100. Multiply that by four classes, and you will be paying at least $400 for the semester. An advantage, however, to transferring to a larger school is that there are more people from whom you can buy used books. Take notice of special discounts for used books in the bookstore and look for flyers on bulletin boards that announce books for sale.

From College to Career

The Benefits of Returning to Work Before Continuing Your Education

There may be a time when you must interrupt your college career to return to your job full-time. Balancing financial and educational goals may be too difficult to handle at the moment, which may mean that your financial needs take precedence. If this happens to you, there are some ways of dealing with the transition back to the world of work while still keeping your eye on returning to college.

First, realize that going back to work doesn't have to be forever. Just because you are unable to return for more than one semester doesn't mean you never will. Be sure to talk with your employer about your desire to get a degree. You may be surprised by his or her support of your goals. There may even be financial assistance for employees who take college classes. Remember to talk with your family and friends about your need to further your education as well. Someone may be willing to help you with finances, scheduling, and family duties. Set a time line for returning to college. If you need to work a semester to earn more money to pay for tuition, then be sure to keep up with registration periods and college announcements.

Finances will be another consideration, so be sure to save your money. Even if expenses were not the reason you returned to work, putting aside money in a "college fund" will make it easier to re-enroll in college. You won't have any excuses for not being able to afford the increased costs. Look for scholarships and financial aid for working adults. Some states are creating grant programs for nontraditional students who work full-time in order to increase the number of college graduates in their states. Finally, keep connected with former classmates and instructors. If you are aware of what is going on at the college, you are more likely to return because you will feel as though you had never left.

Chapter Review Questions

1. What activities will you participate in at the end of the semester and why are they important?
2. What should you consider when planning your degree?
3. What should you consider when you plan to transfer to another college or university?
4. What are the different methods of paying for college?

Chapter 11 Case Scenarios

1. Anja is considering transferring to the university nearby after she graduates with her associate's degree. She is very nervous and is not sure what she needs to do to plan a successful move once she completes her degree. What advice would you give her about making the move and getting involved in the transition now?

2. Ramielle has paid for her first semester of tuition from her savings, but she is looking for other ways to pay for the rest of her college. She doesn't qualify for any grants and is not sure what her options are. Explain to her what choices she has to pay for college without incurring too much debt.

3. Riley has had a difficult time getting used to the expectations in college. He has not had a successful semester so far, and he is getting pressure at work to quit college and take a promotion. It means more money, but less time to get the degree that he wants. He could always come back, he knows, but at 25 years old, he is afraid that if he doesn't go to college now, it will be even harder when he earns a bigger paycheck. What would you tell him about quitting college?

Research It Further

1. As an individual, or within a group, research the qualifications and requirements for the different loans and grants that your college offers. With the information, create a one-page sheet for each type of financial aid that can help students remember the differences between each type.
2. Investigate the entrance requirements of two four-year universities in your area. Find out GPA requirements, available types of scholarships and financial aid, and what kinds of degree programs they offer. Make a brief presentation to your class.

3. What, if any, alumni services does your college offer? If they offer very few or none at all, brainstorm a list of ideas that you would like to see implemented and present them to an administrator at your institution who can give you feedback on what is possible. Then, report to your class on which suggestions can be implemented and which cannot.

Reference

U.S. Department of Education. (2008). Types of federal student aid. Retrieved 14 May 2008, from http://studentaid.ed.gov/students/publications/student_guide/2006–2007/ english/typesofFSA_grants.htm

12 Preparing for a Career and a Life

Evan and Michael's Story

The big red arrow points to the ballroom. The smell of popcorn fills the large space, and red balloons wave back and forth when students walk through the double doors. Evan and Michael feel as though they have walked into a carnival instead of a career fair.

"Hey, Michael. Did you see that clown in the corner juggling bananas?" Evan asks.

"Where?" Michael asks as his head swivels around to find what he has missed.

Evan bends forward, places his hands on his chest, and starts laughing.

"All right, all right. You got me," Michael says, softly punching Evan in the shoulder.

Instead of people with red rubber noses and big shoes, there are dozens of booths inviting students to leave their résumés and learn more about a variety of local and national businesses and industries. The only jugglers are students who are picking up flyers, business cards, and chocolate candy from the bowls on each table.

Fresh from class, in jeans and a golf shirt, Evan stops to pick up a piece of candy. "I'm planning on going to all the booths. Are you?" Evan asks.

Michael has done a little research and knows the two booths he wants to visit. He runs his fingers down his pressed pants and checks his crisp dress shirt for any spot for the tenth time since he put it on this morning.

"No," he says, "I plan on finding the two companies I checked out on the Internet last night. The plan is simple: Introduce myself, tell 'em what I know about the open positions, and leave them my résumé."

"Man, aren't you afraid you will be cutting yourself short? Shouldn't you hit every one of the booths just in case? You can't be *that* sure of what you want to be when you grow up," Evan asks in rapid fire.

"I don't know. I guess with all my time in the military, I have a lot of experience doing different jobs. I definitely know what I *don't* want to do," Michael replies. "Besides, I am applying for that internship at the nursing home. My advisor says I will learn a little something about the nursing field and get to know some people."

"But there are so many options," Evan says. "How do I know that I am going to make a lot of money with whatever I choose? I don't want to waste any time doing something that will get me nowhere."

"Well, what degree can you earn that will get you a job that pays well?" asks Michael.

"That's my problem. I don't quite know. I mean I know what I like to study, but how do I know that is going to get me a job where I don't have to wear a coat and tie?" Evan says.

"I am certain you won't be landing any jobs like that the way you are dressed today!" Michael replies. He slaps Evan on the back and laughs.

Evan looks down at his jeans, and shrugs his shoulder when he notices a spot on the left leg. He pulls out 30 copies of his résumé from his backpack and starts with the booth near the door.

"Watch this! They will all remember Evan," he says. He strolls to the first table and introduces himself.

"I am Evan. It is a pleasure to meet you," he says to the woman representing an aeronautics firm. He gives her a firm handshake and a broad smile.

"So, tell me what your company does and what I would do if I worked for you," Evan says. The woman pulls Evan closer and shows him photos of aircraft interiors.

Michael walks straight to one of the two healthcare companies at the fair. Because his girlfriend works in healthcare, he already knows what he needs to do to get a good entry-level job. He also knows how to progress in the field.

"Here goes nothing," Michael says to himself. He looks over his shoulder to see that Evan is working his way down the line of booths and wonders if he should do the same.

In This Chapter

Deciding where you want to go and what you want to do, as both Michael and Evan demonstrate, can be characterized by uncertainty. After reading this chapter, you will have a better understanding of your choices *after* you have taken courses at your community college. Even though you have just begun your journey toward a certificate or a degree, you may want to keep in mind your options and the different paths you can take. Ideally, you should read this chapter thoroughly and then refer to it as you complete each semester, ensuring that you are on the right track and reminding yourself of the different choices you have.

Once you complete this chapter, you should be able to

- List your options after you complete your degree.
- Discuss the steps in transferring.
- Recognize the elements of a good cover letter and résumé.
- Identify career services at your college and in your community.

Time to Move Forward

Why should you be concerned about what you will be doing after you graduate or transfer from your community college? The answer is simple: Although it may seem as if it will be an eternity before you complete your education, the time will go by quickly. If you have one eye on the future and what you want to do after college, you can make wiser choices while you are there. Therefore, it is a good idea to take some time to envision what life *after* college will be like for you.

Although there are many options open to you once you graduate from a community college, this chapter focuses on three possibilities of "life after college," some of which may overlap: transferring to a four-year university, joining (or rejoining) the workforce as a graduate, and becoming involved in the community as an ambassador for the benefits of higher education.

Reflection   EXERCISE 12.1

What four questions do you have about your future? What can you do to find answers to your questions?

PRACTICE

Deciding to Transfer

Neither Evan nor Michael is considering a four-year degree right now, but they both may be interested in returning to school to get more education down the line. Even if you do not plan to earn a four-year degree any time soon, it is never too early to begin thinking about transferring to a four-year university. You should have noticed that the end of each chapter in this book has a section called "From College to University," which focuses on issues in transferring to a four-year university. Those sections provide you with specific information that will help you cope with the move, if you decide to do it. When you do transfer, you may want to review those sections. The following information will help you prepare to transfer. Your first step is talk to counselors and professors at both schools well before you graduate from your community college and enroll in another school. They will be able to advise you about the details of transferring, from getting your transcripts sent over to choosing a major and degree plan.

Before you make any decisions about continuing your education at a four-year university, you should start searching for one that meets your needs. If you have several in your area, then your best bet is to start looking at their degree programs, their student population, and their tuition—to name a few considerations. First, you should request a catalog from each university and take note of the requirements for admission (they may be a little different from your community college's admission standards), their basic classes (to compare with what you have already taken), and their financial aid and student services. Once you have narrowed your search to a few viable options, you should consider visiting the campuses. Before you visit, call and make appointments with the department chair, admissions counselor, and financial aid officer. If you have time, write a list of questions to ask when talking to these individuals.

When you are on the campuses, check out the layout of the buildings and take note of the differences you see between your community college and the universities. Getting familiar with the campus you will attend will keep you from getting confused—or from being late—during the first few days after you transfer. Figure out where student parking, the library, the bookstore, and the student union are located. If you have time to wander around the campus, look for notices on the bulletin boards of student organizations that pertain to your interests and majors. You may find that the college you are visiting has strong membership in an important career club. Those kinds of extracurricular activities can be as beneficial as a program with a good reputation in the community.

Another consideration when transferring is the acceptance of the courses you have taken. Articulation agreements ensure that students can complete degree requirements at one college and can transfer smoothly to another institution and have their courses credited. Your community college may have articulation agreements with universities in the area, which means you can complete an associate's degree and then transfer as a junior to complete your four-year degree. A benefit of an articulation agreement is that you don't have to worry about matching community college courses exactly with their counterparts at the four-year university. Instead, you can concentrate on completing the requirements needed for a two-year degree, and then move straight into upper-level courses at a university without having to retake basic courses. It is always wise to check articulation agreements between the institutions; knowing ahead of time that you need to take a few more classes because they won't transfer will reduce your stress once you get there.

Preparing to Make the Leap to a Four-Year University

If you have made the decision to transfer and are getting yourself prepared for the change, here are some tips for transferring. Use them as a checklist once you have made the decision to continue your education.

- Request a catalog from the transfer school. Read through it carefully and write down any questions about the courses you need to take to complete a degree.
- Apply for financial aid early. Your transfer school may have earlier deadlines to complete financial aid forms.
- Explore the possibility of transfer scholarships. Talk with counselors and financial aid officers at both institutions for possibilities. If you have chosen a major, talk to the department's chair about tuition assistance for majors. Some programs provide financial aid to entice people to major in a certain field.

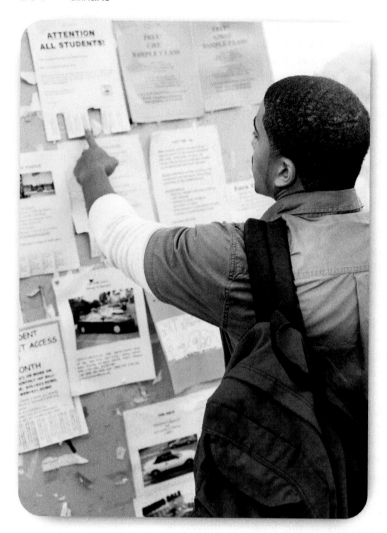

- Request that your transcript be sent to your transfer school after graduation.
- Request that your transfer school evaluate your transcript when they receive it.
- Ask for recommendation letters, if they are needed, as soon as possible.
- Take note of student organizations, honor societies, and activities that could help you network in your field.
- Get involved as soon as you can.

Making that move from a community college to a four-year university is a big step, but it is no more difficult than the step you took to start school. With some help from your family and friends, you can make that leap.

Going to Work

For those who are not moving from one school to another, graduation from a community college means getting into or back into the workforce. Even if you have been working the entire time you are taking classes, it is still a good idea to review the process for finding and getting the job you want.

When planning your college budget, it may be worth your time to investigate part-time work, internships, and other opportunities.

Career Values and Goals

Before you begin delving into the resources and services available at your college, take some time to reflect on what your career values and goals are. They may not be much different from the ones you recorded when you read Chapter 2. However, it is worth considering what you value in a career and what kinds of experiences you want to have. For example, do you value working with others in projects with strict deadlines or would you prefer to work alone with little supervision? Your answer to that question and others can help you determine what you value and what careers work best for you. If, for instance, you have a strong interest in writing, but you prefer working with others, you may decide to choose a career that has many opportunities for collaboration when writing.

In addition to considering your values as they relate to your career, you may also want to consider what your career goals are—it is never too soon to think about them! For example, is your goal to move up quickly in a company or to find a business that will allow you to indulge in one of your values, to travel and meet a diverse group of people? When you create clear, realistic, and reachable career goals, your values will inform what you write down or tell others. Your values and goals will also help you talk with a career counselor, search for a job, and interview.

If you are not sure where to start when considering your career values and goals, then you may want to check out the various career assessment programs, such as DISCOVER or Kuder, at your career counseling center.

Career Counseling

Long before you think about graduating and finding a career, you should visit the career counselors at your college. Preparing for a career takes longer than a few weeks, and the more planning you do, the smoother the process will be. Each college offers different services in its career center, but most provide access to interest inventories, which can help you pinpoint the careers that best suit you. Most career services also provide "career libraries" that include information about different types of careers, their responsibilities, and their pay potential. In addition, career centers may offer help with writing a cover letter and résumé and tips on interviewing for a job. Evan could spend some time in his college's career library to learn more about careers before he visits all of the employers at the career fair.

Don't forget that your professors can also be great career counselors because they often have connections with people in the field (or have friends or relatives working in different industries). You never know when your welding instructor may have a contact at an accounting firm or a biology instructor may have a connection with the human resources department at an advertising firm. Tell professors what you want to do as a career whenever you have a chance. They may be likely to remember you and your goals when they meet someone in your field of study.

Résumés

Another part of career counseling is résumé preparation; you may be able to attend a workshop on how to write an effective résumé. There are two parts to an effective résumé: the résumé and the cover letter. A résumé is a page or two that lists your qualifications and accomplishments. A cover letter, on the other hand, provides information to a specific person that highlights your strengths that may not be apparent in your résumé. Both should be printed on high-quality paper using a good printer. A résumé, as well as any other document you send to a potential employer, should be carefully proofread for errors.

When writing a résumé, the first thing you will include is your name, address, phone number, and email address. Make sure your voicemail has an appropriate message on it and that your email is professional as well: ejcantu@abcmail.com is preferred over bananafreak72@chunkymonkey.com. Double check that there are no errors in your address, phone number, or email address—one number or letter off can cost you an interview because you won't get the message. Michael's résumé contains a new email address to replace his more personal one that he uses for friends and family, because he wants to separate career email from more casual correspondence.

A successful résumé will also contain a clear objective, or statement that tells others what your career goals are. Think of it as a mini–mission statement for your career! Objectives are not always written in a complete sentence. For example, your objective may be "To join an aircraft maintenance team at a highly rewarding company" or "To use my knowledge and skills to manage employees in the retail industry effectively." Writing a good objective takes time and consideration, and you may need to develop more than one if you plan to apply for different types of jobs or jobs in different industries. At least, be sure that your objective matches the job for which you are applying. If, for example, your objective says that you want "To have a fulfilling career working with infants and toddlers in an accredited daycare center" and you are applying to teach classes at a nursing home, then you may not get a second glance, much less an interview. Counselors and professors can help you craft an appropriate objective as you build your résumé.

EXHIBIT 12.1   Sample Résumé Entry

2006–2008   Dental Assistant   No Worry Dental Group   Tacoma, WA

- Cleaned clients' teeth and identified problem areas.
- Took X-rays of clients' teeth and updated their charts.
- Provided guidance for preventing tooth decay and improving gum health.

Once you include an appropriate objective, you will need to include information about your educational accomplishments and job history. If you have not completed your degree at this point, you can write down the anticipated date: "Associate of Arts, May 2010." Be sure to include any other certificates or degrees that you have earned. The most recently earned certificate or degree should be listed first. Information about your work history may be placed either before or after the information about your education. Again, list most recent job first and include the date you worked, your position title, the name of the company and location, and a list of bulleted items of job responsibilities. Exhibit 12.1 is a very basic format for reporting your work experience on a résumé. Depending on what kind of format you use, the order of the information may vary.

For community college students in particular, the first few parts of a résumé are easy to complete. Many students have previous or current work experience and know what educational experiences they have. However, the part of the résumé that is sometimes more difficult is listing extracurricular activities, organizations, or awards. If you are early in your college career, you may not feel as though you have been able to participate in extracurricular activities that would help you add to your list of accomplishments. Nonetheless, with just a little creative thinking, you may be able to create a list of activities and endeavors. For instance, if you received a college scholarship, you can list it as an award. If you volunteer regularly with your child's school, you can list it. If you have participated in a fundraising event, organized a community meeting, coached a sport, or sat on a committee at your church or synagogue, you can list it. You may not realize all the ways you have been involved with others that can show that you have other interests than college and work.

Your college will also provide you with future opportunities to add to a résumé, so be sure to keep your eyes and ears open for chances to participate in a one-day event or a semester-long program. The key is to get involved at any level and record your involvement so that you can remember it when you need to develop your résumé. Here are just a few opportunities for students to get involved that colleges often provide:

- Dean's List or President's List for specified grade point averages
- Student ambassadors' organization for promoting the college in the community
- Student Government Association for representing the voice of students
- Honor societies for community colleges such as Phi Theta Kappa as well as honor societies for specific disciplines such as Sigma Kappa Delta, an English honor society
- Special events such as fundraisers, cultural events, political or community rallies, and celebrations

One last part of the résumé that you will want to include is a list of references or a statement that says references are available upon request. As you meet people in college, you may want to create a list of potential references. A professor whom you got to know well, your advisor whom you see each semester as you plan your degree, or a campus official with whom you have worked closely on a project are good candidates for letters of recommendation or references. People you have worked with—either on the job or through a community project—are other excellent possibilities for references. Make sure these people know you well enough to speak of your strengths and potential in the workplace. Getting their permission before you list them is essential to getting a good reference.

Exhibit 12.2 is an example of a résumé showing one way you can list the information. There are many ways to grab an employer's attention, and résumé books will provide you with examples of the various formats. However, a format that is concise, easy to read, and professional is usually best.

Collaboration

Working in a group, discuss and list all the types of activities your college provides for students to get involved with events that could be included on a résumé.

EXERCISE 12.2

EXHIBIT 12.2   Sample Résumé

Juanita Cook
1234 Broadway Street
Anyplace, US   01234
555–555–1234
jrcook@anyplace.edu

Objective: To use my experience and education to work as an accounting manager.

Education	Associate of Applied Science in Accounting, Juno Community College, May 2009
Experience	Bookkeeper, Mays and Associates, August 2007–present

- Send invoices to clients
- Pay invoices from clients
- Maintain general ledger
- Supervise one staff member

Work-Study, Financial Aid Office, Juno Community College, January 2006–July 2007

- Filed financial aid applications
- Maintained communication with students through newsletter

Honors and Awards	Accounting Award for Outstanding Student, May 2007
	President's Scholarship, August 2005–May 2008
	Volunteer of the Year, Humane Society, October 2003

References available upon request

INTEGRITY MATTERS

Always provide accurate, truthful information in your résumé and cover letter. Highlight your accomplishments without overexaggerating them. Lying on a résumé is called "résumé padding," and it can get you in serious trouble. At the very least, you may not get the job; at the very worst, you could be fired after you are hired if the company finds out that your résumé contains false information.

Cover Letters

A cover letter accompanies a résumé and explains in detail how your qualifications match what the employer is looking for. As with a résumé, keep a cover letter brief and to the point, usually no more than a page unless you have enough work experience that you believe needs to be detailed in the letter. Often, the reason that cover letters should be short and to the point is that many employers simply scan these documents to see if candidates meet the minimum qualifications and then decide, pretty quickly, whether or not to interview them. The more concise your résumé and cover letter, the easier it will be for potential employers to determine whether you are right for the job.

When writing a cover letter, be sure to address a specific person. Avoid starting your letter with "Dear Sir or Madam" or "To Whom It May Concern." If you do not know to whom to address the letter, call the company and ask for the appropriate person's name, along with the correct spelling. If you are responding to several different job advertisements, double-check that you have correctly matched each letter with its corresponding addressed envelope. Also be sure that you have not made any references to people or companies other than to whom you are sending the cover letter.

The basic format of a cover letter is simple. After you type in your address, the date, and the potential employer's name, company name, and address, you can follow this format:

1. Introduction paragraph
   a. Introduce yourself.
   b. Tell where you learned about the job (Internet, newspaper, person at the company).
2. Background paragraph
   a. Tell more about yourself and how you are qualified.
   b. Relate your education and skills to the ones that the company is looking for.
3. Closing paragraph
   a. Tell potential employer how to contact you.
   b. Thank the person for her time and say you are looking forward to hearing from her.

Exhibit 12.3 is an example of an effective cover letter that could accompany the résumé in Exhibit 12.2.

EXHIBIT 12.3   Sample Cover Letter

1234 Broadway Street
Anyplace, US 01234

June 1, 2011

Dr. Judy Pile
Ingram Enterprises
6789 Levi Lane
Anyplace, US 09876

Dear Dr. Pile,

I am responding to your advertisement in the *Tonitown Times* for an accounting specialist at your company, Ingram Enterprises. As you will see from my résumé, I have earned an Associate of Arts degree in accounting from Juno Community College, and I have experience working as a bookkeeper for a local company.

My additional experience as a work-study in the financial aid office at Juno has allowed me to improve my people skills as well as to understand how an organized and efficient office works. I have also learned to use the following computer programs effectively: Microsoft Word, Microsoft Excel, and QuickBooks.

I am sure that you will find both my education and experience fit the position that was advertised. If you would like to interview me, I can be reached during the day at 555–555–1234. I look forward to hearing from you.

Sincerely,

Juanita Cook

Career Fairs

Career fairs are another way to get information about jobs and employers in your area. If your college sponsors a fair off campus or provides one to students on campus, then be sure to take advantage of it. Whether or not you are graduating next month or next year, it will pay to approach a career fair with the goal of making contacts and learning more about area businesses.

When you attend a career fair, there are several steps you can follow to make the most of your visits with potential employers. This list is just a start; you can get even more tips from your college counselors about how to maximize your time at a career fair:

- Dress professionally. Also, carry a professional-looking bag (no backpacks!) and a folder with copies of your résumé. Neatness counts.
- Do your homework. Find out what companies will be present at the fair and research the ones that interest you. You can find out more about them through their websites or through searching in the library.
- Avoid asking, "And what does your company do?" Your research should tell you what the company does.
- Choose a few booths to attend. Instead of blanketing the fair and hitting every representative, be selective and limit yourself only to companies that you would like to work for.

- Write a standard introduction, practice it, and then use it when you meet someone at the fair. Make sure the introduction is brief (state your name, your interests, and any relevant experience you may have) so that you maximize your time at the fair.
- Be energetic and positive. Recruiters and employers want to meet eager, exciting potential employees.

If you cannot make your college's career fair, you may be able to participate in a virtual career fair, which allows job seekers to "meet" participating companies and send résumés. Virtual career fairs are usually linked to a college's website and coincide with the actual fair. For example, the Virtual Career Fair link may only be available while the on-campus fair is open. Some colleges and organizations, however, provide a perpetual Virtual Career Fair so that students can investigate potential careers and companies at any time. One such website is http://www.careersinoilandgas.com, which offers an abundance of information and resources for anyone interested in a career in the oil or gas industries. Other sites, such as http://www.collegegrad.com/careers/, offer more general information about careers as well as advice and preparation for job seekers.

Internships

Another work option for community college students is an internship. This is a supervised position that allows a student to receive on-the-job training. Usually, internships are unpaid, which makes them less attractive to students who need to work. However, even if you need to make money while attending college, think about an internship anyway. Your college may offer course credit for internships, or you might even get paid for your work. This may be a good way to get closer to your degree *and* explore careers. Another idea is to volunteer once or twice a week at a place of business. If you have a few extra hours a week or can trade college credit for an internship, then you should investigate the benefits of interning.

Why are internships such a good opportunity for college students? One reason is that they allow you to work closely in a field that you may be interested in pursuing. In addition, internships can help you explore different ways to use your major in the workforce. For example, an English or journalism major may want to participate in an internship at a newspaper or as a proofreader at a company. A networking major may want to intern at a small business to get practical experience with computer networking issues on a small scale. These opportunities can give you firsthand experience with using your degree.

Internships also allow you to network with others who can help you find a job once you graduate. Even if you decide that you don't want to work in the same area as your internship, you will have contacts that may help you find a job in other fields. If you decide to intern, you should treat it as a job. Some employers rely on interns to complete certain projects each year, and they will expect that you be serious about the position, even if you don't get paid. Keeping a good attitude and being self-motivated are excellent ways to shine during your internship. In addition, you should meet regularly with your supervisor to ask questions and get guidance on projects. Most of all, make the best of your unique opportunity, and add that experience to your résumé.

Interviewing

Another important component to a successful career, if not the most important, is interviewing for a job. If your winning résumé gets you an interview, you are about halfway to getting a job. Consider the following tips to maximize your performance at the interview. Do a little research by checking out the company's website or search for other company information that may have appeared with the job advertisement. The goal is to find out what the company does and where it is going.

Don't forget to practice interview questions with your friends or family. Try to simulate the interview process by sitting across from the person who is practicing with you. Ask that person to make note of any fidgety habits and unclear answers. When you interview, you will want to dress professionally and pay attention to the details. Keep your fingernails clean and short. Check hems and cuffs for tears. Make sure your clothes are clean and pressed and your shoes are polished. For women, be sure that there are no runs in your hose and that your heels are not scuffed.

When you score an interview, be sure to arrive early. Introduce yourself to the receptionist and prepare to wait. If you are offered a drink, decline; you may end up spilling it on your clothes. During the interview, listen carefully to the interviewer's questions, pause before answering, and speak slowly and carefully. Be sure to look the interviewer in the eye when speaking, sit up, and lean forward slightly. Show by your body language that you are interested and relaxed, even if you are nervous. And speaking of nervous, if you are, that is normal, but be sure to avoid fidgeting with a pencil or paper and tapping your fingers or feet.

When you are speaking of what you can do, be sure to highlight your strengths. Even if you don't meet all of the job's qualifications, you may be able to persuade the employer that you can do the job. It may be a good idea, however, to avoid asking about the salary at the beginning of the interview. Instead, ask about the job responsibilities and benefits—the interviewer may provide a salary range as part of the information. As a last question, you may want to ask what the time line is for filling the position. Knowing when the company will be making the final decision will help you prepare for the next step.

As you leave, thank everyone you meet and follow up with a thank-you letter to each interviewer (see Exhibit 12.4). If you do not know how to spell their names, call the receptionist the next day to get the correct spellings.

Interviewers want to hire people who are energetic, polite, professional, and appreciative. Put your best face forward and try to relax and enjoy the process.

Other Considerations

All college career counselors want students to walk into high-paying jobs the day after graduation, but the reality is much different. Students who major in sought-after fields, such as information technology and health services, sometimes do not find the jobs that they thought were plentiful. Fluctuations in the economy are usually the cause for changes in the job market. Being prepared in case the job market has changed is your best defense.

To keep yourself grounded, formulate a plan for what you will do if you don't waltz into a dream job immediately. When writing your plan, be sure to answer the following questions:

* Are you willing to take less money if the opportunity is good?
* Are you willing to relocate for a better job?
* Are you willing to take a job in a different field from what you expected?
* Are you willing to repackage your skills and knowledge to be considered for different types of work?

These are all questions that both Evan and Michael would do well to ask themselves. Even though Michael is very sure of the kind of job he wants, he may want to have an

EXHIBIT 12.4   Sample Thank-You Letter

Juanita Cook
1234 Broadway Street
Anyplace, US 01234
555–555–1234
jrcook@anyplace.edu

July 12, 2011

Dr. Judy Pile
Ingram Enterprises
6789 Levi Lane
Anyplace, US 09876

Dear Dr. Pile,

Thank you for interviewing me yesterday. I enjoyed meeting you and your colleagues and learning more about how your company works.

After speaking with you, I am more firmly convinced that I would be a good person for the job. My education and experience would be a great match for what the position demands. I enjoy professional challenges, and I think your company provides the type of opportunities I am looking for.

Please feel free to contact me at 555–555–1234 or jrcook@anyplace.edu. I look forward to hearing from you.

Sincerely,

Juanita Cook

alternate plan in case those jobs are not readily available when he graduates. Evan can ask himself these questions, too, to help him focus on what is most important to him in a job.

In addition, start building up your network of friends, family, coworkers, classmates, and acquaintances, if you have not already been working on it. Let them know that you are about to graduate and will be looking for a job.

Finally, consider the process that you must go through if you are to be successful in finding the right job for you. Getting a job, then, requires that you

- Consider what field best suits your skills, personality, and dreams.
- Attend workshops and information sessions that provide assistance with résumé writing, interviewing, and networking.
- Prepare a solid résumé.
- Network with friends, family, and acquaintances.
- Actively look for work.
- Respond to job advertisements by sending out your résumé and cover letter.

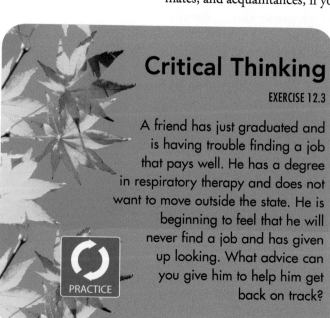

Critical Thinking

EXERCISE 12.3

A friend has just graduated and is having trouble finding a job that pays well. He has a degree in respiratory therapy and does not want to move outside the state. He is beginning to feel that he will never find a job and has given up looking. What advice can you give him to help him get back on track?

PRACTICE

- Follow up job interviews with a thank-you letter.
- Remain positive and flexible but stick to your goals.

Asking for a Recommendation Letter

When you make that decision to transfer, you will probably need a recommendation letter for scholarships, financial aid, or admission into a special program. If you have taken the time to cultivate a good relationship with a professor or an administrator at your community college, you will have an easier time asking for and receiving a recommendation letter that is full of specific information about the quality of your work and your character.

When considering someone to ask, choose a person who has had the chance to see you at your best. If you worked closely with a professor or spent many hours talking with a counselor, ask him or her to write a recommendation letter for you. The better the person knows you, the better the recommendation letter will be. In addition, give this person plenty of time to think about the quality of your work, recall specific examples, and write a polished letter. If you are on a tight deadline, such as a week, be honest with the person and give him or her a chance to decline the opportunity. If the person does agree to write a recommendation letter on such short notice, be sure to provide him or her with all the necessary materials to complete it properly, including an addressed, stamped envelope and the correct forms. You may want to include a brief résumé so that the person can speak specifically about your accomplishments.

Once your recommendation letter has been written, write a thank-you note and show your appreciation for the favor. Consider a handwritten note that expresses your gratitude rather than a verbal or email message of thanks. Finally, when requesting a recommendation, you should take the necessary steps to ensure that you do not read the recommendation letter. If you must hand-deliver the letter, ask that it be sealed in an envelope first. The reason that you should not request a copy or attempt to read it is that doing so jeopardizes the honesty of the individual who is writing it. Committees that evaluate recommendation letters want truthful descriptions of your abilities and strengths; if they know that you have seen the recommendation letter, they may doubt how accurate the description is.

Considering the Community

Although your focus during college will be on yourself and either moving on to another degree or to a new job, consider looking for opportunities to improve your community. One of the purposes of higher education is to improve the lives of individuals so that the community benefits as well, and it is essential that educated community members give back and make improvements.

Professional clubs, social and civic groups, churches, and volunteer organizations are other ways you can get involved in the community after college, if you have not done so already. The people you meet in these groups and the connections you make, both professional and personal, can enrich your life and your career. If you are not part of a community group, seek out one whose interests are similar to yours; also, look for ways to participate in events in your community, whether it is in a 5K run or a recycling drive. Participating in strengthening your community will allow you to give back to those in need, improve your community, and gain friendships and business connections that may last a long time.

Now may not be the time to encourage you to help your college financially, but think about how you can continue to support your school after you have left. In order for a college—or any educational institution—to be successful in improving the lives of the people in its community, it must depend in part on its graduates to make a good name for themselves and to give back with their time, talent, and financial resources. There are a variety of ways that you can contribute to the education of those who will surely follow in your footsteps.

Walking Billboard

By being a productive, educated member of society, you are already giving back to your college. Because higher education's mission is to improve a community by increasing the knowledge of its population, we all benefit from students who complete graduation requirements for degree and certificate programs and continue to lead productive, happy lives. The skills and knowledge you have obtained in college are a good advertisement for the school. Alumni who make a difference in the lives of others through their jobs and community service fulfill the college's mission to not only provide education to strengthen the local economy, but to also graduate people who demonstrate the ideals of higher education.

Mentoring Others

As you know, community college students are a special group of people. They often have overcome overwhelming personal and financial obstacles to attend college, and some get lost along the way, thinking that college is too difficult for them. Many of them may need a mentor to help them stay on track. Once you are confident that you can manage

Reflection

EXERCISE 12.4

In what ways have you already mentored others who want to attend college or are just starting their college careers? How have you influenced others to value education?

PRACTICE

college or once you graduate, you may want to seek out others who need a mentor. Some obvious candidates are people in your family who could benefit from enrolling in a certificate or degree program. Maybe you have friends or coworkers who are apprehensive about returning to school because they don't know if they can handle the responsibilities, or they may believe they cannot afford to go to college. As a mentor, you can share what you know about how to manage going to school with other obligations. You are proof that others can do it and do it successfully.

Giving Time and Talent

Colleges do not survive by tuition and fees alone; the reality is that educating students is expensive, and thankfully for students, colleges receive money from other sources in order to cover the total costs of education. Funds that are raised by companies and individuals as well as federal, state, and local monies all help the college function and keep tuition low. The college, then, depends on the generosity of others to make it possible to provide a low-cost education.

With this said, you may want to consider giving back to your college after you graduate. It doesn't have to be any time soon and doesn't have to be a monetary contribution. For example, you may consider creating an alumni network that encourages employers to donate to the college, or you may consider sitting on a panel that looks at ways to increase the college's visibility in the community. In other words, you can donate your time and your knowledge to help the school raise more money, which will benefit even more students.

The End is the Beginning

It is now a cliché to say that "commencement"—the ceremony you participate in when you graduate—means "a beginning" rather than "an ending." Many graduation speakers address that point each year: When you graduate from college, you are not just ending your academic career, but you are beginning the rest of your life. For community college students, however, the difference between being in college and going off to a career may not be that clear. In fact, career and college, for most community college students, are very much intertwined. Therefore, it may seem that there is no distinct beginning and ending for you. However, once you do graduate with a certificate or degree or even a group of credits, you can think about a brighter future as a beginning.

What will be left for you once you graduate? Beyond transferring, there is always graduate school or a professional school. Why not go as far as you can with your degree? With each semester, you are getting closer. Once you meet your goal of graduating with an associate's degree or certificate, you will see that all it takes is goal setting, time management, and a desire to meet your goals.

Another "beginning" to the end of your degree at your community college is lifelong learning. Not only will you be able to use the research and information literacy skills that you learned in college, but you will also have access to materials through alumni borrowing privileges at the library. In addition, you may be more interested in and informed about guest speakers and community events that are sponsored by your college. At the very least, you will have a network of instructors, counselors, and advisors to call on when you need advice and information.

Mission, Values, and Goals Revisited

In Chapter 2, you wrote down your values, goals, and mission statement. Do you still have that information in a convenient location? If so, get it out and reflect on how well you have met your original short-term goals and how far you have come to reaching your long-term goals. Have your values changed any? Or have they been strengthened by your achievements? Have you followed your mission statement? Is there anything that you would change about your mission statement?

To answer these questions, you will need to reflect on your achievements over the past semester. Your mission and values should not have changed much in the past weeks, but if they have, you can make a new list of values and rewrite your mission statement. Most definitely, some of your short-term goals should be met, and you have no doubt moved on to a new list of them as you make your way to your long-term goals. Now is the time, then, to revisit your long-range plans and make adjustments if you need to. Also, you should keep a record of the short-term goals you have reached and create a new list. Keeping up with what you have accomplished will serve as a reminder of your success if you ever feel unsure about your progress. Here is an example of a new list you can make:

GOALS I HAVE MET

1. Completed my courses with above average grades.
2. Created a study group with classmates.

3. Kept up with my commitments on the job.
4. Paid my tuition.

NEW SHORT-TERM GOALS

1. Get registered for next semester.
2. Speak with a counselor about career possibilities.
3. Make at least two A's in my classes.
4. Take more time to relax.

Once you revise your short-term goals, you may notice that your time line for reaching your long-term goals needs adjusting as well. Keeping your list in a convenient location and looking at it every day or week will help you stay on track.

What Do You Know . . . Now?

Do you remember answering the question "What do you know?" in Chapter 2? You were asked to make a list of all the things that you know something about. The point of that exercise was to help you realize that you do know more than you may think you know. The point of asking the question now is to show you how much you have learned during the semester. Take a few minutes to write down five new things you know and to reflect on how much you have learned about college, yourself, and what you can do to be successful. At the very least, your professors, counselors, advisors, and even this author hope you have learned that you can make it through your classes (you have almost done it already!) and that you have many people around you who are there to make sure that you do succeed. All you have to do is communicate your needs, seek out help if you need it, and use the resources that you have in front of you at your college to help you make your community college experience a success!

PLUS

EXERCISE 12.5

(Personality + Learning Style = Understanding Situations)

Let's consider Evan and Michael's career fair adventure. Evan is a kinesthetic learner and very outgoing, which may be why he is visiting every booth. Michael, however, sees this opportunity to make his time count, which is why he only chooses two booths to visit. Evan seems to lack focus and confidence in what he wants to do. What advice would you give him before he hands out his résumé to all the attending companies? Michael knows exactly what he wants to do and how to get there, but he lacks the confidence to go for his dream. Taking into consideration his personality type and learning style, what is the best course of action for him?

Now, considering your own learning style, personality type, and special circumstances, how would you approach a career fair and making a decision about what you want to do with your degree?

PROFILE

MY STORY
Learning Plan

Directions: Using what you have learned in this chapter and what you know about your learning preferences, choose a task or assignment that needs to be completed soon and create a learning plan that will help you accomplish this task. Then, write your *My Story* Summary, a one-sentence synopsis that crystallizes your newly created plan.

LEARNING TASK	
Time of Day	
Intake Preference	
Social Preference	
Task Management Preference	

MY STORY SUMMARY:

Path of Discovery

Journal Entry

What, if anything, would keep you from completing your degree? What would be your plan for getting back into college to meet your educational goals?

HOMEWORK

From College to University

Hold Off on Starting Your Career Until You Have Met Your Educational Goal

It will be very tempting to head back to work before you have completed your certificate or degree because of changes in your family or financial situation. However, remember that if you can hang in there, the further you go toward your ultimate education goal, the better opportunities you will have in the workforce, and you will have an easier time going back if you find yourself "stopping out" of college for a while as you work.

Another idea for helping you stay in college before returning to work is to look for ways to break your ultimate educational goal into achievable, realistic shorter-term goals that will move you in the right direction. For example, if you need to return to work before completing your registered nursing (RN) degree, which is often a two-year degree, you may be able to complete a licensed practical nursing (LPN) program in a shorter amount of time. Completing a shorter program first, working in the field, and then returning to complete a longer program may be a good fit for your educational and financial needs. Be sure, though, that you speak with an advisor to make sure that you don't take too many classes that will not fit into your longer-term educational goal.

From College to Career

Practicing What You Have Learned to Earn the Job Will Help You Progress

Time management, goal setting, long-term planning are all skills that you have learned during your college career, and these skills will take you far in the workplace. If anything, knowing that you can juggle multiple responsibilities, such as taking care of yourself, family, job, and college, should give you the confidence to tackle other challenges that you will face in the workforce. For sure, practice those skills on the job, but also know that you may need to improve upon those skills as you complete new tasks, take on more projects at work, and change positions.

Don't forget that your college, even long after you have graduated, can help you while you are in the workplace. You may still have access to their career services as a graduate of the college. You may also be able to use the library to do research. For sure, you will have the connections that you made while in college, people you can call on for advice and friendship. Look into what services they offer for you before you graduate, services that you can utilize as a successful graduate.

Chapter Review Questions

1. What questions do you need to ask before you transfer to a four-year university?
2. List and describe three considerations when applying for a job.
3. What is the difference between a cover letter and a résumé?
4. Describe four tips for a successful interview.
5. In what ways can a college student mentor others who are considering enrolling in college?

Chapter 12 Case Scenarios

1. Rudy is getting a degree in business management, but doesn't have any idea how to look for a good job. He is not even sure if that is what he needs to break into financial planning. What advice can you give him to make sure he is starting his career planning on the right foot?

2. Brian's dream is to own a horse farm, but he doesn't think he can afford his dream, so he is in his second semester as a radiology technician because it is a job with a steady income. Also, Brian doesn't want to quit school to follow his dream because he values an education. What advice can you give him about following his dreams?

3. Lawrence is ready to graduate with a degree in networking, and he has been circulating his résumé with the hope that he can roll right into a job after graduation. Because Lawrence lacks experience in his field, he has decided to exaggerate some of his responsibilities as a work-study student in the information technology department and as an intern at a local advertising company. What should you tell Lawrence before he sends his résumés out to prospective employers?

Research It Further

1. Search for a Web site that is devoted to helping you discover the right career for you, such as http://www.solutionskills.com/index.html. Research a career that interests you and collect information about the education needed, the pay you can expect, and the career potential. Present your findings to your class.

2. Will your career allow you to live the lifestyle you want? Use the lifestyle budget calculator at www.real-life.arkansas.gov and determine if the career you want will allow you to reach your goals. What surprises you the most about how far your salary can go? What changes may you have to make to live within your means?

3. Interview at least five students about their career goals and what kind of lifestyle they want to live. Ask them what services they have used to help them along the way. Is there anything that your college could provide in addition to the services they already have that would help students make a smooth transition between college and career?

Appendix A: Glossary

Academic calendar—A list of important dates. Included are vacation breaks, registration periods, and deadlines for certain forms.

Academic probation—A student whose GPA falls below a designated number can be placed on academic probation. If the GPA does not improve, then the student may be prohibited from registering for classes for a designated number of semesters.

Articulation agreement—A signed document stating that one college will accept the courses from another college.

Associate of Applied Science—A degree that consists of about 60 credit hours of courses. Not intended to serve as a transferable degree to a four-year university.

Associate of Arts—A degree that consists of about 60 credit hours of general education courses. Often considered as the equivalent of the first two years of a four-year degree.

Audience—In essay writing, the audience is the person or persons whom you are addressing.

Catalog—A book that provides students with information about the college's academic calendar, tuition and fees, and degree/certificate programs.

Corequisite—A course that you can take at the same time as another course. For example, if intermediate algebra is a corequisite for physical science, then you will take both courses during the same semester.

Cornell System—A note-taking system in which a student draws an upside-down "T" on a sheet of paper and uses the space to the right for taking notes, the space to the left for adding questions and highlighting important points, and the space at the bottom for summarizing the material.

Course objective—A goal that the instructor has identified for the student to meet once the course is completed. For example, a course objective could be to use MLA documentation properly.

Cover letter—A letter accompanying a résumé that describes how a person's qualifications match the advertised requirements for the job.

Creative thinking—Thinking that creates or generates ideas.

Critical thinking—The ability to use specific criteria to evaluate reasoning and make a decision.

Curriculum—A term used to refer to the courses that a student must take in a particular field, or it can refer to all the classes that the college offers.

Developmental classes—Sometimes referred to as remedial classes, developmental classes focus on basic college-level skills such as reading, writing, and math. Students who earn a certain score on standardized tests such as the ACT and COMPASS exams may be required to take developmental classes before enrolling in college-level courses.

Family Educational Rights and Privacy Act (FERPA)—A federal law that ensures that a student's educational records, including test grades and transcripts, are not accessed or viewed by anyone who is not authorized by you to do so.

Full-time student—A student who is taking at least 12 credit hours of courses per semester.

Full-time worker—A person who is working at least 40 hours per week.

Grade point average (GPA)—The number that is used to determine a student's progress in college. It refers to the number of quality points divided by the number of hours a student has taken.

Knowledge—This comes from taking in information, thinking about it critically, and synthesizing one's own ideas about what one has read or seen.

Long-term goal—A goal that takes a long time to complete (within a year or more).

Major—The area that a student is focusing on for his or her degree. If a student wants to teach third grade, for example, his or her major can be elementary education. (*See also* Minor.)

Matching question—A test question that provides one column of descriptors and another column of words that must be matched with the appropriate descriptor.

Minor—A second area that a student can emphasize in his or her degree. A minor usually requires fewer classes and is not as intensive as a major. For example, if a student majors in marketing but also wants to learn more about running his or her own business, the student may want to minor in business or accounting.

Mission statement—A declaration of what a person or an institution believes in and what that person or institution hopes to accomplish.

Multiple-choice question—A type of test question in which an incomplete sentence or a question is given and the correct response must be chosen from a list of possibilities.

Objective question—A question that presents a limited number of possible answers.

OK5R—A reading strategy developed by Dr. Walter Pauk: overview, key ideas, read, record, recite, review, and reflect.

Part-time student—A student who is taking less than 12 credit hours per semester.

Prerequisite—A required course or score that must be completed or achieved before enrolling in a course.

Priority—Something that is important at that moment.

Purpose—What a student hopes to accomplish with his or her writing assignment.

Quality points—The number that is assigned to each grade. For example, an A is worth four quality points and a B is worth three quality points.

Remedial classes—*See* Developmental classes.

Résumé—A page or two that provides a person's educational and work experience, career objective, and contact information.

Short-term goal—A goal that can be accomplished in a short period of time (within a week or a few months).

SQ3R—A reading method that consists of the following elements: survey, question, read, recite, and review.

Stress—A physical and psychological response to outside stimuli.

Student handbook—A publication of the college that outlines what the college expects of the student.

Subjective question—A test question that requires a student to provide a personal answer. Usually, there are no "wrong" answers to subjective questions.

Syllabus—A document that contains an overview of the course, including objectives, assignments, and required materials as well as the instructor's policies for attendance, exams, and grading. It may also contain the college's policies on disability accommodations and academic dishonesty.

Time management—Strategies for using time effectively.

Topic—The subject of a piece of writing.

Transcript—A record of the courses a student has taken and the grades the student has earned. Transcripts also note the student's grade point average.

Transfer—Refers to moving from one school to another. Students who transfer must apply for admission to the second school and must request that their transcript(s) be sent to the new school.

T System—*See* Cornell System.

Values—Part of a person's belief system that provides the foundation of what the person does and what the person wants to become. If a person values financial stability, for example, then the person will look for opportunities to earn money and provide a secure future.

Work-study—A federal program that allows students to work at their college while taking classes. Students must qualify for work-study money and must meet college department requirements for work.

Appendix B: VARK Learning Styles Inventory

As discussed in "Read This First" in the Preface and Chapter 2, there are a variety of ways to view yourself and how you learn. Although you are encouraged to explore your learning styles preferences and multiple intelligences, one inventory stands out for its ease of use and the empowerment students feel when they discover that they have a visual, aural, read/write, or kinesthetic learning preference or more than one.

Neil D. Fleming and Charles Bonwell have developed the VARK inventory, which uses the following categories for the learning styles preferences: Visual (V), Aural (A), Read/write (R), and Kinesthetic (K). If you have strong preferences in more than one mode, you are considered multimodal (MM).

VARK Inventory

Choose the answer which best explains your preference and circle the letter. Please select more than one response if a single answer does not match your perception.

Leave blank any question that does not apply.

1. You are helping someone who wants to go to your airport, town center or railway station. You would:
   a. go with her.
   b. tell her the directions.
   c. write down the directions.
   d. draw, or give her a map.

2. You are not sure whether a word should be spelled "dependent" or "dependant." You would:
   a. see the words in your mind and choose by the way they look.
   b. think about how each word sounds and choose one.
   c. find it in a dictionary.
   d. write both words on paper and choose one.

3. You are planning a holiday for a group. You want some feedback from them about the plan. You would:
   a. describe some of the highlights.
   b. use a map or website to show them the places.

  c. give them a copy of the printed itinerary.

  d. phone, text or email them.

4. You are going to cook something as a special treat for your family. You would:

   a. cook something you know without the need for instructions.

   b. ask friends for suggestions.

   c. look through the cookbook for ideas from the pictures.

   d. use a cookbook where you know there is a good recipe.

5. A group of tourists want to learn about the parks or wildlife reserves in your area. You would:

   a. talk about, or arrange a talk for them about parks or wildlife reserves.

   b. show them Internet pictures, photographs or picture books.

   c. take them to a park or wildlife reserve and walk with them.

   d. give them a book or pamphlets about the parks or wildlife reserves.

6. You are about to purchase a digital camera or mobile phone. Other than price, what would most influence your decision?

   a. Trying or testing it.

   b. Reading the details about its features.

   c. It is a modern design and looks good.

   d. The salesperson telling me about its features.

7. Remember a time when you learned how to do something new. Try to avoid choosing a physical skill, e.g., riding a bike. You learned best by:

   a. watching a demonstration.

   b. listening to somebody explaining it and asking questions.

   c. diagrams and charts—visual clues.

   d. written instructions—e.g., a manual or textbook.

8. You have a problem with your knee. You would prefer that the doctor:

   a. gave you a Web address or something to read about it.

   b. used a plastic model of a knee to show what was wrong.

   c. described what was wrong.

   d. showed you a diagram of what was wrong.

9. You want to learn a new program, skill or game on a computer. You would:

   a. read the written instructions that came with the program.

   b. talk with people who know about the program.

   c. use the controls or keyboard.

   d. follow the diagrams in the book that came with it.

10. You like websites that have:

   a. things you can click on, shift or try.

   b. interesting design and visual features.

   c. interesting written descriptions, lists and explanations.

   d. audio channels where you can hear music, radio programs or interviews.

11. Other than price, what would most influence your decision to buy a new nonfiction book?

   a. The way it looks is appealing.

   b. Quickly reading parts of it.

   c. A friend talks about it and recommends it.

   d. It has real-life stories, experiences and examples.

12. You are using a book, CD or website to learn how to take photos with your new digital camera. You would like to have:

   a. a chance to ask questions and talk about the camera and its features.

   b. clear written instructions with lists and bullet points about what to do.

   c. diagrams showing the camera and what each part does.

   d. many examples of good and poor photos and how to improve them.

13. Do you prefer a teacher or a presenter who uses:

   a. demonstrations, models, or practical sessions.

   b. question and answer, talk, group discussion, or guest speakers.

   c. handouts, books, or readings.

   d. diagrams, charts, or graphs.

14. You have finished a competition or test and would like some feedback. You would like to have feedback:

   a. using examples from what you have done.

   b. using a written description of your results.

   c. from somebody who talks it through with you.

   d. using graphs showing what you had achieved.

15. You are going to choose food at a restaurant or cafe. You would:

   a. choose something that you have had there before.

   b. listen to the waiter or ask friends to recommend choices.

   c. choose from the descriptions in the menu.

   d. look at what others are eating or look at pictures of each dish.

16. You have to make an important speech at a conference or special occasion. You would:

   a. make diagrams or get graphs to help explain things.

   b. write a few key words and practice saying your speech over and over.

   c. write out your speech and learn from reading it over several times.

   d. gather many examples and stories to make the talk real and practical.

Scoring. For each question, mark your answer below and then add up how many V's, A's, R's, and K's you have. The largest number of V, A, R, or K indicates your learning style preference. For example, if you marked "A" for question number 2, your learning style preference for that question is V. If you have more V's than any other letter, your learning style preference is Visual.

QUESTION	CHOICE A	CHOICE B	CHOICE C	CHOICE D
1	K	A	R	V
2	V	A	R	K
3	K	V	R	A
4	K	A	V	R
5	A	V	K	R
6	K	R	V	A
7	K	A	V	R
8	R	K	A	V
9	R	A	K	V
10	K	V	R	A
11	V	R	A	K
12	A	R	V	K
13	K	A	R	V
14	K	R	A	V
15	K	A	R	V
16	V	A	R	K

Calculating Your Score

Add the number of each letter and write the totals in the spaces below.

Total Number of V's circled _____

Total Number of A's circled _____

Total Number of R's circled _____

Total Number of K's circled _____

Look at your calculated score. If you have more V's than any other letter, then you have a strong visual learning preference. You may also have another learning style preference that is the same or close to your dominate learning style preference. For example, if you recorded 8 R's and 7 K's, you have both a read/write learning style preference as well as a kinesthetic learning style preference. Record your preference (s) in the space below.

My VARK Learning Style Preference is _____.

Index

General Education

Required for Major

Other Hours Required

Total hours completed _____

		Course Description & Textbooks
Course ID/Section		
Course Location		
Instructor / Professor		
Course Time		
Lab Hour		
Group Meeting Time		
Office Hours		
Office Phone #		Course Requirements
Office Email		
Office Address		
Midterm		
Final		
Grading / Goal		
Grades		

Course Title

		Course Description & Textbooks
Course ID/Section		
Course Location		
Instructor / Professor		
Course Time		
Lab Hour		
Group Meeting Time		
Office Hours		
Office Phone #		Course Requirements
Office Email		
Office Address		
Midterm		
Final		
Grading / Goal		
Grades		

		Course Description & Textbooks
Course ID/Section		
Course Location		
Instructor / Professor		
Course Time		
Lab Hour		
Group Meeting Time		
Office Hours		
Office Phone #		Course Requirements
Office Email		
Office Address		
Midterm		
Final		
Grading / Goal		
Grades		

Course Title

		Course Description & Textbooks
Course ID/Section		
Course Location		
Instructor / Professor		
Course Time		
Lab Hour		
Group Meeting Time		
Office Hours		
Office Phone #		Course Requirements
Office Email		
Office Address		
Midterm		
Final		
Grading / Goal		
Grades		

		Course Description & Textbooks
Course ID/Section		
Course Location		
Instructor / Professor		
Course Time		
Lab Hour		
Group Meeting Time		
Office Hours		
Office Phone #		Course Requirements
Office Email		
Office Address		
Midterm		
Final		
Grading / Goal		
Grades		

Course Title

		Course Description & Textbooks
Course ID/Section		
Course Location		
Instructor / Professor		
Course Time		
Lab Hour		
Group Meeting Time		
Office Hours		
Office Phone #		Course Requirements
Office Email		
Office Address		
Midterm		
Final		
Grading / Goal		
Grades		

		Course Description & Textbooks	
Course ID/Section			
Course Location			
Instructor / Professor			
Course Time			
Lab Hour			
Group Meeting Time			
Office Hours			
Office Phone #		Course Requirements	
Office Email			
Office Address			
Midterm			
Final			
Grading / Goal			
Grades			

Course Title

		Course Description & Textbooks	
Course ID/Section			
Course Location			
Instructor / Professor			
Course Time			
Lab Hour			
Group Meeting Time			
Office Hours			
Office Phone #		Course Requirements	
Office Email			
Office Address			
Midterm			
Final			
Grading / Goal			
Grades			